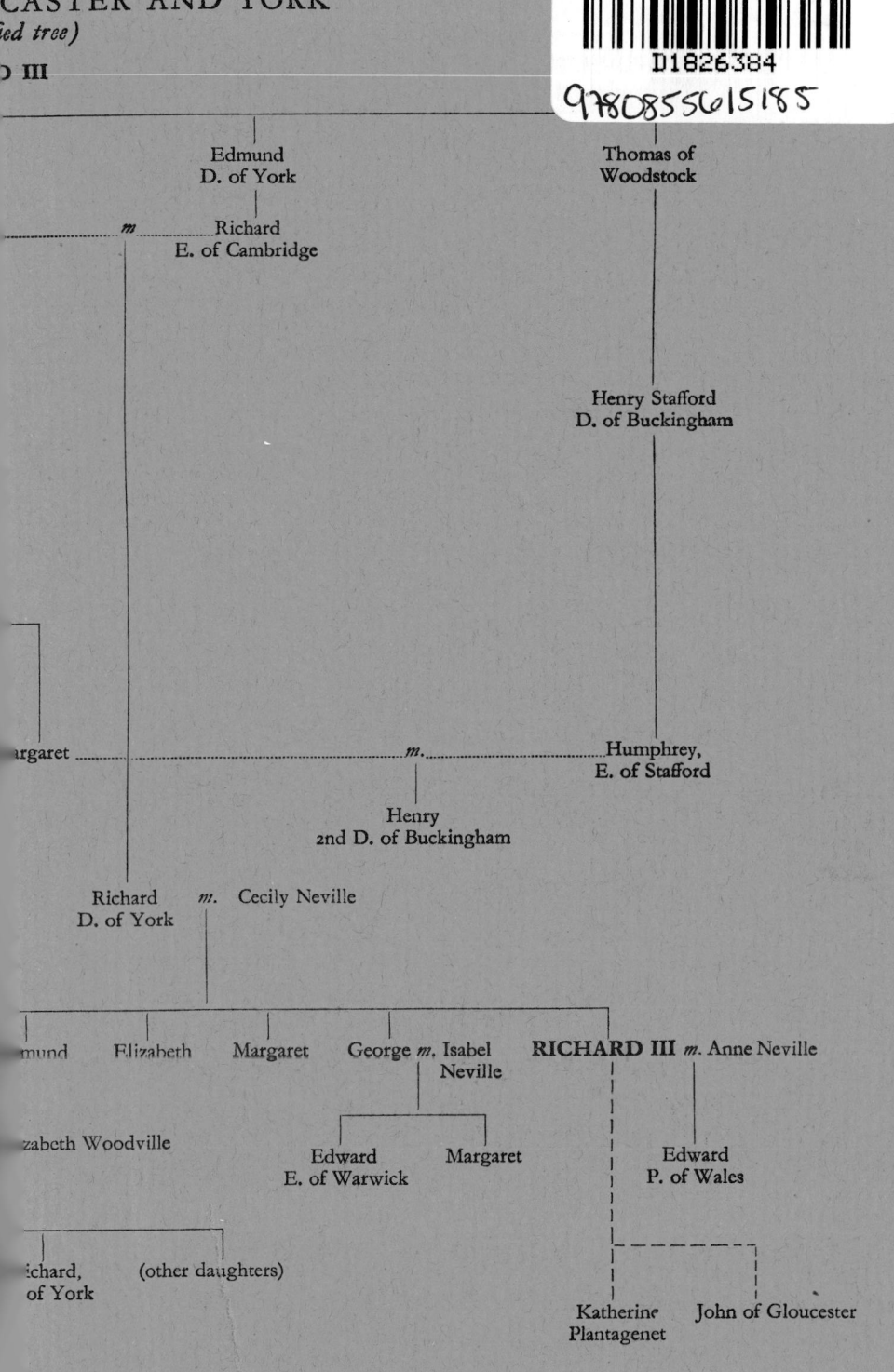

THE LAST PLANTAGENET

THE LAST PLANTAGENET

A Study of Richard the Third
King of England, France and Ireland

Tyler Whittle

HEINEMANN : LONDON

William Heinemann Ltd

LONDON   MELBOURNE   TORONTO

CAPE TOWN   AUCKLAND

First published 1968

© Michael Tyler-Whittle 1968

434   86481   1

Printed in Great Britain by
Cox & Wyman Ltd, London, Fakenham and Reading

To
Jean Denham

Author's Note

Though a fictional treatment, *The Last Plantagenet* is entirely faithful to the known facts. Nothing has been deliberately distorted or omitted simply to make the writing easier or to suit a preconceived idea. No character has been invented save those who are representative of people who must have existed. The few small liberties taken to bridge gaps in the documentary evidence lie always within the seemliness of historical probability.

T.W.

Contents

Endpapers: A simplified tree of the houses of Lancaster and York.

PART ONE

Lord Richard Plantagenet

I

His hand was hot and clammy; her hand, warm but dry as a lizard's skin. He brushed her knuckles with his thumb, trying to get magic from her, the magical power to be brave.

'Madam . . .' he began in a whisper, and stopped.

The noise was increasing – the rattle of wooden drums, shouts from the castle and questions and curses and orders, the tramp of feet, wheels and hooves on setts and cobbles, the creak and rumble of harness, wagons and war pieces.

His mother bent her head a little though she still kept her eyes on the advancing soldiers. 'Dickon,' she murmured. 'You've little to fear. Face them like . . . like a prince.'

Almost she had said 'like George' – like her plump ten-year-old son who stood on tiptoe to see the banners coming, but Cecily Neville knew how vain he was already and she would not willingly puff his conceit.

George, who was always so alive to anything which concerned him, immediately noticed the pause in her voice. He guessed what lay in her mind, and decided the comparison was just. He squeezed her right hand as if to show he agreed that Richard could do no better than look to his example of princely bearing. Was he not fair, and healthy, and handsome – as they were always telling him? while Richard, well, his brother was dark and small and sickly.

'Dick,' he said – and loudly enough for many to hear. 'Dick, you're a Plantagenet. A Plantagenet.'

Anger reddened Richard's sallow face. He straightened himself; tightened the grip on his mother's hand; forgot his dread of the Lancastrians. . . . All this because he hated George and not simply to prove that he was Lord Richard Plantagenet, youngest son of the Duke of York.

From down the street a single trumpet sounded; the notes uncertain and feeble. Was this to herald Henry of England, France and Ireland? There must be fog or river water in the trumpet to make so ribald a noise.

By now three sides of the market place were filled. The Duchess, her small sons and their three attendants made a lonely island before the market cross. The soldiers still marched in, ranking themselves in front of the silent townsmen. Drumboys beat time for the marching feet. Then again came a fanfare from the trumpet – truer than the first and the royal household of lords and servants streamed past the market cross. At last guarded by a file of pikemen came the king. Henry was beaming with a childlike eagerness to please, his wife and queen, Margaret of Anjou, and his young heir, Edward Prince of Wales beside him.

Richard fixed his eyes on the prince. It was easier to look at a boy of his own age than anyone else in the Lancastrian army. Or so he believed: but, though the prince's face was an expressionless blank, his half-closed blue eyes were not. From beneath hooded lids Edward returned Richard's look, and it spoke wordlessly the malice and contempt in his mind. Better hate than scorn. Richard turned away and looked instead at the queen's horse barely three yards from him – until, suddenly, he caught the stallion's eye and saw that he was as savage and wilful as the woman he carried. Again he looked away; first up at the sky; then, as the king spoke, down to the ground at his feet.

'Fair cousin!' It was unlike Henry to speak first in any company, but he was overjoyed that the town and fortress had been surrendered without a battle.

Silence met his exuberant greeting. Then Cecily, Duchess of York, made a sweeping curtsy to the ground. Her sons bowed stiffly.

'Your grace,' she said. 'I surrender myself, my children, and my people to your good mercy.'

Her attendant stepped forward and offered the castle keys to Henry.

'Edward,' said the king, and his heir accepted the keys with a slight bow to the duchess.

'Fair cousin!' said Henry once more.

His queen played impatiently with her finger-rings. 'Your grace is pleased to accept their submission,' she prompted.

Henry took it as a question, not a reminder of his duty. 'Yes,' he said. 'I am pleased, fair cousin. Stand. Stand. Stand.'

'With certain conditions,' said Queen Margaret sharply.

'Certain conditions,' echoed the king

Richard had heard in household gossip that the queen was like a

4

jackdaw trainer with her lord, teaching him what to speak; snapping out words and phrases for him to repeat.

The duchess stayed where she was, looking up to Henry on his quiet gelding. 'Your word, as king, that my people shall have quarter?'

'My word,' promised the king, nodding – but only those nearest heard him because simultaneously Queen Margaret began to speak in a shrill, indignant voice.

'You mistrust the king's mercy, Madam?' she cried. 'You kneel before us to demand guarantees; you, a traitor to your king and the realm!'

The duchess at once stood up to her full height. "I am loyal to my lord and husband,' she said clearly and loudly. 'To his vassals and his people here of Ludlow. I know little of treachery, your grace, save that taught me by the knave in your train who until yesterday was my own guest.' Her eyes were on a large, puce-faced captain sitting his horse not far away. 'Andrew Trollope of Calais will regret his broken word, your grace.'

'Calais is our domain,' shrilled Margaret. 'Sir Andrew and his men returned to their true allegiance.'

'Being too gross to fight, too cowardly to be loyal to my nephew Warwick, Captain of Calais.'

'Madam,' the queen lashed. 'Your husband, your nephew, his father, and your two great sons with all their train have bolted showing scuts to Ludlow, and you talk of cowards!'

She laughed outright. Or rather, thought Richard, she cackled like a beldame; like the black witch he had seen in the castle home of his childhood at Fotheringhay. Could this queen be, as some men said, a true black witch? He crossed himself protectively.

The action caught the queen's eye; and viciously she turned on him. 'I see York's withered runt is holy! But then he needs be. Only the cloister could swallow and digest a crippled, sickly lord spawned by a treacherous coward.'

King Henry, astonished, opened his mouth to a little O, and closed it again.

But Duchess Cecily needed no one's help to protect her youngest child. Instinctively she held Richard to her. Proudly and angrily she regarded the queen. 'Madam,' she said. 'You are ungentle. You lack the manners of the English!'

Margaret at once was the virago men feared. She whipped the

Yorkists with bitter words, and her anger passed to the restless stallion beneath her. He turned his head; tossed it. The reins were drawn taut, cutting and spiking his mouth to a bloody foam. The king's general, Somerset, thrust his horse forward to catch the stallion's armoured bridle and hold him in. But with a scream, his eyes rolling, the beast sprang on to his hind legs and pawed the air. With the great hooves above her even Cecily Neville quailed. She flinched and stepped backwards as Somerset and the queen between them wrenched the rearing stallion down again to submission.

'Dickon!' cried his mother, her face the white of milk.

Richard clung to her hand. His mouth was sandy. There was cold sweat in his groin and armpits.

Through the hubbub he heard a whisper from the body-squire behind him. 'Is all right, Lord Richard.' Tom's voice. Old Tom – always solemn, tight, withdrawn, preserving his words like coins, using them so rarely that when he repeated himself the boy was reassured. 'Is all right, Lord Richard.'

The queen's frenzy had died. Now in wintry anger she spoke to the duchess, briefly, starkly, with no word of apology.

'You will return to the castle and keep to your solar, Madam. Tomorrow we shall meet again.'

King Henry opened his mouth to add a word; but he had no opportunity. His horse was turned away. He merely had time to nod kindly to the duchess and her sons.

Cecily's eyes followed him. They showed half disgust, half pity for the feeble Red Rose of Lancaster: a dotard hag-ridden by his queen: naif as well, for when told of the birth of his heir had he not gaily clapped his hands and sworn the child must be by the Holy Ghost because he'd played no part in his begetting. Or was he too short of sense to understand that Margaret pleasured herself with Somerset, the general of his armies? Crazed certainly, for long periods at a time; holy, they said . . . always at his prayers; wise sometimes, but in few matters; and disinclined to wash or clean himself at all unless they forced him. Son of great Harry of Agincourt! – that bird-witted, dirty, downtrodden simpleton. He had no place on any throne. . . . Yet at least he had guaranteed the safety of the town and mercy to the dependants of his rebellious lords.

An order rang out. The troops began to march back to camp. One detachment of footmen moved towards the Market Cross.

6

'Come!' the duchess said to her sons. 'We return to the castle. Little Margaret will be anxious for us.'

Richard let go her hand. He could hardly believe it but the worst was over. His father had been right to depend on the king's mercy. All his terrors died. No one had spitted him on a lance – as George had foretold. Nor had they slashed his cheeks; nor ripped out his heart. He had not been touched. Not once. And they were to return safely to the castle. . . .

II

The October evening was keen. Looking down from the gallery
of the great chamber to the tables below, Richard shivered in the
raw air. There were few at table and the hall was quiet: very different
from the night before when his father had sat in council there.
Then there had been shouting – from his uncle of Salisbury, from
Edward and Edmund his own elder brothers, most of all from his
cousin and godfather, Richard of Warwick . . . all of them cursing
the Calais men who had slipped treacherously to the enemy . . . not
one of them willing at first to accept the Duke of York's decision;
that they must fly instantly, keeping the sharp edge of their swords
for another day.

'The world will hold us *craven*!' Warwick had roared – so loudly
that he terrified the hounds who were picking and scratching in
the rushes. 'Craven, I say!'

But Salisbury had been persuaded to see the wisdom of York's
decision, and between them the older men had won the day. Rapidly
they had prepared and split into two companies; Richard's father
and brother Edmund to ride west to reach Ireland; his eldest
brother, Edward, to make for France with Salisbury and Warwick.

For almost twenty hours now, ever since their departure, the
hall had been unnaturally quiet.

Richard hugged his favourite hound for warmth and comfort; a
little brachet bitch named Bat. She was a happy reminder of his
real home at Fotheringhay so many miles away. Bat had played
with him there in the water meadows beside the river Nene. Bat
had whelped puppies there. Bat had coursed hares for him, chopped
conies for him, brought anything he wished to his hand. Bat had
been with him always except in the mews, at Mass, at board and in
bed; and when word had come that he and George and Margaret
should be moved to the safety of Ludlow, nothing would do but
that Bat should accompany them. His mother had forbidden it;
then, for once out of character, she had changed her mind. So Bat
had followed the party all the way from flat Northamptonshire;

8

through the great forest of Rockingham to Market Harborough; then, across the midland downs and skirting the Lancastrian headquarters at Coventry, to Warwick, over Severn, by the three hills of Clee, and finally to Ludlow and this great fortress above the river gorge. Bat had raced all that way. Richard hugged her again. She, with Tom his squire, was all he really cared for. He honoured and feared his father, but York was too bright a sun in Richard's world to earn his love. In much the same way he admired his elder brothers; but he was only just seven years old and they were strangers, and belted earls at that, each a remote and brilliant planet. George and their youngest sister Margaret he heartily disliked. Only old Tom and Bat the brachet had his love; though if he had dared he would have liked to have offered it to his mother too.

He peered down at her through the balustrade where she presided at supper. 'More a queen than that other – the witch,' he whispered to himself. Bat cocked one ear.

It was true. Cecily sat regally at the head of the board; eating little as was her custom, and talking to the castle chaplain at her right hand. Some of her people guessed perhaps that she spoke more loudly than usual in order to make certain everyone knew she was talking of ordinary, every-day castle affairs; but everyone in the hall drew confidence from her air of calm unconcern.

When the noise began outside they all looked instinctively at the duchess, not towards the doors.

She raised her voice to command: 'Be still. Do not move.' She stood up. 'Two of you, see what is the trouble.'

As they went to the doors Richard ran across the gallery to the wall slit which overlooked the town, and saw a muddled picture which made no sense; just flames and smoke against the falling dusk. And an equally senseless noise came through the slit as well; a confusion of muffled shrieks and screams and cries.

He ran to the gallery-edge and shouted: 'Madam, Ludlow is afire! Ludlow is afire!'

His mother had time to look up at him before the doors crashed back and a fully-armoured figure flailed his way into the hall, using the flat edge of his battle sword as a staff.

There was a scream; then shouts, curses, the crash of overturned forms. Bat had begun to yelp excitedly. Richard still shouted from the gallery.

The duchess's voice cut through it all. 'Be silent, all of you!'

9

she cried. 'Richard, come down here at once.' Then she turned to the armoured figure whom she had recognized immediately by his emblazoned surcoat. 'Well, my lord of Buckingham?'

'Call off your men, sister-in-law,' he cried.

'This is a surrendered garrison. No one will harm you.' Then she added scornfully: 'Not with fists and table-knives!'

The Duke of Buckingham was clanking towards her when Richard came through the gallery door. He ran to his mother. 'Madam, take care!'

'Softly, Dickon! It is your uncle. Your Uncle Humphrey of Buckingham.'

Richard began to bow stiffly, then stopped. 'But Uncle Buckingham . . .'

'Is Lancastrian,' finished his mother coldly. 'Yes!'

Buckingham lifted his nose-guard. 'Proud Cis you always were and always will be,' he muttered, but not bad-temperedly.

Cecily stiffened. 'York needs no help from Margaret's lackeys.'

'On the contrary, you do.' Buckingham looked up and down the hall. 'You'd best be out of here directly, Madam.'

Cecily, as if to prove her right, sat down again. 'This is a surrendered fortress. We are under the king's protection. I have his word.'

'Cecily,' urged the duke good-naturedly. 'Our interests are opposed. We follow different loyalties. That we are cousins is of no account. Cousins fight cousins by nature. But your sister, shrew though she is, happens to be my wife. And I owed it to York to come and warn you; if necessary to protect you and your little ones.'

He smiled at Richard. Immediately Richard smiled back.

'Margaret would not dare . . .' began Cecily.

'She has dared,' continued the duke. 'Henry is my anointed king and has my sword, but his queen . . .' He shrugged. 'She is a vengeful woman. The Calais men have been restless all day. They claim the town and castle as their right.'

Cecily stared at him unbelievingly.

To convince her, Buckingham shouted to the men at the great doors: 'Open the doors! Open the doors! You will see and you will hear.'

Richard squeezed his mother's hand. 'Ludlow is afire,' he repeated. 'I saw it.'

And then they all saw, through the open doors. Not in detail: merely a red glow above the dark outline of the keep and Mortimer's Tower. And from beyond they heard the shrieks and screams, the terrifying sounds of pillage.

For a moment there was a silence in the hall. The servants and the household still looked to Cecily, each thinking of what he had heard of the sack of French towns by the English. Then a girl began to wail.

The duchess turned to Buckingham. 'Our thanks to you, brother-in-law, for your warning and your protection.' She turned back to her people. 'Hide where you can away from the castle,' she cried. 'The woods are thick —'

Suddenly her voice was drowned. A yell from outside, and then another, told them that the Calais men had come. At once the hall was in confusion. Both men and women panicked. Some rushed to the chapel – in the pathetic hope of sanctuary; others instinctively ran to the main armoury although it was stripped of weapons. The cooler heads waited in shadows by the gate, hoping to slip out into the castle yard and thence to the woods. Some were too crazed to do anything but run here and there like frantic sheep; others stood still and sat still, one even lay prone waiting: all of them human rabbits mesmerized by a horde of human stoats.

Buckingham slammed down his nose-guard when the first red-faced Calais man appeared at the doors. 'Your solar, madam,' he suggested calmly. 'You can do nothing for your people now.'

George and Margaret and Richard slept sometimes during that long night of slaughter; huddled together in the truckle at the foot of their mother's bed. They slept because they were children exhausted by fright – but then they dreamed, and their dreams were knitted with reality.

Richard found it impossible to tell where one finished and the other began.

Did he dream that the Frenchmen attacked the solar door although Uncle Buckingham and Tom and other men were standing guard outside? No, this was no dream because his uncle's voice was clear,

11

his menaces too real to belong to dreams. Yet, at the same time, his mother made them all get up and stand behind her in a row . . . a stupid long row, long row, long row . . . as though they were dancers.

Certainly he must have dreamt that Bat barked from beyond the door. Why was she not in the solar? Surely she had come with them from the hall? She and Tom? Tom would fetch her. . . . But no, Tom was with Uncle Buckingham; swinging swords, cutting flesh . . .

Awake now, surely? – because their nurse Anne Coux and all his mother's ladies were heating possets. He could smell the milk and spices. Such a strange sense to have in the nostrils when in the ears there was that din, that din, that din . . .

Then, equally strange, the clear voice of a priest broke through the pandemonium: '*Suscipe, Domine, servum tuum in locum sperandae sibi salvationis a misericordia tua . . .*'

Amen! Amen! Say it aloud: 'Amen! Amen!' Listen . . .

'*Libera, Domine, animam servi tui ex omnibus periculis inferni . . .*'

From every danger of hell.

Lord Jesu!

Day broke at half past six. Through red-rimmed eyes Richard looked from the solar casement into the inner bailey. It was littered with the bodies of men and women and children. The glitter of red hair caught his eye. He knew whose it was. No one in Ludlow had such carroty hair as Hob the chief porter's son. But the head was by itself – complete, like a red-topped turnip – unattached to anything. Hob's head had been chopped from his body. Quickly Richard turned away, and his eye stopped at a body spreadeagled on the curtain wall. It was a woman; half naked. Her throat had been cut, and her knees. . . . Richard looked away again.

'Lord Richard!' It was Anne Coux behind him, her round face crinkled with sadness. 'Come, love, from the casement. You must break your fast before we go.' She gave him a cup of beer and bread.

He pushed it away. He still felt sick. Where were they going?

No Mass? Were the priests dead, too? No Mass! And where could they go?

Impulsively the nurse hugged him. She cried a little.

'Anne, I feel sick,' he said.

Behind him they were talking, talking, talking. Endless talking. . . .

'I shall escort you myself to Coventry,' Buckingham was saying. 'The bulk of my footmen lie south of the town. The few who came with me last night—' He stopped, and shrugged.

'Thank you, my lord.' Cecily's voice was toneless. She turned to her ladies. 'The castle is . . . The castle has been stripped, and these are our sole possessions. But select the baggage carefully. Bring only what is necessary. Anne Coux, will you carry Meg? And George, take your young brother's hand.'

Richard backed away. 'Not George,' he said. 'Tom shall take me, Tom.'

George tried to seize his hand. Richard yelped. 'No! no! Not you! Tom shall take me.'

Cecily and the nurse exchanged glances, then both looked to Buckingham.

Suddenly he chuckled, caught Richard by the waist and sent him spinning in the air; caught him again, and sat him on his shoulder. 'You're too particular, young Dickon! So I shall carry you to Coventry myself.'

Half-frightened, half-delighted Richard hesitated. 'But you are a duke, my lord. I have a man to carry me.'

'And you are a prince, young Dickon! Right burden for a duke to bear.'

George began to howl with envy until Anne Coux, with her one free hand, shook him to silence. 'Yellow-for-yolks-and-butter-cups-and-jealousy, Lord George,' she cried, shaking him up and down.

And quickly the duchess said to Buckingham. 'Now, my lord. Now. We must leave at once. The ladies will follow.'

'But Tom,' Richard was saying as his uncle carried him through the door. 'Tom – and Bat. We cannot leave without . . .'

And then he saw why the great Duke of Buckingham carried him from Ludlow.

As though it was from a long distance he heard his mother crying: 'I told you! Holy Mary! I *told* you to move them!' He heard her, just, though he was pleading at the same time, the same time, the same time to the duke: 'Oh, stop! I beg you, uncle. Stop! oh, stop!'

But Buckingham went on; and they left outside the solar door all that Richard had ever loved: Tom, with a long, wide gash across his face, and the carcase of a brachet bitch with blood upon her teeth.

III

Ann, Duchess of Buckingham, rated everyone: first her husband, for risking the queen's displeasure; then, like an angry wasp, she turned on her sister Cecily, for being the cause of so much vexation; then George, for speaking out of turn; then Richard, for not speaking at all; and, in passing, poor Anne Coux, merely for being there; then back again to Buckingham.

'Idiot! to bring them direct to Coventry! The greater part of our family is out against the king, and you act like a moonstruck squire, a loon. So far our loyalty has not been questioned.'

Cecily pursed her lips. 'No,' she said icily.

'You sneer at loyalty, Madam?' flashed back her sister. 'I believed you valued it – or else you would not have come to this. And is yours to York more righteous than ours to Lancaster? of higher quality? a finer, rarer, more constant virtue?'

'Have done, ladies,' murmured the duke.

But his wife had not finished with him yet. 'Idiot!' she repeated. 'To bring them away without the queen's consent . . . !'

'I sent her word,' he put it mildly. 'Henry gave them to my custody, and this is his headquarters.'

'It was folly. . . .'

'It was gentle, sister,' interrupted Cecily. 'I had no wish to meet your hell-cat queen so soon after the slaughter of my people.'

Ann paused. Then she smiled. Like much else about her it was lop-sided, but it showed her real concern. 'Cecily,' she murmured. 'You know well we fight for Henry not his queen. She . . . she does much wrong to England.' Then, abruptly, she was her old self. 'Come, we must be doing!' She pushed her lord. 'Be stirring, Buckingham. There is much to do. Come sister, we shall find room for the children. . . . Nurse! I declare you are in my way! Standing there clutching your baggage like an old carpenter! And, boy; yes, you, the fat one, do not ogle me. I am your aunt.' She began to sweep from the hall, and snapped to Richard. 'Don't lag, boy, stir yourself!' Then to Cecily: 'Is this your youngest? a pallid prince to be sure.

But then, if this nurse has had the care of him I am barely surprised. . . .'

Anne Coux glowed like a cinder with indignation, but she knew her place. Richard, too, was alarmed by his formidable aunt. Only George, generally so sensitive to criticism, found her a fascinating addition to the family.

Unaware of his admiration, and, in any case, indifferent to it, the Duchess prodded him before her through the door. 'Move faster, porker. We shall have that fat off you in Coventry. Bread and water, sister, eh?' She chuckled; then added seriously to Cecily: 'We may expect the queen here soon for Parliament, and I shall ask if I may be your guardian.'

When the king returned to Coventry he sent his squire Sir Richard Tunstall with kind messages for Duchess Cecily, and gifts for the boys. There was a half-sword for George and a jewelled pomander in which to burn strong herbs against the plague. Richard received a Missal.

Buckingham smiled when he saw the gifts, and swore they were proof the queen had had no hand in Henry's action. His lady was equally certain that the queen had prompted it. Margaret was subtle, and quite aware of the storm she had raised by the sack of Ludlow. An inexpensive expression of goodwill through the king was good insurance – and, if necessary, she could deny any part in it.

But Richard used his Missal to pray for Tom, and sometimes, secretly, to pray for Bat as well although he knew this was wrong. He was for ever begging coins: from his mother, from the duke's steward and chaplain, from his uncle Buckingham: so much so that they called him the little almsman and asked if he was amassing gold to outweigh the royal treasury. He never explained, merely thanked them, and ran off to buy candles for Tom. Candle after candle before Our Lady, with the same, same prayer: *Requiem aeternam dona ei, Domine, et lux perpetua luceat ei. Requiescat in pace. Amen.*

This was all he did and all he thought about as October gave way to November and the Coventry Parliament formally condemned his family to beheading, deprivation or imprisonment.

Lacking squires the boys were wholly in Anne Coux's care, and she was overworked. Her days were filled, and then each night her sleep was broken by the need to comfort Richard. 'Tom! TOM! TOM!' he would scream, awaking from his nightmare – and there was Anne to soothe and comfort him; tell him he had been dreaming, that the dark night was real and dreams were not, that what had happened was done, finished with, completed, for nothing can be repeated. She would light a second rushdip and coax him to look at the painted pictures in his Missal; point to the glittering picture of Our Lord in Glory, of His Mother hearing the angel's message, of Mary Magdalene weeping on Christ's feet, her head encircled by gorgeous butterflies, of holy Father Benedict in his cell. But Richard barely glanced at these, and turned quickly to dwell on other pictures – of Laurence roasting on his gridiron, Edmund stuck with arrows, Lazarus rising from the tomb, Barbara being beheaded by her angry father in a tower room, her long hair a vivid scarlet. 'Hob!' said the boy whenever he saw St Barbara. 'Hob!'

So Anne went to the Duchess Cecily with her anxieties. 'He is sick, my lady.'

'How, sick?'

'He will talk of nothing but Ludlow . . .' The nurse hesitated. 'He dreams foul dreams, wakes screaming, calling for his Tom. Nothing else ever touches him, good or bad. He barely listened to the good news from Ireland and that Lord Edward is in France. Nor did he pay any attention when I told him we were soon to move to Tonbridge. He is oyster-shut to everything, my lady.'

The duchess considered. Then she said: 'He has been too much alone; and, of all my children, he is . . . he is the most sensitive.' She stood up and walked away from the nurse. 'I should have kept him to me at this time, and taught him to love me as he loved his Tom.'

'It is not too late, my lady.'

'But it is, Anne, it is.' The duchess turned and went back to her chair. 'What am I to him now? A source of authority, and some-times a source of coins to buy his little candles.' She was silent for a time, then asked more questions. Finally she said. 'Both boys have been over-idle here. With George it did not matter.' She shrugged. 'He has filled his time with eating. But with Richard it was different. He needs the lessons, exercises, something to occupy his mind and fill the day.' She stood up. 'At Tonbridge it will be easier. I shall appoint a squire for both boys and a clerk to tutor them.

And you shall have the rest you deserve, Anne Coux. You have served us well in these difficult days. Be sure it will be different at Tonbridge.'

✳

Cecily was right in this. Everything was different at Tonbridge. Being accustomed to ample freedom and the liberty to order her own affairs, she found imprisonment tedious. It was also uncomfortable because Buckingham had remained with the king, and – lacking a target for her nagging – Ann took to scolding Cecily when she felt ill-humoured. But there were compensations: chiefly the good news from York in Dublin, that soon he would return to claim his rights; and the news from France where her eldest son, Edward, and her nephew, Warwick, were gathering an army. The burghers of Calais had received their Captain warmly, much to the concern of the soldiers home from Ludlow. Their faint hope of being left alone proved futile. Warwick had sworn vengeance, and he had it. He weeded the traitors out from the citizens of Calais, lined them up before the Castle, gave them short justice, and hanged the lot, over three hundred of them. Secretly Cecily was a little shocked at his cold-bloodedness, but she defended it when her sister railed at him as a ruthless savage. 'He learnt your queen's lesson, that is all,' she said, and left the room to visit her children.

They were with their tutor, a clerk named Sparrow.

'You are keeping them busy, Master Sparrow?'

'I am, my lady.'

'And they have made progress?'

'In grammar a little.' The clerk hesitated. He was a good scholar, but worldly and ambitious for preferment, and knowing this would come faster from an elder brother he was inclined to favour George more than Richard. 'I may say that Lord George is quick to learn, and shows an aptitude. Yes, an aptitude. But Lord Richard is withdrawn, my lady. He daydreams, is somewhat sulky.'

Cecily looked at him sharply. 'Then we shall see,' she said, and to his astonishment she at once catechised the boys in their Latin syntax.

George stumbled and made great blunders, while Richard barely

18

faltered. The clerk was scarlet with embarrassment; and indignation, too. It was unheard of for great ladies to have learning and such learning.

'Your face betrays you, Master Sparrow,' said the duchess when she had finished. 'You find it alarming for a woman to be lettered and know more than the Book of the Knight of La Tour-Landry?' Her eyes narrowed. 'In fact I think you believe it is indecent.'

'No no your grace!' The tutor fluttered his fingers like iris leaves.

'At Raby in my childhood the winter days were short,' she went on. 'We learnt, of course, the gentle arts, but our father had the odd notion that ladies should be adorned with jewels of knowledge as well as jewels of gold.'

'Commendable,' stammered Master Sparrow.

'And so we learnt the rudiments; no more. We did not for example hear much of this Aristotle.' She regarded him shrewdly. 'The ornament of your New Learning, is he not?'

'Hardly, my lady. Barely.' The tutor had no idea how to answer such a perilous question. Did she, could she possibly know that the master's logic and metaphysics still threatened Christian theology? Or was she subtly warning him: bidding him keep her sons fast to orthodoxy and free of his Oxford nonsense? It was impossible to tell, and he could be sure of nothing save that his own position was delicate and that she was the world's abomination, a learned woman.

Richard answered for him. 'We have learnt of St Thomas Aquinas, Madam.'

Amused, his mother turned to him. 'So, Dickon! And what did you learn? No; George, you tell me.'

Her third son regarded her with dumb dismay.

'Your pupil with aptitude, Master Sparrow!' snapped the duchess. 'Tell me, Dickon.'

Like a trained bird he repeated: 'The *Summa Theologica* of St Thomas Aquinas joins faith with reason.'

'Good!' she nodded. 'And what does it mean?'

'I – I do not know, Madam.'

'But Master Sparrow will teach you, eh?' said his mother eyeing the frightened tutor.

He did not dare to commit himself and so he merely muttered, ducked a bow to the duchess, plucked at the bands on his scholar's gown, and scowled at George.

'Your tutor is displeased with you,' said the duchess to George.

19

'And after his account of your quickness in learning I am barely surprised. You are an idler, George. Correct it. I shall hope to hear of an improvement in your progress very soon.'

George had the wit not to reply. Instead he smiled at her – that dazzling, charming smile which always softened anger. But this time it did not affect his mother. Having said her piece she looked away to Richard.

'Well done, Dickon. Keep to your books. They are friends even in prison, and they never turn traitor.'

Encouraged by her approval Richard found the words to ask: 'Madam, what is the book you spoke of? the Book of the Knight . . .'

'Of La Tour-Landry,' she finished for him, and with a smile she explained. 'An abcedary of manners, little one. But for ladies only.' She tapped him lightly on the cheek but to her distress he flinched.

Why should he do this? She forced the smile to remain on her face, and then abruptly left the room, pausing beyond the heavy curtains at the doorway to wonder at the boy's instinctive reaction. Was she, his mother, so distant a figure that he feared her touch?

Her train of thought was broken by George's voice behind her.

'Our scholar! Our own saucy schoolman!' Anger made the boy's voice shrill. 'Dick, you fawn like a beggar . . . a beggar!'

'Lord George!' It was the tutor trying to mollify his angry charge.

George turned on him as well. 'I care nothing for your learning, master clerk. Nor anything for you. Get me the dish of apples from the window.'

There was a brief silence. Cecily found herself clenching her fists.

'Obey me, dog,' George cried. 'I am your lord. Fetch the apples!'

Cecily spun round and put out her hand to separate the curtains. But something made her hesitate, and she heard George round on his brother for the second time.

'You sicken me. You scrape the favour of our lady mother like a mealy-mouthed clerk! Jesu! the queen was right to say only Holy Church could stomach such a sickly, crippled carcase.'

Cecily winced as she heard George hitting Richard; winced as though she felt the pain herself. But she did nothing to stop it, and merely walked softly away, knowing full well that George's malice and vengeance would only be enlarged if she showed herself at that moment. There were other, easier, more effective ways.

She returned to the small solar and sent for her chaplain.

'I have a task for you, Sir John, if you will be so kind.'

The chaplain bowed.

'First, Master Sparrow must be sent back to Oxford, and directly.'

'Very well, your grace.'

'And for the time being you will keep my sons to their lessons. But there is something further. Would you make inquiries in the tiltyard and discover how things lie between Lord Richard and Lord George?'

'How things lie?' The chaplain was puzzled.

She explained; told him all she had just heard; asked him to be discreet in his inquiries.

He bowed a second time and left her. Within an hour he had returned.

'It is as you feared, your grace. Lord George misses no opportunity to humble his brother in their daily exercises. Misses no opportunity.'

'So!' said Cecily. 'He is a bully.'

'As many are,' said the chaplain evenly. Evidently he considered she was making too much of the matter. 'What shall you do, my lady?' he asked, more in politeness and to humour his mistress than out of any interest. Yet, as she slowly revealed her plan to him, he found himself admiring her sagacity.

'I will write the letter at once,' he promised when she had finished; and not long afterwards a courier was galloping north-west with a plea from Cecily to one of her many Neville cousins. It asked that his son, a boy of Richard's age, should be allowed to learn his lessons with the young Plantagenets in their confinement.

So Peter Neville came to Tonbridge – a bright-eyed, laughing lad of seven – and very soon the duchess's neat plan had proved successful. Peter and Richard became fast friends and presented a united front to George's bullying. They were friends not simply because they were of an age. The reason was more subtle. Each of them had a handicap: Richard his tiny stature and his raised right shoulder; Peter, a stammer which sometimes was hardly noticeable, but which up to that time had always been painful to him. Their handicaps bound them together with a close tie of sympathy.

IV

In the spring of 1460 Richard dreamed his last Ludlow nightmare. He confided it to Peter, and Peter shyly returned the confidence by confessing his own hell.

'I used to dream of hounds. Great hounds that tore me all about my head. But here at Tonbridge the dream has gone.'

Richard nodded sympathetically, but he was thinking what a world of difference lay between dreams and the nightmare of recaptured reality. 'But mine, too, came from what I once saw,' Peter added, sensing what Richard was thinking.

'What you saw?' Richard was horrified.

'Once. Yes. At h-h-h-home.' The memory was making him stammer.

'No need to tell me,' said Richard quietly, and quite genuinely he did not want to know.

But Peter told him all the same, stammering painfully – how his father's brother, a crazed old veteran from Agincourt, had sometimes hunted men with mastiffs for his pleasure; setting the quarry off an hour ahead of hounds; scenting him out of hiding places, even battering down doors to give the mastiffs their reward; and how, once, a wretch had gone to ground in a cruck-house not far from Peter's home and he by accident had seen his uncle's huntsmen fire the cruck-house and wait till the hunted man burst from the door – to be bitten, clawed, savaged, and eaten.

Richard crossed himself at the end of this awful tale. Then he asked. 'But why did your father allow it?'

Peter stared at his feet. He did not answer.

'Why did he allow it?' repeated Richard.

'My uncle was not always mad,' said Peter slowly. 'But cruelty c-c-c-crazed him. And . . .' He spread his fingers. 'And he was the l-l-l-lord; not my father.'

Richard accepted this; for even if the lord is a fiend, he is still lord. 'How did he die?' he asked at length.

Peter gave a wan smile. 'At Mass. Right in the middle of Mass. Like a true, noble, g-g-g-gentle lord!'

They lay in silence after this; then Richard thumped Peter on the back.

'Come to the tiltyard,' he invited. 'We'll practise at quarter-sticks.'

'On such a spring day?' Peter objected, closing his eyes. 'Let us rest here. The grass smells good.'

'No!' Richard sat up. 'I mean one day to be as strong as George.' Peter noted the real seriousness in his friend's voice and opened his eyes. 'As strong as anyone,' went on Richard. 'I shall exercise and practise swordplay and tilting and fighting with mace and staff and pike. I shall work at riding, running, leaping, wrestling and swimming till my body grows and I'm the tallest in the kingdom. I shall train until my arms are strong as iron bands, my legs like tree-trunks. I shall be a giant.'

Peter closed his eyes again. 'Much easier to pray for it,' he suggested.

'That I shall do, too.' He jumped to his feet. 'Come to the tiltyard!'

'No!'

Richard seized Peter's arms and heaved. 'To the tiltyard!'

'No!'

They struggled, pulled and tugged at each other, and rolled like puppies on the grass until a long shadow fell across them. It was Sir John the chaplain.

'Richard,' he said. 'Your lady mother asks for you. And Peter Neville.'

'Now?'

'Now!' The priest walked away.

The boys looked at each other. Richard shrugged. Then they both followed the priest into the castle.

Cecily was brisk. It allowed her to hide her feelings.

'George, Richard. Your uncle the Cardinal has sent word you are to go to Canterbury.'

Quickly she told them the rest; how, unknown to her, Edward of March had requested the Archbishop to care for his young brothers, and they were to leave at once for his household in Canterbury. They would not see her until York won his rights in England.

George was gleeful. Tonbridge bored him and he craved for fresh excitements. But Richard was downcast. Cecily wondered if he could possibly share a scruple of her feelings. Never before had she been so close to her younger boys. There would be heart-ache for her in

23

the separation; and Tonbridge with only her ladies and bad-tempered Ann for company would be more tedious than ever. That Richard was so crestfallen showed his attachment to her.

'You do not want to go, Dickon?' she prompted, taking a mother's comfort from his unhappy face.

He looked at the ground when he replied. 'Not without Peter, and . . .'

He hesitated, and Cecily shut her eyes to conceal her disappointment.

'And?' she said.

'Madam,' he burst out. 'I have something. . . . It is hidden. Nothing of value . . . But I wish to take it with me.'

'Then you shall,' she said, adding with a smile. 'And Peter goes with you.'

'Why?' burst out George.

'It is my wish,' said his mother coldly. 'Your manners, George, are gross.'

George reddened; then wore his sulky, pouting look. He tried to follow Richard from the solar, but was bidden to stay where he was.

When Richard returned he carried a small wallet of coarse cloth. George eyed it curiously until his mother sharply called for his attention. She warned them all that they would find many king's men in the household of the Cardinal. 'Be courteous and obedient, but never hear anything against your House, and never speak against it. Be loyal, always, to York.'

They bowed, and kissed her hand in turn.

'George, you will take my greetings and my humble duty to your uncle of Canterbury. Now, make your farewells to your aunt . . . No, Dickon, stay one moment longer.'

George and Peter bowed again and left the solar.

'Is it a great secret from me?' she said, gently, nodding at the wallet.

His face pinkened. 'It is nothing, Madam.'

She turned to the chaplain. 'Sir John, if you would kindly leave us?'

He moved away towards the window.

'Truly, Madam,' said Richard breathlessly. 'It is nothing.'

Then he showed her.

Her heart moved as she was taken back so many years to her

childhood in the north country, where she too had made a magpie collection. Hers was of ribbons, bits, a brooch, the treasures of a little girl. His treasures were less gaudy: a pine cone, a red pebble and a white pebble, a scrap of parchment, a thong-end, the tip of a drinking-horn, a goose's breast-bone, and two little slabs of wood bound round with cord. She picked this out, and gravely looked to him for his permission. He nodded. She undid the cord, and found between the boards a fresh-pressed orchid flower.

'It is pretty, Dickon.'

'From by the stream,' he explained. 'Peter and I have found an army of them.'

She bound up the boards again, returned them to the wallet. 'Thank you. Keep them all safe.'

'Yes, Madam.' Richard turned to go; stopped, and suddenly kissed her lightly on the cheek.

❋

George was as cunning as he was curious. He dearly wanted to know what Richard had in his wallet, yet he was willing to wait until time made his brother less careful. But Richard was equally determined to keep his treasures hidden.

In fact both of them forgot the matter in the busyness of their new life at Canterbury because every fraction of the day was accounted for from daybreak till dusk, and they were in the company of other boys being schooled at Christchurch Priory. Theoretically these boys, like Peter Neville, were entirely free, whereas the young Plantagenets were not; but they all had to endure the same strict regimen.

Though George's easy and idle existence had so far depended entirely on his skill at charming the ladies, in the company of other boys he soon began to enjoy himself. He had the good sense not to try lording it over them as a prince of York, and being adept at games despite his fatness he soon won their approval. This meant that he saw less and less of Richard and Peter, which allowed them to enjoy themselves as well.

Most of all they enjoyed the daily half-hour between compline and bed when Dom Antony, the junior chaplain, told stories to the younger boys. Sometimes they sat round him in the cloister, but more often, because this was the no-candle time of the year and the days were very long, he led them outside to the priory garden where they all sat on the ground beneath a walnut tree.

Dom Antony had a passion for radishes, and all through the summer he ate them with the gusto of a heron swallowing fish: but though his stories were invariably punctuated by the munching and crunching of his favourite vegetable no priest in Canterbury was better at telling them.

More than anything else he loved to tell them about his own native village in Norfolk where there was the famous shrine of Our Lady of Walsingham, at its centre a simple cottage, just like the Holy House at Nazareth. Each boy who heard about it longed to go to Walsingham, as much as anything because Dom Antony had a younger brother there called Edmund, an Austin canon at the Priory who – and this seemed hardly believable – could tell better stories than Dom Antony.

One evening he had been retelling this story and was insisting on his brother's powers as a story-teller when Peter suddenly plucked at Richard's sleeve. 'Look,' whispered his friend; and Richard, following his eyes, saw George walking quickly beside the wall at the other side of the garden. He must have slipped away from the monk who supervised the bigger boys at that time of the evening.

'Look!' whispered Peter more urgently. 'Look in his hand!'

Then Richard was on his feet. George was carrying his wallet of treasures.

'I had it hidden!' He clenched and unclenched his fists.

'Then he must have seen you hide it,' said Peter quietly. 'Sit down, Richard. We'll get it from him later.'

'Later —!'

Richard was already running across to George – through raised herb plots and beds of marigolds.

George heard him coming, and at first looked alarmed. Then he grinned. 'Little Dick has come for his bag of rubbish!' he mocked.

'Give it to me!' Richard was sweating, his voice hoarse.

George held out the wallet, snatched it back again. And he did this twice before Richard hit him as hard as he could in the chest. George was not hurt, but suddenly he was angry. Deliberately he threw the wallet on the ground, and when Richard bent to pick it

26

up, kicked him hard in the buttocks. But Peter was at him now; tugging at his arm and shouting. And another small boy was on his back. George hurled them off and, crimson with rage, he stamped again and again on the wallet; pulping it, altering its shape.

'Lord George!' It was Dom Antony, spluttering small shreds of white and scarlet as he shouted.

George turned on the priest with fist upraised – and what he might have said or done in his hysterical rage no one could guess, but just at that moment his eye was caught by two men hurrying through the garden door from the outer cloister. It was the sub-prior, leading a gentleman in half-armour. They looked round the garden, saw Dom Antony and the knot of boys, and ran towards them.

'There is word for the Lords George and Richard,' panted the sub-prior.

'They are here, Father,' said Dom Antony, nodding curtly at the brothers, and was about to add a complaint when, to his astonishment, the gentleman in half-armour fell on to one knee.

'Lord George, Lord Richard, I bring you news!'

Richard heard it all wearing an expression of stone: that his brother Edward, with Warwick and Salisbury, had landed at Sandwich and taken London. That they had smashed Queen Margaret's army up in Northamptonshire; killed Duke Humphrey of Buckingham, and captured the king himself; that the Yorkist lords had established a government and now only waited for the Duke of York to come from Ireland.

'My lords, your imprisonment is over,' finished the messenger. 'You are free!'

There was a crackle of excitement amongst the boys, but Richard merely turned away and went to where his wallet lay. He said not a word. Peter followed him.

'It's good news, Dick,' he said eagerly. 'You're free.'

'Free!' Richard began to sort through the wallet. 'Don't you understand? I want to stay here. I don't want to leave Canterbury.' He threw aside the goose's breast-bone which was broken, and he added bleakly. 'But they'll make me. Oh, yes! they'll make me.'

'But I'll be with you, Dick; that is, if your lady mother lets me come. And London's a fine place.'

'Maybe!' Richard went on sorting through his treasures, and then suddenly it occurred to him that the uncle who had been kind to him at Ludlow now lay dead. He crossed himself.

V

For two long months it rained and rained and rained. No one alive could remember such weather in high summer. The swollen streams and rivers made fords impassable, smashed moorings and staithes, and washed away bridges and houses. The peas and beans, the wheat and rye were rotting in the ground; and the poor were silent in their sooty hovels and cruck-houses, thinking of the lean winter that lay ahead, worse still, of the famine-gap that must follow in the spring.

The Lancastrians, adept at propaganda, made good use of the disaster, letting the rumour run that the saints slept and God wept over England to see her anointed king imprisoned. But the rumour dried up abruptly with the weather late in September, when the Duchess of York sent to Canterbury for her sons and Peter Neville.

Together they rode north to London, and their progress showed what a difference it made to be right at the centre of the party in power. All along the route they were welcomed, fêted, and presented with gifts of plate, and wine, and honey, and flowers, and cobnuts and fruit from the Kentish orchards. Gentlemen rode out with their families to meet the Duchess at every hamlet and village along the way.

Sir Favor, Peter's father, met them at Eltham to escort the party the remainder of the way. 'Cousin,' said the duchess, 'you come at the right moment; my chaplain and I are tetchy with each other. He knows my life story, my views, my private likes and dislikes, and my habits; and, believe me, I know his. He, I'll guarantee, thinks of me as a temperamental witch; and to me he is a staid black mole!' And turning to her smiling chaplain she asked: 'Am I not right, Sir John?'

'Of course, your grace,' he said, and added a neat sting, 'But, then, you always are!'

She laughed and turned back to Sir Favor to tell him her freshly widowed sister had lost all spirit. 'Poor Ann! She mopes at Tonbridge. Send your lady to her, Favor, if you will. It would be a kindness.'

She told him how much Peter had done for her taciturn Richard, drawing him out, prodding him out of his graveness into laughter, helping him defend himself against George's bullying. And sharp – why, Peter was a needle, and more than a match for George. Only that morning one of her ladies had overhead George teasing his younger brother, mocking his homesickness for Canterbury, and suggesting that Peter's father might exchange Richard for Peter – hunchback for stammerer, a fair bargain. And while Richard sat his horse silent and miserable, George had continued the attack by asking Peter in all seriousness if his father would agree to the suggestion. 'And, Favor,' Cecily went on, laughing at the memory, 'your boy showed equal seriousness, and said no, he thought it unlikely you would agree to house the brother, be he so good and gentle, of a fat-bellied lout.'

'Eh?' muttered Sir Favor, mildly alarmed. 'He should not have said that.'

'Why not? Peter is good for both my sons. And he said more, Favor, with his charming stammer on the d's and p's, calling George a dumpling, and the plumpest prince of pigs in Christendom.'

Sir Favor had certain views on what is and what is not due to a Plantagenet prince, but at this even he himself could not refrain from chuckling.

He looked ahead where the three boys were riding together in the van. 'They seem happy enough in each other's company at present,' he said.

'Indeed, yes. It is as I told you, Favor. Peter is sweet medicine for both my sons. They bear each other when he is there.'

'Then he shall stay with you, cousin. That is, as long as you wish.'

She chuckled. 'It might be for ever, I warn you,' she said.

❋

Richard gasped when they came up to London Bridge. Never before had he seen such a marvel. It had mercers' and haberdashers' shops on either side of the highway with living-quarters above them, and was longer and grander than any bridge in the world.

Peter described it as proudly as a proprietor. 'It's sitting on twenty pillars,' he shouted. 'And listen to the water roar!'

The current breasting the piers did indeed roar, and navigating through the arches was dangerous work, only for skilled and licensed watermen.

As they clopped to the north side Peter pointed to a fortress with battlements a little way upriver. 'There's Baynard's Castle!' he shouted.

George nodded. He had been there before. This, though, was Richard's first sight of his family's London house. But even standing in his stirrups he could not see it properly because of the forest of masts and cranes which sprouted from the wharves on that busy reach. Peter distracted him by shouting out that the white keep not far away was the Tower of London, where they said the king was being held, a prisoner in his own capital. Richard barely had a chance to gaze at this fascinating dungeon before Peter was calling him again. 'Come, Dick, we go left.'

The party turned down Thames Street close by the river; past the steelyard, a stone warehouse-cum-fortress belonging to the Easterlings, and past the pool of Queen Hithe. Many alleyways broke on to the street – most of them unpaved, filthy, and clamorous with people, but Richard longed to explore them.

Scavenging kites and ravens wheeled about their heads, and gulls from the river.

'Who lives there?' he shouted to Peter above the noise.

'Everyone!' replied Peter, laughing. 'Half the world!'

George was complaining of the stench, but Richard was too busy to notice it. There was so much to see – the wharves and warehouses, the merchants' halls, so many houses, big and little, some thatched, some tiled, some roofed with wooden shingles; all those spires and towers.

'Only three less than a hundred churches,' yelled Peter as proudly as if he were Bishop of London. 'A score of religious houses. And look at the spire of Paul's!'

They were closer now to the cathedral and, looking up, Richard caught his breath. The spire pointed heavenwards like a forefinger, soaring five hundred feet above Ludgate Hill.

He shook his head like a swimmer getting the water from his ears, for the volume and size of everything was by now almost frightening. The noise, too, was tremendous; the colours rich and glittering; the press of people thick and stinking; the shops and selling-booths stacked and heaped and overspilling with goods.

Richard noticed that the nature of the merchandise changed as they moved west along Thames Street. At the Tower end were the vintners. Then came the honey-merchants, the sea-chandlers, the corn-chandlers. And then they found themselves in the stinking province of the fishmongers and at the gates of Baynard's Castle, their father's London fortress.

'York! York! York!' cheered the citizens excitedly.

'Fishguts!' moaned George, and pinched his nose.

VI

The Duke of York was a rare man amongst his peers. He was neither greedy nor ambitious. In fact at first only a natural wish to vindicate the memory of his attainted father had driven him into the service of the king. But in this service he had succeeded too well and the brilliance of his government in France and Ireland held him to the centre of courts like a fly caught fast in a honeypot. Given his own will he would have liked to live simply at Fotheringhay, to supervise the great collegiate church he was building there, to hunt his own demesne and go eeling in the marshy fens, and there he would have the leisure to enjoy his family and comfort his mind with books and learning. Queen Margaret had made this impossible. Her malice and the misgovernment of her favourites had compelled him to resist them. And as the wars he hated dragged on and on, the men of his wife's family drove him to consider the only safe and lasting solution: to claim the supreme power for himself, both by the force of his arm and by lineal descent. So reluctantly he had come from Ireland with the full arms of England blazoned on his banners and an upright sword borne before him, to go to the Painted Chamber in Westminster and there, urged on by the Nevilles and the needs of England, to lay a hand at last upon the throne. But he would not reign as king, only as Lord Protector. A puzzled parliament had ratified his wish, and then, of its own accord, had enacted that Edward of Wales was disinherited, and that when mad Henry died York himself should wear the crown by proper title.

York demurred at this and had to be persuaded. Eventually they moved him to accept the will of Lords and Commons, and as a sign of his consent he feasted the notables of London at Baynard's Castle.

He sat at the head of the board; a stocky, quiet man with a pugnacious jaw that belied his mild nature. He made great attempts to be affable, but without success. Cecily at his right hand sensed his deep uneasiness.

'My lord,' she said privately. 'Wear your larger smile.'

He pressed her hand. 'Because I am Lord of England, Cis? No: rather because we are together.'

'We are together,' she pointed out, 'only because you *are* Lord of England.'

'Vain, ambitious Neville,' he taunted, chuckling. 'You relish your rank and dignities.'

'Yes,' she said with candour. 'But I enjoy more your company, my lord. We have been separated too long.' She returned the pressure of his hand. 'And this is the first time our family has been grouped at one board.' She could not resist quipping him. 'You see, I have defied the custom of table and arranged them for you in order.'

This was true. There was a space between the Duke and Duchess and the Lord Mayor, but otherwise the other side was filled with their children.

York gave a great roar of laughter. 'In case I should have difficulty in recalling them?' he asked.

She nodded.

'Jesu! I am not so vague a father. Hear me, Cis.' And he proceeded to recount their names. When he reached his youngest son he gave the boy an extra nod. But Richard was always receiving pity. He recognized it at once in all its various disguises, inside and out, upside and down; and not for one minute did he mistake that extra attention from his father as a sign of special favour. He bowed politely to the Duke across the table, but the bleak look in his tiny face betrayed his hurt.

His father was puzzled; he smiled once more at the boy, and again he received the same stiff bow, the same hurt look.

'Cecily,' he said softly. 'Young Dick's a strange lad.'

'Not at all,' she replied evenly. 'He is just eight years old and quite unused to banquets. Probably he is bored. Certainly he dislikes having to sit next to George. And who, at present, would not?' she continued, frowning with distaste at George who was attacking a fowl as though his life depended on it. 'I expect he is missing his friend, young Peter Neville. Moreover, you, my lord, alarm him!'

'I?'

'Of course. You are too mighty altogether.'

'Madam, he is my son.'

'Too mighty altogether,' she repeated, almost as though he had not spoken. 'You are the White Rose himself, and poor Dickon

33

feels he is but a slender little root hidden away in the darkness of the earth.'

Such a poetic fancy put York right out of his depth. He grunted; nodded at his youngest child and gave him a smile so forced that it was half a snarl. Then he turned to do his duty by the Lord Mayor.

Richard sat petrified for a moment, until he realized that his father had already forgotten him, and then looked quickly at his less fearsome mother. She was talking to her brother Salisbury. He relaxed a little; chewed at a piece of meat, but put it down again. His small appetite had been satisfied over an hour before, and his head buzzed with the wine. He wished for the thousandth time that they had not put him with his back to the entertainments, and facing his godfather the Earl of Warwick. Nervously he crumbled pellets of snowbread and flicked them below the table to the hounds which squatted there. He rehearsed what he should say if Warwick did speak to him; prayed hard that he would not. Then, by accident, he himself drew the earl's attention. His finger slipped too quickly from his thumb; a bread pellet meant for the hounds scuttered over the board and landed beside Warwick's plate. Richard flushed crimson.

It was a sign of the earl's acuteness that he noticed something as small as a bread pellet in the middle of so much activity and noise. He picked it up.

'So, Dick,' he said. 'You would feed me!'

'Indeed, my lord . . . I beg your pardon.'

'If you had thrown your knife – as some would like to do – I should have considered it discourteous.' He drank from his jewelled cup; and Richard, believing that was the end of the matter, lowered his eyes and cursed himself as a fool. But Warwick went on talking and asked him about Ludlow and how he had found his life at Tonbridge and in Canterbury.

Richard replied in monosyllables.

'Come, Dick,' urged Warwick. 'I am your godfather and your mother's nephew. You have no need to fear me.'

George's mouth was stuffed with meat, but he managed to cut in: 'My lord, he is frightened of everything.'

Warwick merely glanced at George's grease-spotted moon face; and turned back to Richard.

'That, I can see, is not true. No Neville is a coward.' He drank again from his jewelled cup and asked: 'Has your father yet said where he will place you as donzel?'

'No, my lord.'

The earl nodded, and drank more wine. The boy had a sudden hope. Being placed in the household of a great lord or kinsman was the rule for all noble children: the girls to learn courtliness and all the proper accomplishments of ladies; the boys to act first as donzels or henchboys then as squires, be kept at their books, and learn the skills of chivalry and the chase. But for the wars George would have been put out as a donzel three years before. Now it was time for them both to go – and, if he had to be placed anywhere, Richard hoped it would be with this kindly cousin and godfather.

'No, my lord, not yet,' he said again.

Warwick noted the eagerness in his voice. 'Then I shall ask the Lord Protector if you may come to me, at Middleham.'

'And I, sir?' George exploded through a wodge of food.

Warwick regarded him. 'Maybe,' he said, nodded a smile to Richard and turned to talk to his neighbour.

George waited for thirty seconds, then pinched his younger brother in the thigh. 'That for your fawning,' he snapped.

Richard was too excited by the thought of going to Middleham to care much about George, but he paid him back for the pinch. He waited till his brother was busy eating again; then having held out a chunk of meat to a hound below the table-edge, he threw it suddenly on George's lap. The hound snatched at it with a snap of teeth. George was so frightened that he burst into tears.

Edward, the Earl of March, had his young brother George by the arm. 'Our cousin of Warwick tells me you lack manners,' he said softly, twisting the arm. 'That you interrupted his talk' – another twist – 'That you lack loyalty to your family' – a third – 'And that you eat too much' – a fourth.

George, determined not to cry, held his lips fast together and turned violet.

Edward let go of the arm: 'And as for that shindy at the feast . . .'

'Like a stuck pig . . .' said Edmund, Earl of Rutland.

'Exactly.'

'I was startled,' muttered George. 'That hound . . . he almost had me.'

Edward chuckled. 'Well, we'll say no more about it.' Then, seriously, he added: 'But remember, George, if there's one man in this kingdom worth honouring it's the Earl of Warwick.'

George nodded. 'I'll remember.'

'And leave young Dick alone.'

Richard at once looked anxious. Already he adored Edward and Edmund who, once so remote, had burst into his life exactly like the heroes of Dom Antony's stories. His brothers were paladins, gorgeous princes, weathered campaigners, handsome courtiers, brave soldiers. They were everything, and he was nothing; and Edward as the elder had every right to say what he wished – but Richard still looked anxious. This was just the sort of thing that George would remember . . . and avenge.

But George had also fallen slave to his brothers' charms. If they wanted him to be polite to Warwick, eat less, leave Dick alone, do anything – why, then he'd do it, and with a smile.

To Richard's amazement George actually put an arm round his shoulders, and said: 'We're not bad friends, are we, Dick?'

Richard eyed Peter who was grinning from ear to ear. 'No,' he said; and then because he could not believe it himself; he said again 'No!'

Edward smiled. 'Good!' he said; and immediately he became bustling with energy; sending a page with a message to his mother; calling for horses, grooms, escorts and men-at-arms. He had to go to the Strand by Charing – where the bishops had their London palaces. George would go with him on a visit to their lordships of Ely and Salisbury. Edmund was to go to the Tower with messages from the Lord Protector to the king.

Richard believed he was to be left at home and looked downcast until Edmund mounted his horse and invited him to the pommel. He was there in a trice.

'You're agile, little one,' said Edmund surprised; then added kindly: 'And if you hold your head like this,' he demonstrated: 'your top-heavy shoulder would be seen by no one.'

Richard first shouted his farewells to Edward and George who clattered out of the courtyard: then said quietly to Edmund, 'They call me crookback.'

'I know.' Edmund ran his hand over Richard's back. 'But they say it when they want to hurt you, Dick. The truth is your right shoulder's higher than the left: and you stoop to hide it.' He paused a moment to tell Peter to mount on the squire's crupper. Then he urged his young brother: 'It's the stooping that makes you look humped. Sit straight. No, straighter. That's it. And tilt your head a little to the left. Good!' He shouted an order to the escort, switched his mount and they set off beneath the portcullis. 'No, don't relax. Keep yourself straight. Hunchback indeed!'

Out in Thames Street the Londoners looked at the arms on Edmund's banner.

'York,' they chanted; and some of them, recognizing him, called 'Rutland. Rutland.'

Young Richard held firmly to the saddle-bow, his back as straight as a board, his head tilted, just slightly, to the left.

VII

For thirty-five days precisely Richard was as content as a boy can be.

Baynard's Castle was the centre of England; the target gold for couriers, ambassadors, captains, abbots and bishops, landowners and merchants, but this was not the chief cause for his happiness. He wore the fresh honour given him as son to the Lord Protector without artificiality or fuss because, more than any of his brothers and sisters, he had inherited York's natural diffidence and lack of ambition. If they, by instinct, chose to wear gold and scarlet, he and his father, by the same instinct, chose black and silver. Like any boy, he enjoyed the splendour and magnificence of his home, but what gave him the greatest contentment was the sense of belonging, of being a part of his family. Busy as they were, Edward and Edmund didn't overlook their delicate youngest brother. When George was invited to accompany them to the butts or the tiltyard, or to spend half a day in falconry, Richard was asked, too, and Peter as well because he was Richard's friend. They encouraged him in his plan to exercise and train his frail body until it hardened and toughened, and never again did he stoop and show the weakness of his spine, unless he was very tired or thoughtful and forgot what Edmund had told him.

Perhaps, a short time before, he would have been suspicious of their consideration; sensing – without being able to phrase it in words – that it was only charitable pity for his sickliness, or – even worse – the amused tolerance of ordinary, healthy men for a curiosity, a mascot; but his brothers gave him confidence, and made it plain that they enjoyed his company and his merriment. Under their smile the shy, solemn Richard could become as merry a boy as any in London, with a wit unusually sharp and salty for his age; and their kindness could have damaged him, and swollen his head or made him into the family buffoon – but he was saved from this by his high shoulder. No one so sensitive about deformity could ever be a clown.

To the end of his life Richard remembered that halcyon time at Baynard's Castle when York was the Lord Protector. He was often with his brothers, often too with his father and Warwick and his uncle Salisbury. Sometimes when they were all in council, he, George and Peter would ask permission to visit King Henry, and ride off with their own escort of pikemen to the Tower. Henry was much happier away from his shrewish queen, where he could pray, make plans for his colleges at Eton and Cambridge, and play with his tame birds, as much as he pleased. There was no one now to force him to wash, or sign documents, or be agreeable to surly lords; and being half-saint, half-child himself, he would clap delightedly when the boys went to see him, and entertain them with riddles and the ingenious puzzles which he himself invented. They, in turn, grew very fond of him, and often took him little gifts from Baynard's Castle; but somehow they never thought of him as the king: he was their gentle, affectionate friend, no more. York drew all their respect for kingship, because he had the power. His council at Baynard's Castle was the English Court, and occasionally the boys would sprawl in the rushes with a couple of scratching hounds or more, beside his chair, and listen to his judgements and decisions. Most of the grave talk on Church and State was outside their understanding – the granting of lands and honours and livings, the plans of campaign, the affirming of laws, the disposition of supplies. When they were bored with listening, they practised King Henry's puzzles or played other silent games. Richard frequently lay on his back and closed his eyes to imagine his own court of law, where he was plaintiff, defendant and judge in the happy cause of 'Why Richard Plantagenet is to be envied'.

Then one day, at the beginning of December, when Richard was playing this very game of make-believe, his thoughts were scattered by a mighty blow on the table above him. It was his godfather Warwick cursing the queen as a festering boil upon the body of the realm. Richard listened to other angry voices taking up the image, declaring that only lancing and cautery could prevent the spread of her infection. Her energy was unflagging, her methods to regain power unscrupulous: offering the manors, lands and holdings of all declared Yorkists as a bait; guaranteeing full pardon to every outlaw and convicted felon north of the Trent in return for their service in her armies; promising all new recruits the right to pillage their fellow countrymen; hiring adventurers from the Low Countries and France, paying with the royal treasury of England for foreign aid to crush the English; pledging the frontier fortress of Berwick for the support of Scottish troops . . .

Richard and George and Peter eyed each other nervously as the volcano of fury and indignation erupted above their heads. York let it spend itself; contributing nothing until his councillors had said their piece. Then, in a quiet, even voice he declared the time had come to meet the new threats to the safety of the kingdom.

'I ride north to Margaret,' he said and he was obliged to pause while every lord on the council thundered his plea to ride with him. He thanked them and said, 'Edmund, my son, you will come with me; and our cousin of Salisbury.' He turned to his eldest son. 'Edward, you will ride west to Wales. Take with you whom you will; but leave London's governor here.'

'London's governor,' repeated Edward, puzzled:

'My lord of Warwick,' said York; 'Who is appointed guardian of the king, our capital city, and the safety of my family.'

'Your grace,' began Warwick, who dearly wished to join one of the two armies. Then he accepted York's command and bowed. 'As you wish, cousin,' he said.

So on the ninth day of December two small armies marched from the city: Edward of March left first, kneeling on the cobbles at Baynard's Castle for his father's blessing, and then, with his lords and bowmen, footmen and cavalry, to ride west from Ludgate.

Richard watched him go with a small knot gathering in his throat. It hardened even more when his father blessed him and said goodbye, and he could only nod at his smiling brother Edmund as the second army rode away to Bishopsgate and out along Ermine Street to Lincoln and the north.

'If,' said George angrily, 'I had that queen here, now, before me, I should . . .' He broke off, stared at the gatehouse, shook his head, and then, linking arms with Richard and Peter he walked them away.

Richard made no sound, but tears were trickling slowly down his sallow cheeks.

'Come, Dick,' said George. 'We shall ourselves be soldiers soon, and weeping is not manly.' He squeezed his brother's arm, found tears on his own cheeks too, and continued with simple logic: 'But then, we are not yet men.'

VIII

A porter ran through the rain across the courtyard. Richard watched him, leant from the window to see him better, and saw a horseman follow him from the gatehouse. He was mud-splashed from head to foot, and ran awkwardly from saddle-soreness.

'There's a courier,' he said over his shoulder; but Peter and George were concentrating on the game of chequers.

'He's waiting for something,' said Richard. 'Or someone.'

Deep in the game, neither of the others paid the least attention. To his astonishment Richard saw the chaplain run from the gatehouse across the yard. Invariably, at this time of the morning, Sir John said Mass for the York almsmen beyond the gate. Had he been sent for? Yes. The courier was talking, pointing. The chaplain had his back to Richard – and his face was out of sight; but suddenly he seemed to slacken, to sag like a man who is about to fall.

'George, Peter.' Richard's voice was sharp. 'Something has happened.'

'I know,' said George cheerfully. 'Peter's made a bad move.'

'Something has happened,' repeated Richard; and Peter, catching the urgency in his voice, left the chequer board to look out of the window.

'It's only Sir John,' he said.

'But Sir John's at Mass. I mean, he ought to be. He's been sent for. And look at him.'

'Yes,' agreed Peter. 'He looks strange – upset.'

'I'm cheating,' called George, trying to bring his opponent back to the game. But, for the moment, Peter was more interested in the three men at the other side of the yard.

'Dick,' he said suddenly. 'They're going inside.'

The men disappeared from view.

'They're climbing the stairs. Look,' said Richard.

Both boys watched the window-slits in the circular staircase. The men passed the second and third, but didn't reach the fourth.

'They've stopped,' said Peter, 'at the first landing.'

'They've gone to our mother's solar,' called Richard.

'What of it?' replied his brother.

Richard began to pull at his fingers nervously, cracking the joints one by one. 'Something *must* have happened.'

'Maybe,' said Peter. Then he shrugged. 'If it has, we'll hear about it later.' And he returned to the chequer board.

To Richard, waiting at the window, each minute passed like an hour. After fifteen minutes he could stand it no longer, and left the window to watch the game of chequers.

Peter had won the first game; lost the second and the third; George had him cornered. He beamed with triumph.

Peter began to make a move.

'No,' said Richard quietly; and Peter paused to reconsider.

'Don't help him, Dick,' said George. 'Let him work it out himself.'

Richard looked carefully at the board. 'You've won, anyway. It's only a question of time . . .' He stopped abruptly, and listened.

There was the sound of footsteps beyond the curtained doorway. He blanched and whispered: 'What did I tell you?'

Sir John came into the room. His face was grey. As soon as he saw the boys he looked away. 'Lord George,' he said quietly. 'Your lady mother asks for you.'

George looked from Peter to Richard, from Richard to Peter and back to Sir John again. 'Why?' he asked, and his breaking voice slipped into a squeak. 'Is there news?'

'She asks for you at once,' said the chaplain. 'Come.'

And with that he turned and walked from the room.

George followed him, still clutching a white chequer in his hand.

When the footsteps had died away Richard went to the window. 'Why George alone?' he asked angrily.

'Perhaps he is . . . he is in some sort of trouble.' Peter's voice died. It was a lame suggestion, and they both knew it.

'We are all in trouble,' muttered Richard, and afterwards he was silent.

Peter put away the chequers and joined him at the window. 'It's stopped raining. Good.'

Richard shivered a little and moved his cheek against his velvet collar. 'Soon it will snow. Look out there beyond Paul's.'

The sky was pewter coloured, and growing darker all the time.

'Good,' said Peter for the second time. 'There are sledges in the gatehouse. We'll go up to Ludgate Hill. I've heard it said the 'prentices try to reach the Cheap from Blackfriars. They pack the snow . . .'

He stopped abruptly when Richard spun round in anger: 'Leave it! Muzzle yourself this once.'

'Dick,' said his friend gently. 'I know something is wrong. But it's no help to fret.'

'*Fret*!' Richard was in such a blaze of anger that Peter stepped away. 'Did you not see the priest's face! The colour of the sky? – and you prattle of sledging and 'prentices!'

'I prattle,' returned Peter, beginning to be angry, 'just because I know there is bad news.'

For the first time they were quarrelling with bitterness, and Richard recklessly put pitch on to the fire. 'Know! How should you know! I have seen such faces with my own eyes. At Ludlow. At the slaughter – when you were safely in your bed at Eltham.'

Peter was within an inch of hitting him. He wanted to hurt back, and savage Richard with the sort of sarcasm he knew would hurt him most. But he still had a fraction of control, and it was strengthened when he saw Richard tilt his head to the left in final defiance.

'Dick,' he said; and distress made him stammer. 'It is f-f-f-foolish to quarrel.'

The stammer moved Richard more than what he said. The tears of anger in his eyes altered their character, and he hugged his friend.

'I'm sorry,' he said thickly. 'I did not mean . . .'

'It is f-f-f-f-forgotten . . .' began Peter; then, determinedly repeated it without a stammer. 'Forgotten,' he said triumphantly, and put his arm round Richard's shoulders.

They both looked out of the window. The courtyard was still deserted.

'It is this waiting,' said Richard impatiently. 'I cannot bear this waiting.'

Braving the cold they sat beneath the window to play chequers. Snow blew in across the board. It settled in their hair and on their shoulders. Though they were a white chequer short, they played game after game; neither cared who won. They blew away the snow and moved the pieces mechanically, each of them keeping watch out of the corner of his eye.

It was an hour before George and the chaplain came from the tower porch. Both boys saw them simultaneously and both were

44

shocked by George's changed appearance. They sat perfectly still while George and Sir John crossed the yard, heard the footsteps approaching.

Then came George's voice: 'No, Sir John. I shall tell him.' George alone drew back the curtain and came into the room. His face was tear-stained. 'Dick,' he said. 'You were right. There is bad news.' He fumbled for words; then, finding his tongue, he poured out the story.

The Duke of York had kept Christmas at his castle of Sandal, but on Silvester's Day, the Lancastrians broke the Christmas truce, appeared before Sandal and attacked a small foraging party from the castle. It tricked York into riding out to save his men – taking with him a handful of soldiers, his son Edmund, and the Earl of Salisbury.

'And they killed him, Dick.' George swallowed hard and told them the rest. That when the skirmish was finished Edmund was taken prisoner by Lord Clifford – and stuck, like a pig, in revenge for Clifford's father. And their uncle Salisbury, too, was captured and murdered.

The horn sounded for dinner from the hall.

'And they cut their heads off, Dick. All three. Our uncle's, our brother's, and our father's – to spike on York gate.'

Peter moved closer to Richard so that their bodies touched.

'And they capped our father's head with a crown; a crown of straw and paper.'

Again the horn sounded.

Richard looked out of the window, Then he said: 'It is time for dinner.'

IX

Cecily, Duchess of York, was torn with grief, but only the old nurse Anne Coux knew of it, and she, who was about to be pensioned off, became indispensable. She knew precisely when to correct, when to be stern, and she had the rare courage of being able to see her adored mistress's agony and not give way to it herself. She was mother, daughter, friend and confidante in those tragic days of January and early February.

When John Skelton, York's body-squire reached Baynard's Castle, it was Anne Coux who stood in his way. She would not let him enter the duchess's apartments until he had answered some searching questions. How had he escaped? How was it that the master died in battle while the man went scot free? If, she told him, he did not have a convincing explanation for this unlikely miracle he had better take himself off. But Skelton's story had the ring of truth, and Anne permitted him to tell the duchess how his master had been tricked, and hand her the small pathetic mementoes which a man carries when he rides to war.

More couriers followed. Only one brought good news: that Edward of March, now Duke of York, had smashed the western army of Lancastrians in Herefordshire. When he had consolidated his position he would ride to London. But the other couriers brought a series of warnings and pleas for help from loyal Yorkists in the line of Queen Margaret's rapid advance south. She was being true to her promise in allowing pillage. Her soldiers were falling on the country like saracens leaving a thirty-mile wide scene of desolation in their wake. Their progress was a red-painted streak down the map of England, smeared from north to south in a line of fire and blood.

Warwick waited in London until he judged the time was right to ride. Lord Mayor Lee and the city fathers urged him to leave immediately and face Queen Margaret as far away from London as he could. He refused. The Londoners were notorious for their fair-weather friendship to both York and Lancaster – their only devotion being to commerce. Warwick's advice to them was short and disdainful: 'Bury your valuables, my lord Mayor!' He would not move until his men were ready for a pitched battle and he could choose the most advantageous ground, and when he did go he took the crazed king with him as an insurance.

Henry did not care to leave what to him was the freedom of being in prison, and he sulked as they rode from Aldersgate up to St Albans. Warwick was courteous, but he had little time to console his prisoner. He was preoccupied. A little beyond St Albans he drew up his army in three main groups right in the line of Queen Margaret's advance. There he waited for the wild northern moss-troopers.

They came: but not as Warwick had expected from the front by daylight, but into his flank before dawn had broken. It was hellish in the gloom and the mist, in the terror of being caught unprepared, and very quickly the battle was done.

The Yorkists' lines were broken, their royal hostage lost, and Warwick himself, with a shred of his army, escaped by a miracle.

Instinctively they rode westwards to meet Edward. London they gave up as lost.

❊

The capital was in confusion. Fugitives poured in from the north with news of the battle at St Albans. The gates were closed – until the rich merchants' valuables had been hidden – and then they were reopened. The city fathers had decided to submit to Margaret's mercy. Within an hour they had changed their minds. Word had come that Henry's queen would give London to her wild men. The gates were shut once more.

Cecily was contemptuous when she heard of this: 'They'll wear out the gate hinges before they're done,' she snapped.

Quickly she made up her mind. Margaret had threatened she would expunge the whole house of York. The children must be removed from London without delay. She sent down-river to where the carracks of Genoa and the Flanders galleys lay, but they had already moved far out of Margaret's reach. And the smaller vessels in London Pool were hoisting sail because Lancastrian horsemen were pillaging the city suburbs. Only one shipmaster could be bribed to wait.

'And his vessel is old and rough,' the messenger told Cecily.

'No matter.'

She summoned her sons and Peter Neville, and Skelton, her dead lord's squire. Briefly she told them they must fly from London; take shipping to Burgundy where the duke was friendly to the White Rose.

'Master Skelton, these princes of York and my cousin's son are in your charge. They will obey you in all things. You have my writ.' She handed him a hastily-prepared document of authority, a sealed letter to the Duke of Burgundy and money.

George protested loudly, Richard no less. Anxiety made their mother peremptory.

'You will do as you are told,' she said sharply.

'But you, Madam . . .' began George.

'Have no fear. They will not harm me. But with Edward you are York's heirs, and I fear for you. Now be gone.' She smiled at them. 'Take your weapons, but little else. Skelton, they are in your charge. I shall send other messengers to Burgundy directly.'

The farewells were brief. Richard lingered for a moment, and was hustled from the solar by Anne Coux.

'Don't fret for your mother, Lord Richard. I'll be here to care for her, be sure.' She hugged him; catching her bodice on the sharp part of the dagger he was holding. 'Mother of God! a babe to carry arms.'

'I am eight, Anne,' he said, much on his dignity.

Skelton was waiting at the foot of the stair. 'Speed, Lord Richard. Into your travelling gear. Speed!'

His man was packing a small canvas bag with clothing.

George told his servant: 'A cloak, no more. Our mother said "Your weapons and little else".' He ran his finger along the sharp edge of his half-sword, the present from Henry of Lancaster. 'This will do for me.'

George was enjoying himself, and so was Peter.

'Ready, Dick?'

'Yes.'

Richard had the dagger in one hand, his Missal in the other.

'Your wallet,' Peter reminded him.

Richard was already following his man through the door. He said briefly: 'It's of no matter.'

'But, Dick!' squeaked Peter in amazement. 'Your wallet!'

'I know. I shall leave it.'

Peter caught him up on the stairs.

'But you value it.'

'I know what I value,' said Richard.

Peter shrugged his shoulders: then laughed. 'And after all the fuss at Canterbury.'

Richard made no reply and went on. He was trembling – and determined not to show his fear. Action made George forget; it made him remember. His whole inside felt loose one second, and stretched taut the next – just like when George had told him. *They killed him, Dick . . . cut off their heads . . . a crown of straw and paper.* He stumbled on a stair, righted himself, and quickly straightened his back as Edmund had told him – Father, Edmund, Uncle Salisbury and Tom and Bat and . . . His mother had said *They will not harm me*, but he remembered her crying at Ludlow *Margaret would not dare*. And Margaret had. He stumbled again. Peter's hand was there to steady him. Why would they not leave him alone?

'And after all that pother at Canterbury,' Peter was saying once more, and he was laughing.

All Richard's fear suddenly hardened to anger.

'Leave me alone.'

Peter lost his smile. 'I only said —'

'Too much.'

George, Skelton, the servants looked at him in surprise; and Peter felt shamed in front of them.

'I only said,' he repeated firmly, 'that at Canterbury you valued . . .'

Dick cut in again, and in a white-hot temper. 'You chatter like a girl. Keep with the servants – where you belong.'

Peter winced. Even George thought that was too much. 'He is our cousin, Dick.'

Skelton intervened. 'Lord George, Lord Richard. There is no time for a boys' quarrel. The shipmaster waits.' He pushed Richard before him through the door into the yard.

Richard flung back at George over his shoulder: 'His father is but a shire-knight, and we are princes.'

Neither he nor Peter said a word as they ran to the dock, and the sight of their transport did nothing to cheer them. She was a small, besalted coast-hugger, with an old-fashioned leg-of-mutton sail.

'Get aboard!' roared the shipmaster as soon as he saw them. He

49

was a French tallow-dealer, yellow with fear and resentful because he was forced to leave with only half a load. He cared nothing for lords and courtiers and had only waited because he was greedy for their gold.

The boys and the servants scrambled over the side. Skelton came last – crossing himself as he stepped on the gunnel.

'Stow your piety! And let me see your gold,' shouted the master.

Skelton held up a purse. 'Which you'll get when we reach the Low Countries,' he said.

The master would have argued but Skelton looked as though he meant what he said and the ebb had begun to run. 'Then get below,' he ordered – and immediately began bellowing to the two youngsters in his crew. They scrambled the sail up and the tallow-tub began to move sluggishly down-river. 'Below!' roared the shipmaster from the helm. 'And out of our way.'

Skelton lifted a hatch cover and peered into the greasy evil-smelling hold.

'We'll stay in the well,' he shouted, his hand on his sword.

'As you will.' The shipmaster shrugged. 'But later my pretty cock, you'll be hungry for shelter.' Skelton picked his way aft with care because the wind blowing strongly from the Kent shore rocked the coaster on the ebbing tide.

'You've a precious cargo, shipmaster,' he warned quietly when he reached the helm. 'If there's foul weather ahead, take no chances.'

The master plucked at his beard. 'There's but three things I value here,' he growled. 'Myself, my ship and your gold. Be sure I'll not risk any of them. Now, get to your pretty lordlings, master squire, and have them pray against a blow. You'll be holding their heads by the time we ride for the night.'

Skelton returned to his party. Richard and Peter were still sulking at opposite ends of the well, refusing to look at one another or talk. George vexed by their silence, turned to the squire for company, until, for a different reason, he fell silent himself.

Above them raced dark, low clouds that spoke of more wind. Beneath them the strong spring tide ebbed to the estuary. Skelton looked anxiously at the squally sky.

'It's freshening,' he said to George, and again – 'It's freshening.' Anything to keep occupied, not think of the rolling. Keep talking, he told himself, as he felt the nausea rising within him. 'Blowing half a gale,' he said between his teeth.

But George made no reply. Sometimes he gulped at the wind, sometimes he pressed his lips together. Abruptly he put his head over the gunnel and vomited.

Skelton grasped his shoulder. 'You'll be all right,' he said. 'All right.' He let go of George, and put his own head over the side.

Within two minutes all of them save Richard were vomiting. He sat there; a withdrawn, tiny figure hunched over his dagger and his Missal. Once or twice he slipped a glance at Peter who was retching painfully and noisily. Suddenly he felt sorry for him. His sullenness was draining away; but a little still remained. He was sorry for what he had said because Peter had meant no harm, but he would not say so. Let Peter learn when to leave him alone and not pester him, not provoke that black anger. Peter had meant no harm but he had caused it all the same.

The ship heaved, her prow riding up, and for a moment Richard had to drop his Missal and the dagger and use both hands to steady himself. When he could he picked them up, sheathed the dagger and half sat on the Missal. The wind blew harder, whipping the stays and halliards and creaming the waves in the estuary. By twilight it had veered astern and strengthened to a gale. The little tallow-tub was pounding along the estuary, knocking up sheets of spray and rolling as well as pitching. Through the scream of the wind Richard heard the shipmaster shouting to his crew, and through the dark he saw them at the mast and shrouds. Down tumbled the leg-of-mutton; and the ship immediately plunged and heaved like a twig on a millrace, her lazy tackle rattling, her prow smacking the wave curls. Then up went a smaller sail which cracked like thunder as the wind caught it. The ship steadied a little, but the waves were still fast, steep and vicious. Richard was grateful for the darkness when it came. At least he could no longer see the following waves which loomed over the helmsman. There was a smudge of light from the Kentish saltings but it quickly fell astern.

Then it began to rain, and the gale hardened. There was more shouting, and the shipmaster loomed beside him. He bellowed at Skelton to get below and wrenched off the hatch cover.

Richard could just make out the squire's face. He was trying to say something but his words were blown out to sea. He tried again, and Richard caught the words 'heave-to', 'nightfall'. He heard a manic sound – the master's shrill laugh.

'Heave-to in this?' he was bellowing: 'We'll run before it.'

Skelton's voice was louder. 'Out to sea?'

'Aye! I can't pinch her in this blow. It's a Cherbourg Kiss – channel gale blowing up from Normandy. We'd not make Sandwich.'

There was a snarl astern as a great wave started to break and then thought better of it.

'Get *below!*'

Skelton with a frightened glance astern heard another snarl. He grabbed George and almost pitched him through the hatch cover. Peter followed. Then one of the servants. The next missed his footing as the ship sledged into a trough between waves, and he fell with a cry into the hold. When Richard got below he heard the man moaning with pain, but he could see nothing. It was pitch-dark and the stench from the cargo and the bilges was indescribable. George, Peter and Skelton had begun to vomit again.

Richard closed his eyes and prayed because he knew that now he would be sick himself. The darkness, the stench, were bad enough, but worse was the noise of grinding timbers and slopping water, and the moaning and the retching.

Then he heard Peter gasping: 'I must! I must!' and his friend was pushing against the hatch cover. He added his small weight. He, too, must get out from this hell. Between them they raised the edge of the cover and, caught by a gust of wind, it was wrenched from their hands and sent scuttering across the deck. Peter scrambled out and Richard would have followed but Skelton caught his leg.

'Stay! Lord Richard.'

'No. I must be in the air.'

'You will stay.' Skelton forced him below into the hold, and ordered one of the servants to keep him fast.

Richard struggled, but the man would not let go. From outside he heard a shout, and another, and the clump of heavy boots on the decking. Then Skelton's shrill agonized voice. An argument . . . the shipmaster crying, 'We'll be broached. Away from the helm. AWAY!' – and, without being told Richard knew what had happened.

The man who held him asked anxiously: 'Lord Richard. What is it? What is it?'; then hugged the boy to comfort him.

From the deck came another roar from the shipmaster. 'For the love of Jesu! He is gone. We can do *nothing!*'

'And we had quarrelled,' whispered Richard, his mouth pressed against the servant's cloak.

X

The nib scratched as Richard penned the last upward stroke of his signature. He dusted the wet ink and began to fold the letter. Then, changing his mind, he handed it to the squire.

'I am to read it, Lord Richard?' The boy nodded; swung his legs over the bench and walked to the window.

Skelton examined the letter to Sir Favor Neville. Richard had asked that it should accompany his own official report of Peter's death; and the formal preliminaries, penned by the professional scrivener, were in striking contrast to the text which followed. Evidently the boy had not found it easy to write. There were mistakes, and some scratchings-out, but his sincerity was unmistakable. Yet one correction was so curious that Skelton said: 'Lord Richard, you had written "my friend was swept away to death".'

Richard nodded again: he looked away from the squire.

'But you have altered it,' continued Skelton, 'crossing out the words "my friend" and putting "your son" in their place.' He hesitated. 'Why?'

There was a long silence.

'Why?' he asked again.

This time Richard replied – slowly and over his shoulder. 'We were not friends . . . not then.'

Skelton sighed, and sat down heavily on the bench to ponder; worried by his inability to convince Richard that his quarrel with Peter had been unimportant; no more than a tiff, a stupid squabble which both of them would have forgotten very quickly. But then nothing, he reflected, had gone well in this venture since the loss of Peter Neville. He crossed himself – not only for the sake of Peter's soul, but also because he was beginning to believe that this disaster had set a pattern for all that happened afterwards. They had been blown right across to the Frisian Islands before the gale suddenly and mercifully spent itself, and then had had to creep slowly south along the coast. At Ostend, after a twelve-day voyage which had been part terrifying, part hideous, expecting to be welcomed, they had met with a tepid reception from the Duke of Burgundy's officials who merely accepted the letters from the Duchess of York, provided them with a dingy lodging in Bruges, and bade them wait. Skelton could resign himself impassively to all this – to the boredom of waiting, the servants' complaints, and George's impatient grumbles – but Richard's long silences and his frozen haunted appearance bewildered him.

He looked again at the boy's letter, and made a last attempt to reassure him.

'Lord Richard,' said the squire solemnly. 'You know that my lord, your father, trusted me?'

'Yes,' said Richard.

'And your mother gave you into my charge because she has confidence in my judgement.'

'Yes.'

'Yet you neither trust me, nor rely on my judgement.'

This made the boy gaze at him in surprise, but he said nothing so Skelton rang the bell for Peter's servant who was waiting beyond the doorway.

He handed over his own dispatches. 'This for her grace at Baynard's Castle; this for your lord at Eltham.' He gave further instruction as to how the man should reach England; then said: 'And this is another letter for Sir Favor. From Lord Richard.' He folded the letter, and was about to seal it when Richard spoke.

'Master Skelton!'

'My lord?'

'I have something to add.'

The boy sat at the table, cleaned the end of the quill nib, dipped it in the well and wrote two words. His sentence now ran *Your son, my friend, was swept away to death.*

Skelton looked with approval at the correction; but, shrewd as he was, he failed to see the deeper cause of Richard's haunted look: that, while undoubtedly he suffered from remorse, he was suffering more from a helpless feeling of being fated to lose everyone he loved; worse still, that perhaps his love carried with it a curse. Bat, Tom, Peter, Edward and Edmund had had all his love. His father, too, and his mother had come within its warmth; and one by one they had been chopped out of his life until only Edward and his mother remained. Each day, each hour, he expected to hear that they, too, were dead and gone.

But Skelton could not know this. 'Well now,' he said encouragingly. 'Our present life is tedious. So we must fill the hours until the noble duke receives us. Should we find your brother and accept Master Caxton's offer?'

There was no reply – and Skelton for the first time showed some exasperation. 'Lord Richard,' he said loudly, and his tone was a rebuke. 'I asked if we should visit the city? Master Caxton has offered to lead us.'

Richard started nervously. 'As you will, Master Skelton,' he muttered.

Until Duke Philip of Burgundy was sure which English rose would flower, he intended to walk the tight-rope which allowed him to claim friendship with both York and Lancaster. Lodgings, a meagre allowance, and permission to inspect the treasures of his palaces when he was absent, was all he would allow George and Richard for the present. This suited the subtle William Caxton well. Intelligent, cultivated, the mercer was an opportunist who at this stage of his career would be agreeable to the devil himself for a groat – or a groat's worth of power – and, with the skill of an oriental, he managed to maintain a confidential relationship with the Lancastrian agents in Bruges while at the same time demonstrate his warm affection for the princes of the house of York. He gave them quiet discreet suppers in his fine stone house – where he introduced them to a selected circle of influential people; some lords of Brabant, a bishop or two, and Prospero Camuglio the Milanese ambassador.

Some of these people deemed it prudent to offer a similar degree of discreet hospitality. The invitations were not accepted. John Skelton had served the Duke of York long enough to learn the folly of burdening oneself with small obligations in times of adversity; tiny favours which, in prosperity, ballooned and had to be returned a thousandfold.

It was sufficient that they had to be beholden to William Caxton who loaded them with obligations, though always with the greatest circumspection.

At a suitable moment – in other words, when it was guaranteed to command the most gratitude – he let out the news that London had so far withstood the queen. She was hesitating north of the city. Events of course, still hung in the balance. Yet there was great hope . . .

'Then our mother is safe!' blurted out the younger Plantagenet, his elf-like face so flooded with relief that the merchant almost regretted not telling the news when he had heard it himself, and that had been some considerable time beforehand.

But the regret was momentary. Mercers with an eye to the main chance could not afford such tender feelings. Caxton continued his discreet bear-leading.

When the Plantagenets were ordered to move to Utrecht and there continue their studies it was Caxton who convinced them it did not necessarily mean Duke Philip had received bad news from England. It was Caxton who found a clerk to tutor the boys in Utrecht; Caxton who found them lodgings there; Caxton who against Skelton's note of hand was prepared to advance any money they might need; and Caxton who persuaded the duke to let them return to Bruges – or so he claimed.

When they were back again, and in better lodgings than before – he appeared to shed his policy of discretion, and was happy to be seen taking them on a visit to the duke's library. He had a great love of books himself and the Burgundy collection of rare painted manuscripts bound in jewelled covers was his particular delight. Then he took them to the duke's country estate at Hesdin where both the palace and the pleasure grounds were studded with elaborate curiosities; among them, bridges which collapsed without warning, bound volumes which puffed out fine sand when they were opened, and a room hung with tapestries where thunder and lightning and even snow and rain were artificially produced at the touch of a spring.

The mechanical marvels fascinated both boys, though, after the first exhilarating demonstration of a controlled snow storm, George's pleasure was dampened by the fact that Caxton took his arm and asked if he had ever seen a more ingenious spectacle. No, said George, resenting the man's hand on his arm. He did not really care for Caxton. George was fining down and had already caught some of the full-blown good looks of his father's family, but he was still sensitive to criticism of his eating and his plumpness. At their first meeting the mercer (presumably in an attempt to show friendliness)

56

had teased him about his appetite and laughingly promised to bid his cook remember it. It had been an unhappy beginning to their relationship which had not endeared the mercer to the boy. George, though, had been canny enough to conceal his dislike. To begin with he sensed rather than knew that Caxton mattered, but in time it became clear that the mercer's attitude to the exiled princes reflected the fortunes of the Yorkists and Lancastrians as accurately as a weather vane showed wind direction.

George managed to smile at Caxton while servants prepared a second artificial blizzard simply because he guessed that the merchant's increased willingness to commit himself was a sign that all was well with the House of York. Caxton returned the smile for he adored the smiles of princes, and, after the blizzard, he made George's guess into more of a certainty by proposing another excursion for the next day; this time to a famous abbey and the cathedral, with a picnic – thoughtfully provided by the mercer – in between.

'Dick,' muttered George, on their way back to Bruges, 'I believe the see-saw's going up in our direction. That old devil knows something, or he'd not be so generous with his time or goods.'

His brother cared less for such subtle thinking than for the marvels of Hesdin.

'I wish,' he said, 'that he'd take us to that storm room again.'

'There's no need,' said George – and loud enough for everyone to hear. 'We'll be home again soon, you'll see.'

❋

George was right, and proved so early the very next morning when a court chamberlain arrived at the lodgings with a first invitation from Duke Philip. He would receive them at noon.

'See-saw up,' cried George exuberantly. 'What did I tell you! Old Caxton can unpack his picnic hamper.'

By any standards their reception at the Ducal court was magnificent. Had they been Pope and Emperor the boys could not have been given greater respect or closer attention. The duke himself walked them up and down, his hand on George's shoulder, as he told them the great tidings from England.

Queen Margaret's hesitation north of London had cost her

everything, and now all her followers could do was play the game of make-believe: beginning at that essential point: *if only* she had captured the heart of England, *if only* . . . For, while she took counsel, rested her soldiers, and waited, she was giving time to Edward of York and his cousin Warwick. They came from the west like the wrath of God, and drove her pillagers and mercenaries and freed felons and moss-troopers back along that scar of desolation which ran the length of England: until, one hundred and seventy miles from London, she turned at bay. There in a blizzard as freakish as the snow at Hesdin, the bloodiest battle ever known was fought and won by York. The Lancastrians were routed, the chief lords killed or taken captive, and only by a miracle had the queen herself, her son, and her poor mad lord fled on to Scotland.

They were on the first rung of the upward ladder, George told himself, when, on an inspiration, Duke Philip sent to the gardens for white roses. They should all wear white roses. And, though it was early in the season, white roses were found and distributed by the Duke's own hand as he recounted the next, and quite unexpected ascent to the second ladder rung.

Edward of York, less diffident than his father and with a surer political sense, had allowed himself to be proclaimed king.

George and Richard eyed one another across the duke, at first nervously, then incredulously. Their admired eldest brother was to be crowned Edward the Fourth of England, France and Ireland.

Rung three: the city of Bruges would give the royal princes a formal banquet, to show their loyal affection to the house of York. A formal banquet because, *rung four*, they were to be escorted soon to Calais and there take shipping on a royal barge for Dover. A royal barge, mark you, not a besalted tallow-tub. On and on, up the ladder: five, six, seven, eight rungs – still more.

There were letters from their mother, letters from their brother; they were to be measured directly by the court tailors for fine clothes of velvet and Flemish cloth – which, promised Duke Philip, would be adorned and jewelled at his expense; and this was but a prelude to a shower of gifts to mark the goodwill of Burgundy.

Skelton could not calm his charges until very late that day. They were beside themselves with joy: George, because the world had turned turtle and he was heir to England; Richard, because Edward was safe, not dead and gone, and not only safe, but king. And now, because there was no danger, he could confess his secret dread to Master Skelton; his fear that everyone whom he loved were cursed by it and doomed.

'It was untrue,' he said. 'I was wrong. My own loved brother is to be king. My mother lives and waits to welcome us.'

The squire put an arm around his shoulders. His feelings were tender for this small, spare child, who in such an illustrious and talented family was but a drab hedge sparrow amongst peacocks; and he was glad to know at last the reason for Richard's strange reaction to the death of his young friend. Aware that soon they would part, and perhaps for ever, he took the chance to encourage the boy and arm him against similar disasters in the future.

'An honourable death is no enemy to anyone,' he said quite rightly. But then he added – and quite wrongly: 'Never fear to give your love and trust.'

Well-meaning Skelton; so anxious to help; inevitably ignorant that this little sparrow amongst peacocks was to be the greatest squanderer of trust in the history of his family.

XI

By command of the king, George and Richard Plantagenet kept their knightly vigil as initiates into the Order of the Bath. The Tower chapel of St. Peter's Chains was small and on a midsummer's night it was uncomfortably warm, but neither boy moved or thought of moving, and neither spoke a word, except to God and his holy Mother.

George was seldom minded to pray very much, but the solemnity of this occasion had moved him unexpectedly and now he felt small and humble; not the Lord George of York, soon to be Duke of Clarence as Edward had promised, but simply George, a boy of twelve, in need of grace. So he meekly asked to be made worthy.

Richard had his eyes on the foot of the altar Crucifix. He was telling his beads as a thanksgiving that he was past the first ceremony of all when two fully-fledged knights, acting as his governors, had stripped him and then placed him in an ornate bath.

Only the kindness of one of them, Thomas, Lord Stanley, had made it at all bearable. The other was a sour young man who did precisely what he had to and no more, and even this he did with reluctance. But Lord Stanley had been more considerate: he understood Richard's shyness and he took the trouble to explain the reason for all the complicated rituals of being knighted. The bathing and sprinkling and drying and dressing in hermit's clothes, the vigil, the confession and penance, the offering of a candle stuck with a gold coin, the Mass and the bedding, the dubbing and kissing, were but the earthly husk of an important event which was really happening in heaven. For while the initiation moved formally from stage to stage, all the time God was polishing Richard's soul and, through the Sacraments, giving him the power to carry out his obligations.

Stanley talked so simply and so naturally that Richard forgot he was puny and ugly and stark naked in a bath, and by the time they pulled him to his feet and had sprinkled him and signed him with the Cross he had lost all his shame. He knew that he was the same boy but he felt different and he thought only of God polishing away in heaven. Thomas, Lord Stanley, had won a new and devoted friend.

When Richard finished his chaplet of thanksgiving he prayed for his dead father and his family, for George and the other boys who were to be knighted with them, for his governors, and for God's blessing on the pilgrimage to Walsingham which his mother had promised they should make together after Edward's coronation. Then, as daylight was breaking, he made a special vow and dedication unknown to anyone else, that he should be a good knight and entrusted to wear the honour of Peter Neville as well as his own.

It was time to make his confession before matins and Mass. The Dominican who shrived him was old and wise and inclined sometimes to despair at man's grossness. Richard's hesitant, stumbling admissions of a boy's guilt rebuked his despair. '*Ego te absolvo a peccatis tuis,*' he said with a light heart – grateful to God for showing himself through the marvellous innocence of children.

XII

It was a fortnight before the duchess's entourage left Baynard's Castle for East Anglia; two weeks in which, despite all the coronation feasts and jousts, the nineteen-year-old king had found time to make provision for his brothers. George, now Duke of Clarence, was considered old enough to stay with Edward and learn at first-hand the principles of government and the duties of kingship, while Warwick had honoured his promise given the year before and offered a place to Richard in his castle at Middleham in Yorkshire. Before the autumn he would ride north to lose his identity in the communal life of a great nobleman's household. He had but a few weeks more with his mother and as they rode out of Bishopsgate on their way to East Anglia she made a silent determination that the pilgrimage should be a happy golden memory which he could cherish all his life.

At first she felt uneasy, even a little guilty, because they travelled in such comfort, and she gently chided the chamberlain for making their pilgrimage too comfortable altogether. 'We are pilgrims, my lord chamberlain, not ambassadors.'

'It is my duty to care for her grace,' he piped in his own defence – third-personing her after the new-fangled style of upper servants at the court of France. 'But if her grace should wish it, closer to the Holy Shrine she may walk barefoot or with dried peas in her shoes to win Our Lady's favour.' And, with a courteous bow, he had concluded: 'Her grace may be certain we carry a supply of peas.'

Probably a bushel of them thought Cecily with amusement, for never was there so efficient or meticulous an administrator as her chamberlain. With wise foresight her chamberlain had arranged the journey north in easy stages so that they had leisure to stop when they felt inclined to rest or talk with strangers on the highway. They met many – stewards, drovers, carriers, pedlars, begging friars, small troops of soldiers, even a heavily-guarded party of lawyers and justices on circuit. At the end of each stage the company lodged at religious houses and manor halls, that is, as many as could be accommodated; and once, to Richard's great delight, they put up at an inn. Sir John did not share his pleasure – catching, so he claimed, both a chill and bed-bugs in the course of the night's lodging.

Each morning they collected other travellers who wished for the protection of the king's mother and her household. These were of all kinds, entertainers and private citizens, riff-raff and men of substance, and the closer they drew to Norfolk and the Holy Land of Walsingham, more and more fellow pilgrims attached themselves to the royal cavalcade. It was a very large company that tramped along the Pilgrims' Way and forded the little river at Houghton-in-the-Dale.

Richard and his mother took off their shoes and left them at the Slipper Chapel. Like everyone else they would carry a lighted candle and walk the Holy Mile barefoot; telling their beads, singing pilgrim hymns, praying the Blessed Virgin of Walsingham to accept their gifts and thanksgivings and grant them the blessings they had come to ask.

Only the chamberlain was mounted so that he could act as marshall but no one seemed to care about place or rank and fell into position without much regard to precedence. First came Sir John and the other priests, the clerks and the singing boys; then the duchess and her son, walking side by side; and behind them the whole household jumbled higgledy-piggledy, and mingled with the other pilgrims who had joined them on the journey.

The chamberlain was mildly shocked by such a straggly demonstration of disorder, but then he, too, ceased to care, abandoned his horse, took off his shoes, and fell in with the rest.

The informality was increased when at another ford across the River Stiffkey they came up with an unattended herd of milch cows twitching flies from each other in the shade of a clump of willows. The cows gazed at the singing pilgrims, and then, either because it was their custom or because they were bored and wanted a diversion, they joined the procession – one of them walking beside Sir John and lowing like the victim of a pagan sacrifice.

Cecily enjoyed the informality. With a dun cow behind her and another beside Richard, it was a refreshing escape from the elaborate ceremony of court and enabled her to feel more like a mother with a large family than a great duchess on progress. It had never been her wish that their pilgrimage should be considered as a formal

63

royal visit to England's Nazareth, but the people of Walsingham were not going to miss the chance of showing their loyalty to the mother and the brother of the king and enjoying an extra holiday at the same time.

They came out in a large company from the town – with the guildsmen, the manor steward, the twelve greyfriars and their guardian, and the Austin canons. At their head was Prior Hunt who eyed the cows with astonishment and the mob – for it was no less – that tailed off behind the Duchess of York. He could not prevent himself from smiling.

'Your grace is welcome,' he said formally: moving forward to kneel and kiss her hand.

But Cecily forestalled him. With a true sense of occasion it was she who knelt to kiss the prior's ring, crying so that everyone could hear: 'Sir Prior. We come to ask your blessing and offer prayers and gifts at England's Nazareth.'

Like a flock of duck flopping to rest her whole company knelt in the highway.

Somewhat astonished, the prior blessed them: then he raised the duchess to her feet and bowed to Richard.

'Your grace. My lord Richard, you are welcome,' he said again.

The formal presentations were made of the Greyfriars' Guardian, local lords, and important visitors on pilgrimage. Cecily expressed her particular pleasure in seeing there an old friend from the north, Sir James Metcalfe of Nappa. 'Sir James comes from Aysgarth,' she told her son. 'Close by your cousin's castle of Middleham.' Richard bowed to the Yorkshire knight – but he was really wanting to hear one name in particular: Edmund, the brother of Dom Antony of Canterbury. But the prior presented his canons by the title of their office, as sub-prior, precentor, sacrist, cellarer, infirmarian and almoner, and before he found an opportunity to ask, the cavalcade was prepared to move on again.

His mother took his hand. 'We go first to the Holy House to offer our gifts and prayers.'

XIII

The duchess's main party lodged at the priory while the rest were put up at one or other of the many inns and hospices in the town. At the first dinner in the refectory Richard asked the prior about Dom Antony's brother: 'Dom Edmund – our almoner, Lord Richard,' he said indicating a canon sitting far down the table. 'I shall instruct him to speak with you later.'

It appeared that after dinner Dom Edmund was about to visit his aged mother in the town . . . a daily duty which he could not neglect. 'But I shall look forward to talking with you when I return, Lord Richard.'

Richard took his hand. 'Could I not come with you, Dom Edmund?'

For a moment the canon hesitated. His mother was barely alive, and a senile old lady would only bore the boy. But he seemed eager to go. 'If you would be so generous with your time, Lord Richard,' he said.

They walked down to the Knight's Gate by which stood a small house. 'Our father was miller to the priory,' explained Dom Edmund. 'And wished and prayed that his sons, all save one, should be priests of Holy Church.'

'You have more brothers than Dom Antony.'

'Nine,' said Dom Edmund.

'And all but one are priests?'

'All, Lord Richard. The one who should have been miller in my father's place was drowned.' He crossed himself. 'It was God's will.'

Richard followed him into the house.

The old lady was almost blind and very deaf, and her son had to bellow to make her understand. Even then, Richard guessed, she had not the least idea who he was. She patted him on the head, told him to be a good boy, mind his prayers, and be loyal to God, Our Lady, and good King Henry.

'King Edward,' roared the canon, and explained that in fact

65

she meant Henry of Monmouth. 'For she's muddled now, poor mother.'

When the old lady tired, and that was no more than twenty minutes after their arrival, she was quick to send them away.

'Until tomorrow, Antony,' she said.

Outside the canon said: 'Nowadays she muddles us all up.'

'How lucky,' said Richard simply. 'For she thinks all her sons are visiting her and not just one.'

'True!' The canon smiled. Then he said: 'Lord Richard, I still have thirty minutes' recreation. Would you be so kind as to tell me about my brother in Canterbury?'

Richard did so, and with all a small boy's hero-worship. 'He told us,' he finished, 'he told us you were a story-teller too. Even better than he is.'

'All my brother's geese are swans,' said Dom Edmund, and then, because the boy looked mystified he continued: 'Which is the beginning of a story.'

He lifted Richard on to a low wall, leant against it himself, and told him about the plain, smoke-grey, sad little bird who believed he was a duckling.

In half a minute the boy was wriggling with pleasure because Dom Edmund had his brother's gift for painting word-pictures and at once Richard could almost see that pathetic, crushed duckling; share its dejection and tears because it was so different, share its wonder at the slow disclosure, and then join in its joy when the remarkable truth became plain.

At the end he said thank you and then was silent because he saw the story as an allegory. He gazed at his feet. Without thinking he flexed the muscle of his right arm and felt it. Dom Edmund saw this, and guessed immediately what the child was thinking, but he did not say anything.

A bell began to chime from the priory tower. It was taken up by another from the friary, and another, and another until all Walsingham was ringing.

'Recreation is over,' said Dom Edmund lifting him off the wall. 'I should return to the almonry.'

They walked hand in hand from the Knight's Gate. When they reached the Priory Gate Richard stopped. 'Dom Edmund,' he asked slowly. 'Does Our Lady of Walsingham always give her favours to pilgrims?'

The answer came instantly: 'She prays that we may be helped to help ourselves.'

'So if I asked her that . . .'

Richard never completed the sentence because at that moment a small boy ran out of the gate. He was being chased by an older boy, and because neither of them looked where they were going they both crashed into Dom Edmund and knocked him down.

They stood back, eyes wide with dismay, while Richard helped the canon to his feet.

'Your pardon, sir,' stammered the little boy.

'Dom Edmund,' said the other. 'We were tigging, and . . .'

'A pair of tom fools,' snapped Richard, brushing down the canon's habit. 'Beetle-headed, and ill-mannered with it. To knock down a priest . . .!'

The younger boy was about Richard's age and, at being told he was ill-mannered, he turned scarlet with indignation. 'Tom fools!' he repeated. 'Beetle-heads!'

His brother tried to pacify him. 'That's right, Miles. We were zanies. Both of us.' He turned to the canon. 'Are you hurt, Dom Edmund?'

'No, Thomas, I thank you.' He retrieved his black square hat from the gutter. 'But, truly, I wish you were less exuberant. Old men scarcely relish such treatment.'

'Old?' laughed Thomas. 'You're not old, Dom Edmund.'

'At twenty-nine I feel it,' returned the canon.

'Aye, he's old,' said the younger boy with a small boy's candour. 'So we're sorry, sir, for knocking you down.'

The canon smiled at him, then, drawing together the loose folds of his habit, he bowed to Richard. 'I thank you for your concern, Lord Richard. Here are two fellow pilgrims come from the north country a bare week ago, Thomas and Miles Metcalfe. . . .' The presentation was cut short by the gate porter who put his head into the street and rebuked Dom Edmund for his lateness. With a promise that he would see them after dinner on the next day, the canon hurried away.

When he had gone the brothers eyed Richard. Now that they knew who he was, Thomas was bashful. Not so his brother Miles.

'I beg your pardon, my lord!' he said, but so defiantly that it made a nonsense of the apology.

'For what?' asked Richard.

Miles squared his shoulders. 'For resenting what you called us – Tom fools and ill-mannered beetle-heads. We were but tigging!'

Thomas was aghast. 'Miles! have done! My lord, I beg you to forgive his lack of courtesy. . . .'

But Richard would not quarrel. For the moment he was more interested in their name. Were they, he asked, sons to the Sir James Metcalfe he had met that morning?

'Aye,' replied Thomas. 'We are from Nappa Hall by Aysgarth.'

'Close to Middleham?'

'Not far away,' said Thomas. 'I am put out with Lord Scrope at Bolton, but Miles here is being schooled in my lord Warwick's household.'

Richard started. 'You are a donzel at Middleham?' he asked Miles.

'I am,' said Miles briefly. He sounded sulky, but he was incapable of staying in a bad mood for long, and he quickly added: 'We have permission from our lords to make this pilgrimage, but soon we return north.'

'And I, too!' said Richard.

Both brothers looked at him in surprise.

'You, my lord?' said Miles.

'Not only north, but to Middleham!' cried Richard in excitement. 'I am to be a donzel in my cousin's household after Hallowmass.'

Thomas grinned. Miles gaped. Then both began chattering at once. Richard managed to stop them.

'Tell me of Middleham,' he begged.

This was exactly like touching gunpowder with a match. The brothers exploded with enthusiasm. They were so excited that once more they talked simultaneously and Richard had to plead with them to start afresh. Then, each in turn, and following hard on the other as though they were singing a litany in praise of Middleham, they described the strength and size of Warwick's massive fortress, the beauty of Wensleydale, the moors and peat-hags, the hunting and coursing, and the fishing in the swift-flowing Ure.

'Nothing,' finished Miles – and he was fast losing breath. 'Nothing can compare with Wensleydale and Middleham.'

'You make it sound like paradise,' chuckled Richard.

'It is,' insisted Miles, and they would have continued their litany of praise but at that moment one of the duchess's pages came from the priory to ask Richard's presence in the refectory.

'Her grace has a letter for you, Lord Richard.'

68

'A letter? For me?' Without waiting for an answer he took the Metcalfe brothers by the hand and dragged them away to meet his mother and repeat all they had said about Middleham.

Richard had never received a letter in his life. 'For me?'

'For you!' Gravely Duchess Cecily handed him the sealed packet.

'It is from Edward,' he said excitedly. 'From my lord the king.'

'Yes.' Cecily smiled at the care with which he broke the seal. She could guess at the letter's contents for Edward had a special fondness for his youngest brother and though George had the right to a dukedom as heir apparent to the throne, she knew it was in her son's mind to do as much for Richard after a discreet interval of time.

Richard carefully read the letter right through. His face was pink. 'Madam,' he asked, 'what is a Commissioner of Array?'

'A gentleman who summons the county levies,' she replied. 'That is, the knights and men-at-arms who are pledged to defend the king.'

He thanked her, and re-read a part of his letter.

'Well, Dickon?'

He blushed. 'Madam,' he said. 'I am to . . .' he hesitated.

'Yes?' she said encouragingly.

He held out the letter. 'At Hallowmass,' he said, and his voice was firm, 'before I leave for Middleham, I am to be made Duke of Gloucester, Earl of Carlisle, Earl of Richmond, and Commissioner of Array for the North Parts.'

Later Thomas Metcalfe soundly kicked his younger brother for having been discourteous to so exalted a personage in the public highway. 'You are witless, Miles, to behave in such a manner to a lord who is to be Duke of Gloucester.'

Miles kicked him back – 'and Earl of Carlisle and Richmond,' he cried with spirit; adding for good measure as he darted out of Thomas's reach. 'And King's Commissioner for the North Parts.'

69

PART TWO

Richard, Duke of Gloucester

D

I

Middleham.

From the first moment he saw the castle keep against the southern slope of Wensleydale Richard had the distinct awareness that he belonged there, that in some sense he was returning home. It gave him confidence as he and his small escort rode through the village market-place and up to the north gate of the castle. The drawbridge was down.

'Way for the Duke of Gloucester!' called his standard-bearer to the guard serjeant. 'Way for the Duke of Gloucester!'

Richard was taken directly to be received formally in the Earl's Presence Chamber. Neither Warwick nor his lady were at Middleham, but their children were there; two little girls sitting on the Earl's dais with the steward, the treasurer, and the comptroller of the household. The elder, Isabel Neville, was prodded into making her rehearsed speech of welcome.

Richard took the opportunity to look covertly at the three men who would be ordering his life, and then at his cousins. Isabel was a prattler, obviously; but her sister was different, demure, shy perhaps.

Isabel finished her speech with about as much feeling as a cook declaiming a recipe for pudding, but Richard gave her a polite smile and a bow before he began his equally rehearsed, formal and uninteresting speech in reply.

Afterwards the comptroller led him from the Presence Chamber to his quarters, and the king's brother became an ordinary lad again, with a dozen others who were being tutored in polite and knightly accomplishments.

Miles Metcalfe was there to greet him, his face a map of smiles: proud, but not vain of his acquaintance with the Duke of Gloucester; eager to present him to the donzels' mess; amongst them to Francis Lovell, a ward of Lord Warwick, to Robert Percy, to one of Blount's grandsons, and a Dynham.

All save Miles were strangers, yet again Richard had the peculiar feeling that he belonged to this place, that, in some sense, he had come home.

※

Warwick's chief officers at Middleham were hard-working, able men, honourable and wise in their dealings with subordinates. That they lacked the imagination ever to deviate from the immemorial routine of castle administration was to everyone's advantage. It gave the household the sort of dull stability which for many years had been a rarity in England.

Richard especially benefited from the unchangeable order of events in each day. He settled quickly into his apprenticeship in chivalry although it was both disciplined and exacting. His secret ambition, to train himself and become as hardy as his messmates, seemed impossible – but, through hard work and practice and Plantagenet stubborness, he succeeded to a remarkable degree. His chest filled out. His skin began to clear of pimples. His pallid face became as weathered as a kennel-boy's. And no one, now, could justly call him Crookback because he never stooped unless he was exhausted at the end of a long day.

Without exception, after a few months his instructors had reason to be proud of him; the clerks who taught him religion and book-learning, his teachers in music and other polite arts, the serjeants and armourers who were responsible for his education in horseman-ship and tilting; most of all the bald Agincourt veteran who in-structed the donzels in the theory of warfare and the chase. This knight sent a highly complimentary report on Richard to the Earl of Warwick who, astonished that his whey-faced godson should have made such progress, passed the report on to Westminster. The king was equally surprised and delighted. He had recently made his brother a Knight of the Garter, but judged it time to give him further honours. A courier arrived at Middleham from London. He carried the Lord Richard's Commission as Admiral of England, Aquitaine and Ireland.

Richard received the news with unusual solemnity, not joining in the good-natured laughter against himself when someone quipped:

74

'A Lord High Admiral with a fleet of one rickety raft on the castle moat!' It was quite unlike him to take himself so seriously; and it was significant maybe that from this time in the eyes of his messmates he seemed to change his attitude towards them. He became more and more detached.

Miles, Francis Lovell and Robert Percy were his closest friends but even they were spared little of his time or his confidence. They tried to draw him out, but he resisted, asking to be left alone – to work.

'Work! work! always it is work!' Francis said impatiently to the others.

Robert Percy nodded. 'Aye! To prove himself.' He sighed. 'He would be first and foremost all the time.'

None of them liked Richard's habit of infusing a spirit of fierce competition into everything they did together – from racing to Mass at daybreak to eating the mess of bread and ale last thing at night. At length, because he was too occupied to regard them they began to disregard him. It was a barely perceptible process. Before he realized it he was being left out of things. Slowly he was pushed out from that intimacy which, on his first arrival at the castle, he had so much valued.

It was brought home to him when, at the king's command he was sent from Middleham to the siege of Berwick. None of his messmates showed more than a polite interest in his adventure. They sent him off on his journey with their good wishes, and when he returned they welcomed him home again – but even as he told them about the siege and the surrender, events which to him were important and exciting, he knew suddenly that they were merely giving him the attention a household gives to any stranger from the world outside – be he pedlar with scandal from York and Ripon or a travelling baron. Somehow he no longer belonged to them.

The realization hurt him, and being hurt he reacted swiftly and disastrously. Dismay gave way to indignation, indignation to a sour arrogance which was really quite alien to his nature. Even his closest friends could not stand this. Within two days he was being ostracized by the whole mess. Within three he was fighting with them physically, and losing; being humiliated in the foul ways boys use to humiliate each other. Then, after a scene when Richard lost his last shred of dignity and became a screaming babe again, Miles wisely said they were simply trying to douse a fire with pitch. Thereafter they

75

totally ignored him, and Richard, nursing his grievances, imagined petty revenges and tried to stand on a dignity they would not allow him.

All this happened just as he was first feeling the uncertainties of growing to manhood. By most standards he was still a child but, like many children with unhappy or unstable backgrounds, he was maturing early. Already his voice was inclined to waver and this enraged him because it seemed to show lack of control. Already he had the longings which he could barely satisfy, and being so precocious for his age he was actually mortified by the visible changes in his body. What to the other donzels was a source of fascination as well as frustration was to him a heavy cross which he carried clumsily and reluctantly and with huge self-pity, and the effects showed themselves in everything he did. He became sour and selfish, truculent with his instructors, increasingly idle and thoughtless. With the arrogant notion that his rank entitled him to do and to take what he wanted, he even went so far as to paw the pretty young wife of the head groom, and when in fright she resisted he treated her cruelly.

Soon he was chafing and vexing the whole household like a bug beneath armour; being quarrelsome, boorish, demanding attention, and apparently determined to make everyone as miserable as he was himself. For a long time those who had liked him found reasons and excuses for his sultry defiance, but their patience ran out and they tried to correct him. Yet whatever they did seemed more of a goad than a check. He was beyond everyone's control and if this state of affairs had been allowed to continue his character might have been damaged permanently. But Warwick and his lady came home to keep Holy Week and Easter, and within an hour of their arrival the comptroller was making a formal report on the Duke of Gloucester.

Warwick was tired, jaded by his travels back and forth to France to arrange a good marriage for the king, and he longed for a rest. But the news that Richard had his tutors gadding like fly-blown cattle was serious enough to command his personal attention. He cursed the comptroller, the clerks and serjeants, the governor, and the music and the hunting masters, and he went himself to the donzels' mess.

II

Richard was sitting in a corner of the mess polishing his falchion, and he did not look up when the door opened. But the sudden silence made him look towards the door. Then all the boys were scrambling to their feet and so eagerly that a bench was knocked over. They had seen the earl ride in but an hour before, and the last place they would have expected him was in their mess, and alone, without even a servant.

Robert Percy, the eldest there, stammered a welcome.

Warwick gravely thanked him, looked at the trestle-table on which lay their oddments and playthings, and said he believed he had not been in the mess for some little time.

'Not since I have served you, my lord,' said Robert.

Warwick cocked an eyebrow. 'So long?'

'Aye, my lord.'

'I regret it,' said Warwick evenly. 'But then I am able to leave you safely to the care of my clerks and serjeants.'

He looked at Richard and continued: 'That is, all of you save one.'

There was a silence while he walked the length of the table until he was standing beside his godson.

'You have grown, Richard,' he said suddenly.

'I thank you, my lord, yes.' The boy was puzzled.

Warwick was still smiling, but now he sighed: 'And you have spoilt my pleasure in returning home.'

Richard said nothing.

'Because since my return all I have had is complaints of your behaviour.'

'From your servants, my lord?' The sly edge on his voice was unmistakable.

'From my servants,' agreed Warwick. 'Whom I trust and honour.' By nature he was choleric and only just prevented himself from boxing the boy's ears. He must be patient, cat-and-mouse him, be deliberate. 'Servants whom I have in the highest regard,' he said again to emphasize the point. Abruptly he changed tack and asked: 'How long have you been my donzel?'

Richard told him.

'So long!' Warwick appeared to be considering. 'And I recall you were becoming an ornament of the household: quick in your studies, a good horseman, skilled enough at tilting and with arms . . . and the rest.'

The boy judged it prudent to keep silent.

'The king, your mother, and I were truly proud of you.'

Richard winced, hating the mockery, this ruthless benevolence. He knew quite well what would follow – a whole catalogue of faults. They'd have told Warwick everything, every single thing, and he would lose his smile, and start to shout, and maybe strike him, as each item fed his choler. Very well then. With a courage that ordinarily would have been commendable, the boy squared his shoulders. Awesome and mighty though his cousin was, he should learn that a prince of York still had a tongue to defend himself.

But Warwick outpaced him and gave him no opportunity to argue or put any points at all. He made no charges, simply left a gap in what should have been a developed argument; not troubling to particularize how Richard had altered for the worse, merely accepting it as a fact that he had. He stood there, silent for a moment, staring until the boy lowered his eyes. Then he said lightly: 'It seems, lad, that I shall have to correct you.'

Richard had the helpless feeling of a dumb prisoner unable to defend himself. It made him angry as well as frightened.

'As my lord wishes,' he said coolly, and was rewarded by his mess-mates' reaction.

They were aghast at such daring impudence to their lord. But Warwick leached it of insolence by repeating with equal coolness: 'Yes, as my lord wishes.' With the smile yet at the corner of his mouth he added: 'Untie your points, my boy.'

Richard whitened beneath his tan. He did not fear the pain, but to be beaten then and there, in front of his hated mess-mates: that he could not bear.

'Your points, my lord of Gloucester,' repeated Warwick. He turned to Robert Percy who stood beside him. 'Get me a rod, boy, if you please.'

Robert went outside and returned with a hazel switch, but Richard stood like a statue, his chin a little higher than usual, waiting for Warwick to lose his temper for only then would he have the courage to defy him.

Warwick felt the fire within him. He kept it down by seeing Richard not as the resentful, healthy boy in front of him but as the frail even pitiable object he had been.

'Dick,' he said quietly. 'I shall whip you, and here before your friends because I guess they have suffered more from your moods and tantrums than anyone at Middleham. That is my intention.'

Richard, sucking up courage to shout his defiance, noticed the earl's eyes change colour: they turned a darker blue, and became dead, almost unseeing, as frozen as his tone when he continued: 'But if you do not untie your points and drop your breeks and take your beating, why then I shall have you flogged by the cookboys at supper; strung up naked in hall before the household. And afterwards, king's brother though you may be, and my own godson and cousin, you will be turned out, denied my hospitality, and sent like a babe back to your mother.'

Richard looked at him in horror. Through his teeth he said: 'My lord, you would not dare!'

Had any of the boys looked at Warwick's clenched hands they would have seen the knuckles whiten, but without exception their eyes were on his face.

'I would, my boy,' he said with an affected easiness of manner. 'Come, Dick; I admire your spirit; but as you are a lad and in my care, I have to master your stubbornness, and you must master your self-will.'

Richard looked at his mess-mates. A few could not help showing their delight at seeing him put down: his friends were full of pity. He hated the crowing triumph and he hated the sympathy. He hated Warwick. He hated everything, and everyone, even himself. And he untied his points, dropped his breech hose and bent over the table.

Warwick whipped him hard, harder perhaps than he intended for the rage he had controlled so well seeped a little into his arm and hand. He whipped him in silence until the boy's frame began to quiver with pain. Then he stopped and said: 'Good lad,' because Richard had not made a sound.

The boy raised his head. His right cheek was yellow where he had pressed it hard against the table; his dark eyes were swimming and his nose snotty. 'My lord?'

'I said, good lad!' repeated Warwick. He sent Francis Lovell to

79

the castle physician for balm. 'Tell him alone why I require the ointment.' He smiled. 'The others may guess I have splintered my finger in your mess, or tripped over your baggage and bruised myself.'

Richard managed to show his gratitude – then cleaned his face with a handkerchief. The other boys said nothing and shuffled their feet. Warwick broke the silence by saying unexpectedly: 'When I quarrel with my lady we are demons.' He smiled. 'Have you not heard this, Percy?'

Robert stuttered. 'No, my lord,' he lied.

'Demons,' said Warwick again. 'And then contented angels. In fact I believe my lady provokes me to anger and to argument, so that afterwards we may enjoy the sweetness of reconciliation.'

The boys were still and silent, but they were thinking.

Then Francis returned with the balm and gently anointed his friend's striped flanks.

'It is mystifying to see so much unnecessary damage done to a friend,' said the earl. 'Would you make it worse, Dick?'

Richard was bewildered. 'My lord?'

Warwick laughed and explained that when a soldier loses a hand or leg in battle the surgeons healed his stump with pitch, and exceedingly painful it was. 'Would your rump stand the same sort of treatment?'

'Pitch?'

Warwick shook his head. 'A saddle. Though you can stand in your stirrups. I've a mind for a gallop on the moors.'

'As my lord wishes,' murmured Richard, and this time there was no trace of insolence in his tone.

'Yes, as my lord wishes,' replied Warwick. 'Come, gentlemen. I shall ride with my donzels – and we'll take a couple or so of hound as well.'

'Richard,' said Lady Warwick when the earl came to escort her to supper, 'I declare you are loose-tiled.' She tutted once or twice. 'To ride here from Bedale: then, with no sight of your daughters to take horse again.' She tutted and sniffed.

'The gallop cleared my head . . .' he began.

'Of sense,' she cut in. 'Poor bird-witted Warwick to ride with his donzels about the moors.'

'Madam, it was for young Dick,' he explained. 'And brought a smile to his face.'

She tossed her head. 'He is but a wilful boy. Your health is my concern, my lord, and you need rest, not exercise.'

Warwick laid a hand on her arm and promised he would rest until Easter. 'And remember, my love, though Dick is but a boy he is yet of consequence.'

'Consequence?' she snapped unbelievingly.

'Aye.' Warwick smiled at his countess, and added mysteriously: 'The house of Warwick might one day need the Duke of Gloucester.'

III

Richard was himself again and so much so that he took it in good part when his mess-mates ribbed him.

'Cured by the rod,' declared Miles – impressed by the proved value of a whipping. Robert Percy said no, it was the effect of a gallop at stirrup-stand: a battering, shattering, rattling, shaking process guaranteed to spill the humours from anyone. Francis, referring delicately to what he called 'the Duke of Gloucester's melancholy' compared it less elegantly to a boil; and boils, he said, must burst one day – be they lanced, poulticed or left to erupt. It was all a question of time.

There were other suggestions – some extravagant, some lewd, some fairly sensible, and Richard listened to them all with good humour, believing himself that life had abruptly become more reasonable and comfortable simply because he had fallen in love.

On the very day of his whipping and the gallop with Warwick he had caught a smile from the Lady Anne at supper, and lost his heart. Timorously he smiled back; then sat fingering a fish back, picking small scraps from it, even forgetting the soreness of his rump, thinking only of that shy and sympathetic smile. It had moved him as sharply as a rowel in horseflesh, driving him to look in an entirely new direction, away from himself. Now he would look only to his little cousin, with his eyes when he could and when he dared – otherwise in his mind's eye. And as often as he saw or thought of her he felt that mixture of sourness and sweetness, tension and relaxation, aching and sea-depth contentment which are the peppery ingredients of love.

Easter passed. On the Octave Warwick and his countess left the castle to make a tedious embassage to France and afterwards join the king in a concerted effort to clear Northumberland of Margaret's men. The castle settled to its stale routine.

Richard, soaked in such strength of feelings that he could not keep them secret any longer, decided to confide in his three particular friends, choosing to tell them in the only place safe from eavesdroppers, that is aboard their raft. There, squatting on the largest barrel, the Lord Admiral of England, Ireland and Aquitaine, confessed his love for the Lady Anne Neville.

Robert and Francis listened sympathetically. In some degree both of them had experienced the same sort of exalted passion. But Miles, who had not yet loved, laughed at their romantic notions. He considered such a nursing of secret love contemptible. And he said so. Why, he asked, was the Lord Richard so lacking in spunk that he dared not seek the company of his cousins Isabel and Anne? He had but to flatter their Lady Governess . . .

Before they threw Miles overboard into the stinking moat they agreed that his suggestion was not without merit.

Emboldened by his friends' encouragement – and a very large horn of wine – Richard made his request.

Twenty-four hours passed before the Lady Governess sent her answer. It made Richard caper then and there in the donzels' mess for, though the moat, the outer baileys, and the village were out of bounds, if the Duke of Gloucester cared to visit the ladies Isabel and Anne at agreed times, and on occasions escort them in the hunting field, he and his friends would be welcomed by the young ladies' attendants.

A week of bliss, that was all they had. For Richard, whirligigging in the joy of his first love, and for Anne herself, glad to find her cousin so agreeable and kind, it was, truly, a week of bliss. And when it suddenly ended it ended in the best way possible.

The king sent word that his brother was to break his studies for the summer and raise levies in the south-west. He must leave at once for the Welsh Marches, summon a power, and meet with the king at Leicester on May 10th.

The comptroller received additional instruction from Warwick that Robert Percy and Francis Lovell were to accompany the Duke of Gloucester as body-squires, together with a suitable escort of household knights, clerks, men-at-arms and servants.

Richard tried to make the separation from Miles easier; first, by promising they would not forget one single particular of their adventures and would report them all on their return; and, second, by giving the Lady Anne into his safe keeping. 'Guard her well for me, Miles,' he said. And Miles, vowing that he would, proved both his understanding and his friendship through obtaining – by means best known to himself – one of Anne's ribbons for Richard to wear as a favour.

✳

At first all was well. It was springtime. This was an adventure any boy would pine for. And Richard, Robert and Francis made the most of it. All three swiftly made an impression on their knights and men-at-arms: the tall and elegant Percy for his gentle courtesy; young Lovell for his salty wit and for his infectious, dog-like devotion to Richard; and the young prince himself, for his scrupulous attention to detail and his natural power of command. There was no denying his Plantagenet blood in the way he drew his men's respect. He set an energetic pace which carried them rapidly down through Lancashire and County Chester to Shrewsbury, Hereford and his own city of Gloucester. Everywhere he went, his brother's subjects came to admire the wiry, tireless little duke – most of all for his ability to attract men voluntarily to his standard who otherwise would have been pressed into service.

Bristol ... Wells ... Mere ... south for more levies ... then north again; and the three friends' spirits flew higher and higher. Then came the news that the Lancastrians had suffered a heavy defeat at Hexham, far away in Northumberland.

It was a victory for the White Rose which brought wild cheers from all the levies, but not from Richard or his two squires. They had the full report before them, and there, listed amongst the Lancastrian dead, was Robert's cousin, Sir Ralph Percy, a knight who had been fully pardoned for former treacheries to King Edward, and had turned his coat again. Robert felt it keenly. And then fresh news reached them – that Warwick's brother, John, Lord Montague, had been given the princely earldom of Northumberland, chief title of the treacherous Percies.

Robert hung his head at this further disgrace to his name, and from that day he began to alter in many ways.

His friends tried to cheer him and make him see and realize the truth: that his own loyalty was not in question and English families had been torn in their allegiances for more than a generation.

He thanked them, and for their sake he went on trying to give an impression that he shared their pleasure in the campaign. But it was more than he could manage. Slowly his private grief ate away all his reserves. He shed his boyhood on that journey north back to Middleham.

And so their return to Middleham, though they were heaped with the good opinions of the king and his captains, and though it brought Richard back again to his Anne, was both quiet and sad.

IV

George of Clarence had every fault and virtue of the Plantagenets to excess, being the handsomest and vainest, potentially the most talented yet in fact the most stupid and feckless of them all.

He had always been the odd one: promising to be paunchy and becoming lean, promising to develop a strong and dominating personality and becoming unstable and easily led. It was characteristic that, as soon as Edward allowed him his own establishment, George chose to surround himself with sycophants, and it was not long before only his confessor, his mother and his brother were in a position to be candid with him. Even this was too much for George. His unruly nature choked on bits. And so, though he had put up with the king, he tended to neglect his mother, and quickly changed his confessor for another – a Dominican with a reputation for softness, for being too heavenly to be of much earthly use.

Being such a contradiction perhaps it was inevitable that he should actually be jealous of his younger brother who, in so many particulars, seemed less fortunate than he. Certainly he envied the grants and honours given Richard for his work as sole commissioner for nine of the twenty-two southern counties, though Edward was scrupulously just and never overlooked George's claims upon him both as heir-apparent and as Richard's elder brother.

Perhaps it was inevitable, too, that, with London as his plaything and all England at his disposal, the one and only place George longed to be was where his young brother served as a donzel.

The news that Clarence had the king's permission to make a progress through the country as heir-apparent, and that he would stay at Middleham threw the castle into a turmoil of preparation. Warwick was occupied with the weighty matter of the king's French marriage, but his countess made a special journey to Wensleydale in order to welcome the Duke of Clarence and stir up her household. This she did as thoroughly and as effectively as if she were prodding a beehive with a stick – ordering the castle to be scrubbed, cleaned, scoured and turned out from top to bottom, fitting a set of apartments with rich hangings, ordering a series of banquets, and arranging tourneys and hunts and extravagant entertainments quite regardless of the expense.

The comptroller and the treasurer had a high sense of duty and they were appalled by the costliness of the preparations. They went to the countess and told her with the candour of loyal servants that, though her lord had great possessions and ranked as one of the richest magnates in the kingdom, there were yet limits to his purse, and that it appeared unnecessary to honour one of the king's brothers with such magnificence when the other was but a donzel at the castle. She swept the objections aside declaring that the 'little one' was of small account, but George of Clarence was England's heir until the French marriage was concluded and the king had sons. Moreover, though Edward was lustier than most and would beget sons with ease, bearing and breeding them to healthy manhood was ever a lottery. Allowing for miscarriages, stillbirths, and all the hazards of lying-in, Clarence might still remain heir-apparent for a good long time, and afterwards be heir-presumptive. Something in her tone, a suggestive nod in the direction of her daughters' apart-ments, told the two men her real and unspoken motive. Very quickly rumour caught hold of the idea that the Nevilles would not be averse from marrying one of their daughters to the Duke of Clarence.

Richard was already downcast when he heard the rumour because Robert, though he had improved in the weeks since their return, was still not the old Robert, and Miles Metcalfe had just left the mess for a lawyer's chambers in York City. The rumour of Neville match-making made his heart sink still further.

Clearly everyone's thoughts were on the Lady Isabel, but what if George's eye should settle on his Anne? and would she not be charmed by George's good looks . . . and prospects . . . and older years . . . and higher position? It was impossible that she could prefer him to George. He whipped himself with memories that belonged to the unhappy past when he had been called the runt of

York's fine litter, the little one, the crooked one, the sickly one to be pitied and patted.

Waiting for his brother to reach Middleham was a long and drawn-out torment, and when the day came, and Wensleydale echoed to the thunder of cannonades and cheers and trumpet fanfares, Richard could not bring himself to be gracious in his welcome.

For this one special occasion he had been summoned to be with the family in the Presence Chamber, and he stood on the dais, a little to the left of the Lady Anne, with Francis and Robert behind him as his squires, racked with suspense and promising Our Lady of Walsingham a dozen yellow candles if George should prefer Isabel to Anne. And George did. He made it obvious that he was taken with his glittering cousin Isabel – and Richard's face first drained white and then flushed crimson in relief.

The Duke of Clarence, in fact, had been caught by Lady Warwick, for not only was Isabel a beauty in her own right but had been dressed in an eye-catching gown of yellow and white so that she stood out like a butterfly amongst moths. It was a showy piece of stage-management which a mature man might have shied away from, but the countess guessed she need not waste subtlety on George of Clarence. He was a great calf too naif to see the obvious, and once caught he could hardly keep his eyes off the coltish and yet voluptuous charms of her elder daughter. She was a well-satisfied mother and, when the formal welcome was concluded, curtsied deeply to her guest and retired with Anne and Isabel through the curtained doorway to her solar.

George was led to the luxurious apartments set aside for him. He insisted that Richard and his squires go with him, and no sooner had he kicked off his long boots than he was talking of Isabel, asking endless questions, gulping at the spiced wine sent up from the buttery, pacing the floor, making plans to bring himself to her notice, and suddenly roaring out for a bath, hot water, scented oils and lenitives, fresh clothes to make him sweeter for his lady – which was such an unusual request for that time of the year that the Middleham servants were temporarily dumbfounded.

George went on asking questions about Isabel, so many questions, one on top of the other, that neither Richard nor his friends had a proper chance to answer any of them. They could hardly get in a word. But when the bath arrived the warm water began to soothe his excitement, and for the first time he had thoughts for his brother.

'Dick,' he said. 'It is months since we saw you at court and I've barely greeted you.' He sloshed water over his knees and smiled at Richard. 'You've grown, lad. And life must be good here for you're as fit as a bowman.'

Richard grinned as George added reflectively: 'But who would not be, living at Middleham?' This almost sent him off into another panegyric in praise of Isabel, but he remembered his manners and asked to meet his brother's squires. Richard formally presented them, and George with the easy charm that he could exercise if he took the trouble had something agreeable to say to each of them. Unwittingly he worked a miracle on Robert Percy by remarking that he knew both his father and uncle and highly valued their friendship. Robert's sad eyes brightened at this recognition of the unbroken loyalty of at least a part of his family. He actually smiled the sort of true smile which his friends had not seen for months, and they were delighted. It was something else for which Richard had cause to be thankful.

This coloured his attitude to George, and for a day or two they were such obvious friends that the neighbouring lords and gentlemen at Middleham for the tourneys and entertainments remarked on the great fortune of their kind in having devoted brothers like the Dukes of Clarence and Gloucester.

It was George who spoilt the picture. He was inconsistent, and under strain he always reacted childishly. He wanted to excel, to show off before Isabel like a vain cock in springtime, and the more his lady approved of his singing and dancing, his wit, his horsemanship, his skill with the bow and his adventures in the tiltyard, the greedier he became for her approval. With the sly cunning of a child he decided that he would shine brightest and show himself to the greatest possible advantage against a butt.

He might have chosen anyone because few at Middleham could match him at any courtly or knightly exercise, but for years it had been second nature for him to bully his younger brother, and he chose Richard without either thought or mercy.

Thus there began the first in a series of misadventures which clouded Richard's last days as a donzel at Middleham, when George his own brother cunningly used him as a butt, showing him up and making a fool of him time after time, drawing attention to his limited skill in dancing and other elegant arts, to his small stature, to his ignorance of the prevailing modes and customs at court; worse still by belittling his considerable talents . . . and George worked all this mischief so playfully and charmingly that hardly anyone at Middleham in those gay and hectic days detected any malice in his actions. He certainly caught and held Isabel's affection, and never lost it all his life; and the countess was so delighted with the success of her scheme that she barely noticed that the Duke of Gloucester seemed to be replacing the castle clown in everyone's estimation. Had it not been for his friends, Richard might easily have tried to protect himself by actually becoming the picture George was painting and ended as a buffoon, but his mess-mates were so angry, and so indignant at his harassment that their sympathy made him suffer the humiliations with a quiet dignity.

George of Clarence reaped a large harvest from his stay at Middleham; the love of a rich and beautiful heiress, the high opinions of all the lords in Wensleydale and beyond, the adoration of the servants he had treated so lavishly, the fury of a score of boys who one day would be influential in the kingdom, and the bitter hatred of his younger brother.

V

Early one morning the porter was woken by the arrival of three mud-spattered horsemen before the barbican. It was Warwick with but two followers. Ordinarily he arrived at Middleham after long notice and with a large retinue, and his sudden, unexpected appearance startled the whole household.

The comptroller, still not fully dressed, hurried to keep up with him as he strode up the keep staircase and through the Presence Chamber . . . Would he break his fast? Would he hear Mass? Would his company soon follow? But Warwick made no reply at all. He merely waved the comptroller aside and went into his private apartments.

No one at Middleham had ever seen him in such a black rage. The reason was quickly forthcoming from the squire and servant who had ridden with him. It passed from mouth to mouth. Warwick and the king had quarrelled.

The matter was so near to Richard that his face blanched when he heard of it.

Edward had allowed and encouraged Warwick to negotiate on his behalf a highly advantageous, dynastic marriage with the French princess, and then – the arrangements actually completed – had calmly announced in Council that he had changed his mind. There would be no French marriage. Warwick allowed the king his little joke, although he did not care for it at all, and politely humoured him until Edward snapped out a second time that there would be no French marriage. Moreover, he added insolently, as Lord Warwick was in such close contact with the French court he could communicate his firm decision to King Louis.

This defiance had made Warwick almost choke with fury. Pounding the council board with clenched fist, he rated the king with base ingratitude for placing his chief councillor in an impossible position of ridicule. But Edward had cut him short, bidding him hold his tongue and remember he was but a subject, and stunned the council to silence by saying he'd no mind to commit bigamy. He was already married to a widow lady well known for her virtue and beauty, Dame Elizabeth Woodville. Which, he finished pertly, was an end of the matter – save that his councillors might now consider a suitable day for the queen's coronation.

Richard was awed by Edward's defiance of his most powerful supporter and quick to realize how this might affect his position at Middleham. He tried, though, to make light of it.

'What is said of Dame Elizabeth?' he asked. 'I know nothing of her.'

Nor did any of the donzels, and the servant who had brought the news from the kitchens appeared reluctant to say very much.

'It is muddled, my lord . . . garbled,' he said.

'Yet I would know,' insisted Richard, and urged it out of the man. As he listened he was dismayed. Even allowing for prejudice and exaggeration the picture of Edward's queen was still an unattractive one. She was neither young nor rich nor even amiable, and being of the menalty she was scorned by the nobles and resented by the commons. It seemed she was a shrewd and scheming beauty with an appetite for power, and an enormous and complicated family which included two teenage sons, a step-father and a step-son – all of whom were equally greedy for grants and honours. Already they had descended on the court and were leeching the good-natured and besotted Edward for titles, manors, estates, appointments and sine-cures with such assiduity that very soon – so ran the tale – England would be ruled by Woodvilles.

When the horn for dinner blew Warwick emerged from his private apartments with the countess, walking stiffly and with his eyes cast down. He looked up while the chaplain intoned grace and at once it was obvious that he had lost none of his rage.

The donzel whose turn it was to wait at the dais, trembled when he offered his lord a silver ewer of water and a napkin. A few spilt drops of water earned him more curses than he had ever heard from Warwick.

The meal began. The minstrels were nervous and played false notes. Down in the hall all voices were subdued. On the dais no one spoke at all.

The donzel made another mistake: spilling wine this time on the edge of his lord's cuff. Warwick cursed and knocked him down.

The musicians stopped playing one by one, and in the hushed silence everyone could hear the upturned jug glugging its contents on the dais. Then, harshly, came Warwick's voice commanding the comptroller to send the boy away and find another less oafish. Abruptly he looked down the hall, and in a lower tone, a voice of ice, he said: 'By the splendour of God, I'll have his brother serve me.'

Richard looked up from his place at the donzels' table, far more frightened now than when Warwick had thrashed him in the mess. It was as though he had been chosen to act the principal part in a play without any warning at all, without having read the script, and without the least idea of what to do or say. He looked at his friends.

'Gloucester!' cried Warwick. 'Gloucester shall serve me.'

The boy stood up and walked to the buttery for a flagon of wine. Hurriedly the minstrels began to play, and a hum of conversation followed.

Warwick made no attempt to cat-and-mouse young Richard. He was outspokenly malevolent, sometimes speaking to him directly, more often loudly expressing his opinion of the king to everyone on the dais: calling him ingrate, puppy, treacherous lecher, soft lad with a crown. If he hoped to provoke the boy he was unsuccessful, and this was simply because Richard was too frightened even to think of Edward; scared out of his wits by the sight of his admired godfather, a choleric man by nature but generally so strictly self-controlled, in the grip of such mad fury.

The meal went on and on, but Warwick ate nothing, merely drank and cursed and excoriated the king . . . cup after cup until it became plain by an alteration in his manner that he was three parts drunk. Under ordinary circumstances this might have made him angrier still but he had reached the limit of his vitality. He was too exhausted by his long ride from court, by the continual spilling out of his fury, by sick disappointment which eats men's vigour like the crab, and the wine soothed rather than inflamed him. Yet Richard was still in danger. As Warwick's manic anger died, so did the boy's terror and his instinct of self-preservation. Now he was able to think of Edward, and unspokenly resent his godfather's rancour.

Warwick somehow sensed this. 'So, our pretty Edward, who has neither honour nor wits commands your loyalty?'

Richard made no reply.

'Does he not?'

'Aye, my lord,' said Richard. 'For he is my brother.'

93

'Whom you love?'

'Whom I love.'

'Yet he is base, asleep to honour, double-faced . . .' Warwick raised his voice. He wanted to make certain every word was heard. But it was unnecessary. Not a sound came from the hall. They were all listening. 'He is an easy fish caught on the hook of lust . . . thoughtless of his friends . . . now prey to the contemptible family of his ruttish woman . . . This, Gloucester, is your brother.'

Richard fixed his eyes on the great salt cellar before Warwick. 'Aye, my lord,' he mumbled. 'And my king.'

'So!'

'As he is yours, my lord.'

There was a pause, an intaking of breath, then for a brief moment the yellow flame leapt again. 'By the Passion of Christ!' roared Warwick – but his voice was drowned by a crash from the hall. A bench at the donzels' table had been kicked over backwards and half a dozen boys were sprawling in the rushes.

The suddenness of it checked Warwick and snapped back his self-control. He was aware immediately that the bench had been up-turned in order to divert his anger; an act which made him admire the loyalty of Richard's friends though he did what was expected of him by cursing the boys and ordering the master-at-arms to correct their boorish manners. At the same time instinct told him that he would but harden Richard's loyalty if he continued to make him a public spectacle. It was not the way to wean him from Edward, not the Neville way.

He looked back at Richard. 'So, you would teach me my loyalties, Dick?' he said softly.

Richard made no reply.

'Tell me that Edward has but been foxed by a mean widow who kept her legs fast tight together till she had him mad as a springtime tup?'

Richard knew nothing of his brother's wife save what he had been told three hours before. Wisely he ventured no opinion of her at all.

'Look at me, Dick.'

Richard did so, reluctantly dragging his eyes from the safety of the salt cellar, but he was agreeably surprised. Warwick had lost his black look of self-pity, and nowhere was there a sign of the rage that had disfigured his face.

94

His smile encouraged Richard to say: 'I know little of the queen, my lord. But Edward, my brother, is our king.'

Warwick looked down the hall before he replied: 'Aye, Dick. You are right. You are right.'

The Earl left the castle as suddenly as he had arrived there – giving it out that he would take himself as far from the royal court as possible. No one knew if this were true or not.

That same afternoon Richard met the Lady Anne in the inner garden by appointment. He was accompanied as custom demanded by Francis and Robert, Anne by two of her ladies. These four attendants sat on turf seats by the wicket-gate and talked while the two cousins walked up and down the paths.

The air was cool but fragrant with herbs, and the wind-beaten flowers still attracted some last bees of autumn. It was a beautiful and tranquil place and Anne's presence would ordinarily have been a balm to help Richard forget the hurts done to him by his brother George and his lord the Earl of Warwick. But it seemed as if misfortunes now were snowballing, that there was a malign Loki sitting on his shoulder prodding him into disaster after disaster.

By accident – for neither intended or wanted it – they quarrelled.

Out of politeness, nothing else, Anne said she was sure her father would quickly forgive the king. It was the very worst thing she could have said. Still raw and unnerved by Warwick's enraged hostility, Richard could scarcely believe his ears. He regarded her with amazement. Such evidence of her Neville pride appeared to inflame his own, and as warmly as a boy in his first love can do so, he corrected her, saying the reverse was truer, that the king might come to forgive her father, but not of course until Warwick had deserved his pardon.

Anne had not set out to offend him. Bewildered, she tried to make amends for her stupidity and, as sometimes happens, only made the matter worse. He was sharp with her, too sharp she thought, and at once she hardened. He hardened as well. Now they were two proud spirits picking at the sores that hurt them but unable to stop. Neither would submit.

'The king,' said Richard, his face white, 'may do as he wishes.

95

He is free to choose a wife. Should he wish to marry any woman in England . . . the basest in his palace . . . a kitchenmaid, he could do so. . . .'

'Is not that what he has done?' she cut in with spirit. 'From all I hear of Elizabeth Woodville she is base enough.'

For the first time she saw his lips thin into a double line of suppressed fury.

'Elizabeth Woodville, as you so lightly call her, madam, is my brother's wife and queen.'

'Yet base!' All the Neville arrogance was in her voice. 'For my father has said she is base.'

'Your father is my brother's subject, Lady Anne.'

'Lord Richard, your brother was helped to his throne by my father. Warwick made him king.'

'He reigns by Warwick's pleasure?' he shouted.

'Aye, sir, by Warwick's pleasure. Is he not called the kingmaker?'

And, turning, Anne called to her startled ladies, and began to walk from the garden.

Suddenly contrite and appalled at what he had done Richard followed.

'Madam . . .' he stammered. 'Anne. . . .'

She walked on and would not turn – until she heard him appeal to Robert and Francis to help convince her. . . . tell her . . . assure her . . . plead with her to stop. Then, because her pride was as dissolvable as his, and his voice betrayed such unhappiness, she stopped and turned back to him.

They walked silently together by a raised bed of costmary; he whitefaced, she with her eyes moist. And spontaneously she touched his wrist. It said more than any words, and promised nothing should come between them again and their quarrel would be forgotten when next they met.

But they were not to meet again for a long, long time.

* * *

After supper at five o'clock the comptroller of the household sent for Prince Richard, to the little chamber which he gravely called the Warwick Chancellery. Purposely he had dismissed his two scriveners so that they should be alone. He gave the boy his chair and walked up and down the room. Richard stirred uneasily. It was not the comptroller's custom to be deferential to a donzel no matter how noble. The reason was soon made clear.

The comptroller had orders to equip the Duke of Gloucester with all necessary arms and provide him with an escort for his journey home.

'Home?' Richard was dazed, for where was his home but there at Middleham?

The comptroller explained. He was to go to court, leave Middleham, be with his brothers.

'For how long, sir?'

'Lord Richard, I regret it, but your time with us is over.'

He went on to give details of the journey south to London, but Richard hardly heard a word. He was too stunned by his godfather's sudden order. Then anger found his voice for him. 'My lord of Warwick is ungentle,' he interrupted. 'He does me less than justice to drive me from Middleham.'

The comptroller looked away from him and fingered the bears and staffs linked to each other in his chain of office. 'My lord does not yet know of this,' he said. 'I am acting on his behalf by carrying out the king's command.'

'The king?' Richard sprang to his feet.

'Aye, my lord.' This time the comptroller looked at him steadily. 'You are not driven from Middleham but summoned to court.' He turned away again, aware that he was but playing with words. It was all the same. If King Edward had not acted Warwick would have done.

'I regret it, my lord,' he said once more, genuinely distressed that a boy's happiness should be crushed between the two heaviest millstones in the kingdom, though he knew his duty too well to say so.

The full realization of what it would mean came home to Richard. If he left the next day at dawn he would not see Anne again.

He forced himself to sound unconcerned. Lightly he said: 'I would go the day after, sir.'

The comptroller shook his head. 'The king's command is explicit. You are to leave within twelve hours of receiving the warrant.'

'But it will take us longer to prepare for such a journey.'

The comptroller raised his eyebrows. 'Us?' he repeated.

97

Richard's heart sank. 'I am to leave alone?' he stammered unbelievingly. 'But Percy and Lovell were with me on the king's affairs this summer . . .' Then seeing the look in the other's eyes he threw his dignity aside and pleaded like a frightened schoolboy. 'Sir. I *must* have them with me. Without them I shall be cut off: alone . . . and let me, I beg you, leave on the day after tomorrow . . . or tomorrow at nightfall. Sir, I beg you.'

The comptroller could not bear to see him so unhappy, and he cursed his duty. But he knew he must do it. His lord would be doubly angry if he permitted Lovell and Percy to leave for court. Moreover, the king would hardly welcome them. For a moment he was seriously tempted to postpone the departure, but no, he dared not risk it.

'Lord Richard, I fear you go only with your servant and with a Middleham escort who will return here. And you will leave tomorrow.'

For a moment Richard wildly thought of trying to use his rank and insist that as a royal duke his commands were law – but he knew the comptroller too well. It would be no use.

'At dawn?' he said, his lip trembling.

'Aye, my lord.'

98

VI

Since his victory at Mortimer's Cross Edward Plantagenet had used a sun in splendour as his personal emblem. It was appropriate. Standing over six feet tall, and said to be the handsomest prince, even the handsomest man in Europe, he radiated charm and beauty, affection and energy exactly like a sunburst.

Richard, fresh to the dazzling court, quickly fell under Edward's spell again. The hero-worship which had budded long before now bloomed profusely. Nothing Edward did, or ever could do, would shake his younger brother's loyalty. It helped to soothe his bitterness at being cut off from Anne and his friends at Middleham, and even made the continual presence of George more bearable.

Love, though, did not blind him to the king's faults.

Edward was a man of huge appetites who loved beauty and luxury and would deny himself nothing: a king who apparently indulged everyone and anyone and allowed liberties to be taken with his prerogatives which no other living prince would tolerate. But this made no difference to Richard's dog-like devotion and Edward spontaneously responded by giving him his confidence. It was a precious reward, given to so few that, in all the kingdom, their number could have been counted on the fingers of one hand.

This privileged company knew the real Edward as a shrewd ruler, aware of most of the intrigues in his court and yet subtle enough to pretend the opposite. Everyone believed the king had defied Warwick simply because Elizabeth Woodville would never consent to be anything less than queen. He smiled and let them think so because it suited him. He saw no reason to tell anyone he remembered the salutary lesson taught by Hotspur and Henry Bolingbroke: that a kingdom must have but one ruler. Nor did he care in the least that everyone believed his new queen was a scold who nagged him into advancing her large family. Privately it amused him to satisfy their greed by showering on them a golden rain of manor lands, peerages, good marriages and military commands. At the same time, by advancing the lesser gentry to positions of influence, he was also reducing the power of the old nobility whose partisanship and pride had been the cause of civil war. Men thought the king degraded his crown by receiving merchants and parvenues at court. He smiled and let them think so, knowing that only through the wealth of his new associates could he keep the Lancastrians in check and his own coffers full. His courtiers said he would lose his vitality and dignity through self-indulgence, but he knew the measure of his stamina better than they, and, as sometimes they found to their cost, the easy-going lecher of one moment could become a man of iron will the next.

Edward was precisely the king England needed after two decades of civil war, but because he was self-dependent, and relied on the counsel of so few, he made some errors of judgement and had blind spots.

One – which cost him dear – was his reluctance to confide any longer in his mother. Initially they had quarrelled over a lady-in-waiting of her household. The Duchess Cecily was no puritan but she was outraged to discover the king had seduced her favourite confidante, a quiet dark girl named Eleanor Butler. To take his lust into her own private home showed scant respect for her as his mother, and she rated him in the haughty, Neville fashion which generally reduced any member of her family to complete submission. But on that occasion Edward had not been of a mind to accept such a scolding, even from his mother, and with a smile that belied his true feelings he reminded her that he was an absolute king, not a nursery babe. She would not let him see how he had wounded her, and thereafter maintained a proud indifference which she certainly did not feel and which only served to widen the gap between them. His secret marriage to Elizabeth Woodville did nothing to repair the damage, nor did his summary action in summoning Richard from Middleham. More galling still, when the queen bore his first child, though it was a little girl and not the longed-for prince, he made the christening the occasion of a sumptuous court ceremony, and did not trouble to invite his mother. He hurt her, too, by naming the princess after his Woodville queen.

It was foolish of Edward for had he consulted with her she would have warned him not to readmit her nephew Warwick to the council. Edward believed it was safe, seeing the earl simply as a clever ambitious magnate who had been put in his place. But Warwick was far more dangerous to the kingdom – a schoolboy whose pricked vanity made him long for revenge. To readmit him to the council as though nothing had happened was as naïve as it was generous. But Edward did just this, and, moreover, gave Warwick fresh responsibilities and honours. In her apartments in Baynard's Castle the duchess heard that Warwick was in favour once again, and she knew what it would mean to England.

✳

Richard was embarrassed by Warwick's first return to court. Emotionally and in every other way he was now committed to the king, yet he knew he owed much to Warwick, and Warwick was Anne's father. On the first occasion they were alone together his godfather surprised him by showing not the least trace of resentment that the king had arbitrarily plucked him away from Middleham.

'It was time you left, my lad, and here they are teaching you what you could never learn in Wensleydale.'

Richard wondered if this was a tilt at the comfort and opulence of Edward's court, and he showed in his eyes what he was thinking.

Warwick chuckled. 'I mean it, Dick,' he said. 'Your place in the kingdom is high, and you must learn to rule as deputy. Attend at the councils and pick what you can from the chancellery officers. Don't miss a single opportunity. England has need of solemn, hard-working viceroys.'

Again Richard wondered, was he tilting at Edward – and George? But Warwick put an arm round his shoulder. 'I'll say it again. Don't miss a single opportunity to learn.' Then suddenly he stared into his godson's eyes. 'You're content here, Dick?'

'Yes, my lord . . .' Richard's voice trailed off. It was in his mind to be frank and say how much he still missed Middleham, above all Anne. But he could not be so outspoken to Anne's father.

Warwick smiled suggestively. 'But like all Englishmen you find the queen's family over-forward for your liking?'

'No, my lord,' said Richard. He was taken aback. 'No,' he repeated firmly.

'Good lad!' said Warwick heartily. 'Spoken truly like a well-taught jackdaw.'

Richard, hot-faced, protested: 'I am not taught what I should say, my lord.'

'No? Then I like your spirit. It shows you value loyalty. Aye, Dick. Keep yourself hooded to the queen and all her brood, and you'll serve the king well.' Richard opened his mouth to make a second protest, but Warwick went on in the same bland, agreeable tone: 'Brothers need brothers, and Clarence, they say, is slow to give anything unless he is baited first with lavish promises —'

'George is but George,' said Richard simply, caught off his guard.

'And you are Richard of Gloucester, my own dear cousin and godson.' Warwick squeezed his arm. 'A courier came from Middleham early this morning.'

Richard tried to keep the excitement from his voice. 'Aye, my lord?'

'And I have fond messages for you from my family and the household.' He smiled. 'But more of that at another time, for I must to the king.' He turned to go. 'Be sure, lad; he needs all our love and counsel in this nest of Woodvilles.' This time Richard made no protest. 'Attend me, Dick, when you will.'

'Aye, my lord.'

It was an hour before Richard realized what Warwick had been trying to do, that he had been attempting to suborn him, to seduce him as cunningly as some of the court women who tried to get him into their beds. The shock of it unnerved Richard for a moment, and he had to clench his hands to prevent them from trembling.

Attend me when you will. It was the old French game of *taquinerie* – teasing with offers, threats, promises, withdrawals, bargains, feints, bluffs – and Anne was to be the prize.

His eyes swam because for many years Warwick had taken the place of his dead father, and though Richard had few illusions and knew most of the earl's weaknesses, he had not guessed their extent. Now, for the first time, Warwick had exposed himself as shamefully and hurtfully as drunken Noah before his sons, and Richard could see him in his true colours: ruthless, deceitful, childish, totally unforgiving. And the unsavoury reality lost Warwick precisely what he had hoped to gain. By using Anne as bait in a game of *taquinerie* he had forfeited all claim to respect and service, and his godson no longer had a problem of divided loyalties. Suddenly it occurred to him that Warwick might have tried to suborn George in the same way. Anne and Richard – Isabel and George.

He sent his servant to inquire if his brother was in the court that day. The boy returned after some minutes with the information that his grace of Clarence was at the Westminster pit.

George was in a sunny mood. One of his cronies had toppled by accident into the pit and when Richard arrived they were just pulling him out. The man was bleeding from a torn cheek, and sweating and cursing with fear. George chided him, ridiculing his terror.

'It's a devil, and you know it, my lord,' said the man hotly.

'The bear? God's head, Ackerley, he's a mangy beast. As are the dogs. I've a mind to throw you back for a tussle.' Then he caught sight of Richard. 'Dick lad!' he called. 'Come and see our sport. Poor though it is.'

When Richard stood beside him he said: 'Now is he not a tame and scruffy brute?'

'Aye!' Richard nodded.

'Yet he can breed daughters,' he added quietly.

'Eh?' George did not follow this, but he had had enough of the bear-baiting and took Richard's arm. 'Come, we'll walk by the river, but someone shall first bring us malmsey.'

It was typical of him that he gave no instructions and merely mentioned what he wanted; typical too, of the place-hunters in his company that they hung so much on his words they needed no commands but sought to please him without being asked. They stayed where they were to let the royal brothers talk in privacy. No less than three pages raced off to fetch their master's favourite wine.

When they were out of everyone's hearing Richard repeated: 'A bear can breed daughters.'

'Aye, of course. But what's the riddle, Dick?' A smile creased George's face. 'I see. A bear and staff is Warwick's emblem – and he has daughters.'

Richard nodded. 'The Lady Isabel,' he began, and stopped for the word Isabel was like a spark in stubble, firing all George's enthusiasm for the girl of his heart.

Richard let him run on until he said: 'Were it not for Edward's blindness she would be my wife.'

Then his brother affected surprise. 'Surely he would not prevent a match?'

It goaded George to give his candid opinion of a king who married as he wished and would not let his brothers do the same . . .

and, through all he said, Richard could hear Warwick's voice, his argument, his persuasions. To be absolutely certain of this he grasped the nettle, saying blandly: 'Yet after his breach with our family I doubt if my lord of Warwick would consent.'

George regarded him with astonishment. 'Not consent? Dick, Dick, your brain's pea-sized. But then' – he added patronizingly – 'you're young and ignorant of the affairs of court. Be sure he will consent, and gladly. That is, he will if . . .' He was interrupted by the arrival of the malmsey. 'Good lad,' he said to the page who had won the race. He took a cup. 'Now one for my lord of Gloucester, and off you go.'

When the boy had scampered out of earshot, he continued. 'Never doubt Isabel's father, Dick. He has a good heart and takes trouble for his children. Already he has promises of a papal dispensation for our marriage . . .'

'You are sure of this?' snapped Richard, interrupting. 'You believe you can trust Warwick?'

George finished his wine and nodded. 'It is Edward who stands in our way. Only Edward.'

✳

Richard's head was spinning as he walked back to his apartments, for he had no idea how to deal with this dilemma. Should he go to Edward? or to Hastings the chamberlain? or to his mother at Baynard's Castle?

His heart jumped when he found a man sitting on the bench outside his door, and recognized him as a courier from Middleham.

The man smiled. 'I waited, Lord Richard.'

Richard forced himself to return the smile. 'You bring messages?' he asked.

The courier nodded. 'From my lord,' he said.

'Yes?'

'Who bids you to sup with him.'

'Today?'

'Today: when he will give you news of Middleham.'

Richard opened the door and beckoned the man to follow. Inside he took off his mantle and walked to the corner seat. He was thinking

104

rapidly. Without looking at the courier he said: 'You could give me news of Middleham yourself.'

'But that I am bidden to keep the pleasure for supper.'

'You are bidden?'

The man bowed. 'By my lord himself. He bade me tell you good tidings are like wine and best enjoyed after maturing.'

'So it is good news?'

The man shrugged. 'My lord also added that if wine matures too long it sours to vinegar.'

Richard sat down, longing for Anne and Middleham, Robert and Francis.

'Tell your lord,' he said briefly, 'that I sup at Baynard's Castle with my lady mother.'

When the courier had gone he gave way to silent bitter tears.

VII

Duchess Cecily had not been herself for a week or more. She never complained but it was obvious to her ladies that she was unwell. They noticed a slight alteration in her speech. Her voice, usually so sharp and clear, was sometimes muffled, and she had developed a habit of touching her temples as though to soothe a headache. Twice she had suffered from profuse bleeding from the nose. On the second occasion her ladies suggested they send for a physician. They at once regretted it. Cecily was still an imperious woman even when her nose was bleeding and she was lying on a stone floor. Thereafter the household pretended that their formidable mistress was as healthy as ever.

It followed that when the Duke of Gloucester proposed himself for supper at Baynard's Castle the ladies were much relieved. One of them was deputed to meet him at the gatehouse and inform him of his mother's illness.

Richard, who had his own troubles, was inclined to be short with her. 'Your task is to serve my lady mother,' he snapped. 'If she will not send for the physician, then he must go to her without being summoned.'

'But, my lord!' exclaimed the woman, so startled that she asked him if he himself would dare to do as much were he a physician.

He relented. She was right, of course. 'No,' he admitted. 'I should not care to risk it.' He threw his reins to a groom. 'Very well, I shall try to persuade my mother to consult her physician.'

After what he had been told he was surprised to find her looking so benign. She greeted him affectionately and teased him for neglecting her. 'I see you so seldom, Dickon,' she chided.

He kissed her hand and then her cheek. It was the best reply he could make.

On his return from Middleham she had hoped he would be allowed to make his home at Baynard's Castle but Edward had refused to consider the idea. His brother must learn government and diplomacy at Westminster. As a result Richard saw less of his mother than either of them wished.

'You have been ill,' he said, stepping back to look at her, making it a statement not a question.

She stiffened, and he knew that he had been over-direct and tactless. With someone so sensitive and proud as his mother it was necessary to exercise a degree of subtlety and hint at such intimate personal matters as illness. But then, after his dealings that day with Warwick and George, he felt drained of all subtlety.

'I shall box their ears!' said Cecily, suddenly reminding him of his godfather on the day he was beaten in the donzels' mess. Evidently it was a habit sometimes with the Nevilles to leave out the whole body of an argument and leap straight from the toes to the head.

Having blundered once he risked it again; 'Tell me truly, madam,' he said.

But the only response he got was another sharp declaration that certain people's ears would tingle for this breach of confidence. In their corner by the doorway her ladies regarded each other with dismay.

At this he wisely decided to leave the subject until she was more bending and ready to be frank with him. He sat on a cushion at her feet and asked if he might have her advice before supper was brought in. 'In private,' he added.

She nodded and glanced at her attendants who were already hurrying to leave the solar.

When they had gone she smoothed her black gown and bent to touch his hand.

'Tell me,' she murmured. 'Do you still fret at Westminster?'

He spread his hands. 'Sometimes,' he admitted, and she nodded understandingly.

She knew he did not fit easily into the opulent surroundings which his brothers loved, and that he tolerated rather than enjoyed the endless banquets and tourneys, and the elaborate ceremonial which turned the simplest function into a feat of endurance. Like her he preferred simplicity, one flower more than a whole garden, one single minstrel singing to a lute rather than a great chorus accompanied by sackbuts, viols, rebecks and shawms.

He smiled wistfully. 'At Middleham the entertainments were less lavish.'

His tone of voice told her a great deal. 'So my lord of Warwick has returned to court.'

'Aye, Madam.'

'He is altered,' she said. 'Like butter melted, then allowed to harden. It is not the same.' Again she touched his hand. 'I find him different.'

'*You* find him different, Madam? He has already been here?'

'Naturally! He is my nephew. Politeness demanded that he should visit me.' She chuckled. 'But, in fact, curiosity brought him. He was out to discover what he could, find which way I lean, probe my feelings towards the queen. So!' She spread her hands: 'I told him to mind his business, mend his manners – and gave him a good dinner.'

'I wish I could have done the same,' said Richard wryly. Quickly, he told her of his own colloquy with Warwick, and how far George had been baited and hooked.

When he had finished she said softly: 'Be cautious, Dickon. Between them they'll prise you from your Anne unless . . . un . . . less . . . less . . .'

Her tongue fumbled for the words and Richard saw her eyes glaze over. With trembling fingers she bent forward for the third time to touch his hand . . . swayed a little . . . and suddenly blood gushed from her nostrils over his upturned face. Slowly she tippled forwards on top of him.

Richard barely knew where nightmare ended and reality began, lying there beneath the dead weight of his mother and drenched in her blood. He shouted – tasted the blood – shouted again. His cries brought in her ladies and the servants. But they stopped dead, horrified by what they saw. After a fractional pause some screamed, others clamoured in distress and wrung their hands, flapping the loose sleeves of their gowns. All were rendered useless until Richard's curses and shouts drove them to move. Then they lifted the Duchess and carried her to the bed.

'A physician!' cried Richard. 'Get a physician . . .' He went to the bed.

One of the ladies turned to him. 'She is insensible, my lord.'

Richard looked at his mother. They had removed her coif and for the first time in his life he saw her hair. It was yellowy-grey, and thin, so thin. It was this more than anything which for a moment almost unmanned him, to see her patches of baldness, and the distinct oval line about her face which marked the frontier between what she appeared to be and what she really was. Deliberately he bent forward to kiss the top of her head, and left there from his lips a slight trace of her own blood.

He threw off his doublet and they were wiping his face and hair when the physician arrived with two assistants.

He bobbed a bow at Richard. 'My duty to your grace,' he said, and went immediately to the bed.

The ladies had already begun to burn feathers, but he waved them aside and instructed two of them to remove the pillows and bolsters from beneath their mistress's head.

When he had examined her, he returned to Richard. 'A catalepsy, my lord. That is, a seizure, caused by a grossness of blood.'

'And this seizure is . . . curable?'

The physician smiled encouragingly but he would not commit himself. 'We shall bleed and purge your lady mother. And her chaplain will assist us with his prayers.' He turned to give instructions to the assistants; and Richard went to the door where his groom waited.

'Send – no – ride yourself to the court. With all speed. The king and my brother of Clarence must know of this.'

VIII

Within an hour both Edward and George had come to Baynard's Castle, and by then their mother had recovered consciousness. She was weak and needed rest, but she insisted on seeing the king. His brothers waited alone in the small chamber next to her solar.

Richard was silent. He was trying to forget the awful circumstances of her attack, yet, though he had washed several times and a servant had brought fresh clothes for him, he still imagined he could feel the warm stickiness of that blood torrent. George was anything but silent. Now certain that his mother was not dying, he was full of complaints because she had not asked to see him as well. He felt left out, unwanted, and he said so.

Edward had a grave face when he returned. He sent immediately for the physician.

'My mother will not die?' he asked.

The physician shook his head. 'No, your grace, I believe not,' he said, and added quickly: 'Though this catalepsy was a warning. It told us that your lady mother will need to rest and be watched most carefully for a considerable time, or – she will suffer another attack . . .' He left the sentence unfinished.

Edward thanked him. 'I will send Master Hobbes, my own physician, to consult with you, but we leave her in your care, and shall expect daily accounts of her recovery.'

The physician bowed and left the room.

'Why —' began George petulantly, but Edward cut him short.

'George, I wish to speak with Richard alone.'

This was too much for George. 'Very well then,' he shouted angrily. 'Dismiss me like a servant! Put me out of the room. Consult with my lord of Gloucester and tell him our mother's secrets.'

'Control yourself,' said Edward calmly. 'And leave us.' But he stiffened with anger when George opened the door and in full view of those who stood outside, he began to bow himself out of the chamber with a haughty insolence.

'By the Wounds of Our Saviour!' he roared, and George stopped his affected prancing and blanched with fear at the sudden fury in his brother's voice. 'One day, Clarence, you will outrun my patience.'

Richard, too, was alarmed and startled by the outburst of rage. When the door had closed he tried to mollify Edward by suggesting that George had intended no harm. He was unsuccessful.

'No harm!' exploded Edward. 'Is the crowned king of England to be defied and mocked by a popinjay? I tell you, brother, his school-boy pranks and petty jealousies, his greed and his ambition, and, most of all, his peacock stupidity threaten our house far more than that hell-cat Margaret or any Lancastrian alive.'

Richard regarded him with amazement. Never before had Edward given him so much as a hint of his real opinion of George.

Edward saw the astonished look, and it cooled his anger. 'Believe me, I'm no zany, Dick,' he said grimly. 'I know George's lunacy well enough, and I would to God he had half your good sense, and but a quarter of your loyalty.'

Richard shrugged. 'He is . . . easily led,' he suggested.

'Carrots to a donkey, aye!' said Edward contemptuously. 'And the Nevilles have a garden full of them.'

Richard looked down, his face crimson. Edward smiled, and chucked him under the chin. 'Why did you not tell me of your love for Warwick's girl?' he asked.

Richard muttered in reply: 'I seldom see your grace alone.' Then he asked: 'How did you know of it?'

'From our mother. It was this she wished to tell me, sick though she is. And she warned me of Warwick's foxiness.' He put an arm round Richard's shoulder. 'So you must run with them, Dick.'

'Run with them?' repeated his brother in dismay.

Edward nodded. 'We'll meet foxiness with foxiness,' he said. 'First, I'll scotch Clarence and refuse his request for the Lady Isabel.' He clenched his fist. 'Both he and Warwick must learn the metal of my will. But at the same time I'll save the old bear's pride by giving his brother George the Archbishopric of York. Yes!' he added with a chuckle. 'And you shall represent me at the enthronement, Dick; a duty I'd find tedious myself but you'll catch a glimpse of your Anne.'

Richard blushed again. 'But how may I run with them as you say?' he asked.

The king took his hand. 'I need a trusty hound of my own in the Neville pack,' he said seriously. 'I've learnt today of the implacable hostility of our noble cousin, but to deal with him effectively I must temporize. I need time to test his strength and call on my own; time to unravel his plots and make his malice impotent. You can help in this time, Dick, by playing his game.'

Richard looked doubtful. 'Come,' urged his brother. 'Warwick cannot harm you as long as you keep your wits. Be suave to him, attentive, even allow yourself to flatter him. It would fetch his confidence if you openly declared your interest in the Lady Anne. And if he should try to commit you to disloyalty, save yourself by appearing gawkish.' He chuckled. 'Yes. Appear to be as lunatic as brother George.'

Richard hesitated. 'Yet I could wish to follow a simpler path to the Lady Anne,' he said.

'It is the only path at your feet,' his brother pointed out. 'And do we not all long for simplicity?' He sighed. 'It is a pity that present circumstances do not allow me to chop off Warwick's head. It would be simpler.'

IX

Cecily's physicians were adamant in their instructions that she must have rest and quiet and receive no visitors who might alarm her and set back her recovery. The ladies of her household were bidden be gentle with their lady yet still firm; a command which at once made them throw up their hands. But then they discovered her imperiousness had gone. She could no longer command or even contradict them. The seizure had killed that power which once made men tremble in her presence.

She who had commanded all her life now had to obey and merely because a little mechanism in her personality no longer functioned as before. Her old friend and chaplain tried to help her, but Sir John himself was ailing. The cold and damp of Baynard's Castle wrung his lungs until they were screwed tight like damp leather. He was too feeble, too ill to help her; and then one day he quietly died. Cecily was not even given the privilege of appointing his successor. One of the other chaplains took his place, a priest she did not know and who, because he was young, she could not confide in.

She became a lonely, anguished old woman who sat listlessly in a chair or lay on a day-bed, taking refuge entirely in the past. Reliving her childhood at Raby Castle, and her life as bride and mother sometimes brought a sparkle to her eyes – a sign, said one physician, that her brain was damaged and soon she would be senile, though another took it as a happy augury for the future. But the sparkle died when they interrupted her happy dreaming to follow the strict regimen of the sickroom by carrying her to bed when she did not wish to rest or forcing her to eat when she had no appetite.

The world beyond her solar was as remote as the moon – and she heard nothing of the great events which were wrecking England's peace until one day a special messenger, a grave young man in a lawyer's gown, arrived at Baynard's Castle from Richard, Duke of Gloucester, and, for the first time since her seizure she was permitted to receive a caller.

It surprised her greatly. She eyed the young man who was brought to her by a physician, and her hand flew to her mouth.

'Now, your grace,' soothed one of her ladies. 'Do not agitate yourself.'

'This gentleman has brought a gift from your son,' explained the physician.

'Of fruit, my lady,' said the messenger. 'Fresh picked this day.' He held out a basket to the wizened old lady.

'Which son?'

'From the Lord Richard,' he replied.

'Duke of Gloucester,' added one of the ladies.

Cecily closed her eyes. She wanted, desperately, to turn on the woman with all the bite and cold ferocity she had once commanded. Did she consider her an imbecile, a senile cretin, that she could not identify her own beloved Dickon? But it was as though a landed fish flapped helplessly in her insides. She was incapable of rebuking anyone.

'Who sends you his loving duty and assurance of his constant prayers for your recovery,' continued the lawyer.

The duchess began to smile, then she stopped. They had drawn her few remaining teeth, to free Aries from poison, as they put it, and she would not bare her gums to anyone, not even Dickon's messenger whom she believed she recognized. She thanked him and asked his name.

'Metcalfe, your grace. Miles Metcalfe.'

'Aye,' she said softly. 'So I thought.'

The physician was at once on the alert. He regarded her with anxiety, and wondered if she was indeed as senile as some of his colleagues claimed. Brain softening could sometimes be preluded by pretending acquaintance with strangers.

But then she said: 'Walsingham. Dear comforting Walsingham!'

And to the physician's amazement the lawyer bowed and replied: 'It is many years since, your grace.'

Undoubtedly they were acquainted, and she had recognized him. Far from being senile she showed an acuteness rare in the elderly. The physician beamed with delight. This would confound his pessimistic colleagues.

The duchess underlined the sharpness of her memory. 'I would know you, Miles, even in your raven gown,' she said, and added: 'You were ever a merry boy and Dickon has told me much of your pranks together.'

'I serve him when I am able —' began Miles, but the physician interrupted to say her grace must not be tired and the interview should end. Her mention of Miles's merriment and pranks alarmed him. She must on no account be excited.

And Cecily, though she had a thousand clamant questions to put to Miles, did not object. She had learnt some of the skills of subservience, and one was to postpone graciously what she wanted immediately. She put out her hand for Miles to kiss. 'You will give my blessing and my love to Lord Richard?' she asked. 'And come again to see me?'

A barely perceptible nod and his eyes said yes he would be back, but with his voice he said: 'Your grace, I would not by so much as a half-second set back your full restoration to health, and only your learned physicians can tell how best I may serve you.'

She nodded and dismissed him, and the physician, charmed by Miles's tact and prudence could hardly wait to get him outside before assuring him that he would confer with his colleagues on the advisability of granting her request. 'As you are acquainted with her grace it might serve to lighten the darker corners of her convalescence.'

Miles bowed: 'I know little of your mystery, sir, but your wise suggestion proves you a worthy follower of Galen and Hippocrates.'

The physician rubbed his hands together. 'We shall hope to see you soon, Master Metcalfe, as our associate in this enterprise.'

It was simply arranged. Thereafter Miles was permitted to visit the king's mother at regular intervals. And he took her surer healing than all the leeching and astrological calculations, and talismanic treatments, and the draughts of crushed gems and powdered gold of her physicians.

At first his visits were short and always under the supervision of a physician, and he was strictly prohibited from mentioning any subject which might excite her; in short, forbidden to talk of the very matters he knew that she longed to discuss. The rule lay heavily on them both, but straight away she conveyed her wish that for the present they should exercise the discipline of self-restraint. She managed this very cleverly when the physician's attention was drawn from them, by quickly calling Miles her Blondel. Miles smiled. The inference was plain. He must be as discreet as the Lion-Heart's page carolling beneath the walls of Austrian castles. He sealed their conspiracy by calling her a lion-hearted lady, and thereafter they communicated by a code of sympathetic understanding which had no real key but served them well enough.

She was entirely in accord with his philosophy, which he never stated but which was as clear as crystal from his attitude, that it is better to meet God merrily in a hurried death than exist bat-like in the close half-light of a sickroom. And he learnt from her, not through words but by small indications, the truth which medicine ignores; that in many circumstances there is small difference between prolonging life and prolonging death.

He told her of his work as lawyer, and by inferring that he was seldom at his Inn of Court, told her he was in fact more often busy in the service of her son.

With his help – for he drew it out of her like a thread from a spider – she developed a germinal plan that, if she was blessed to catch all her old health, she would take the veil and devote herself to a life of prayer.

With his infinite tact and solemn flattery he won the full confidence of the physicians, and the duchess's recovery was so marked that at last they were given the reward of their patient waiting and allowed to talk freely.

X

Blondel and the Lion-Heart became Miles Metcalfe and Cecily, Duchess of York.

First, because she demanded it, he told her about her family.

She heard him out, then laid a hand on his arm. 'You plead well, master advocate,' she said. 'But it is not necessary to whiten my children. I know well enough their greys and blacks.'

Miles looked doubtful for a moment. To encourage him she said: 'You are my eyes in this and I have no other. You must tell me the truth.'

'Aye, madam,' he agreed. 'It is just.' Then he added wryly: 'But first I should present my credentials as ambassador from the world at large.'

He told her how he had been sent south from York to an inn of court and there had renewed his friendship with the Duke of Gloucester. Now he was a full-fledged attorney and attached to Richard's household.

'His household?' interrupted Cecily.

'The king has allowed him a small following,' explained Miles. 'And my lord has chosen to be served by old friends.'

She did not recognize some of the names he mentioned but she recalled Dom Edmund, almoner of Walsingham, who was now Richard's chaplain and confessor, and she knew of the household chamberlain, Robert Percy. 'The sad Percy?' she asked.

'Aye, he, but sad no longer, being in a fever of love and daily in sight of his Joyce – who serves the queen.' Miles grinned. 'We give the court a serious face, but indeed we are a merry company. And would be merrier had Francis Lovell come from Middleham, but, having a rich inheritance, he is already married to Lord FitzHugh's daughter Anne, and both are kept in the north. Lord Richard did have a mind to ask for him, but Lovell is my Lord Warwick's ward—'. He spread his hands expressively and added: 'These are my credentials, your grace. I learn of affairs from Lord Richard's court and do not depend on rumour.'

'Excellent,' said Cecily. 'Then tell me of my Lord Warwick. How does he with the king?'

Miles laid one forefinger across the other to show they were still at variance, and then, standing, he asked her permission to leave. 'We are tied to time, your grace, and I shall return when the physicians permit.'

So Cecily was obliged to wait impatiently to hear of the continued quarrel between her nephew and her son, but true to his promise, Miles returned at regular intervals to answer her many questions and tell her piecemeal of much that had happened in England during her seclusion.

He had sufficient regard for the physicians to be cautious, and he larded bad news with the tiny inconsequential details which any mother wants to hear about her family, but he quickly discovered it was unnecessary. The renewal of her contact with the world began to act on Duchess Cecily like sun and air and moisture on a withered plant. She brightened visibly, and soon proved by her shrewd questions and judgements that her mind was as alert as ever. Moreover, to their amazement and in fact to their dismay, the members of her household discovered she was fast recovering the power she had lost. She was peremptory again, each item of news serving to strengthen her.

Miles told her everything he knew; how the king had attempted to sweeten Warwick by making his brother chancellor as well as Archbishop, but the gesture had been futile. The earl would not tolerate the continued advancement of the hated Woodvilles, and his hurt vanity made him obstruct all Edward's policies in council until, enraged by such high-handed, spiteful, and unreasonable opposition, Edward had asserted his independence by making a treaty with Burgundy at the precise moment Warwick was concluding a treaty with France. It was a show of strength which the kingmaker found intolerable. To return home after contriving what amounted to a diplomatic triumph, and with his bags heavy with French gold, and discover he had been made a laughing-stock for the second time, was past belief. Simultaneously Edward deprived the Archbishop of the Chancellorship and made it plain that no Neville, save John, Earl of Northumberland, was welcome at his court. It was almost a duplicate of what had happened before, but this time, when Warwick returned angrily to Middleham, he took with him George of Clarence. The significance of this was plain, and Edward would have crushed them both and without mercy, but he was suddenly faced with other threats to his throne – puzzling and sometimes alarming reports began to come in from Brabant and France and Brittany, and from Wales and Scotland. The Red Rose had lain dormant for more than two years, King Henry having been captured wandering in Lancashire and taken back to the Tower, but Margaret and her son were still free to plot and bribe and cause ferment.

The reports turned out to be rumours not based on fact, but they held Edward fast in London until his fury had cooled down. Warwick at Middleham had time to reflect, and considered it expedient to accept the king's olive branch of a place in the escort of the king's youngest sister, Margaret on her way to be married to the Duke of Burgundy. His real motive was not clear, but he carried out his duty and thereafter kept at court, not committing himself in any way. Edward watched him warily, but when news came of a small rising in Yorkshire led by an agitator named Robin of Redesdale, Warwick wore an inscrutable countenance which did not alter when he heard that his brother John had promptly crushed the rising. A fresh Robin, of Holderness, then led a riot to air local grievances and shout for the restoration of Henry Percy as Earl of Northumberland.

When Cecily heard this she frowned: 'Though John Neville is my nephew,' she murmured, 'the king did wrong to give him Percy's earldom.'

Miles pointed out that it had kept him loyal to the house of York. 'He quelled this new revolt, and hanged Robin of Holderness before the gates of York.'

'For the king, or for his earldom?' asked Cecily, and added: 'Percy *is* Northumberland. It cannot be altered by a word, even the word of a king . . . as Edward may find to his cost.'

Miles smiled. 'My lady, your nephew has every opportunity to prove his loyalty. The old Robin, of Redesdale, has appeared once more at the head of a rebellion in Lancashire.'

'So!' she said. 'It is pop Robin time in the north country.' But her tone was serious. She did not smile like Miles; and evidently she was relieved when he told her that the king had decided to go north himself and investigate these persistent disturbances.

'Taking the Earl of Warwick with him?' she put in.

'Why no, madam. His grace has Lord Richard with him and two

great captains, Sir John Howard and Louis de Bretaylle . . .' Her gasp of dismay made him pause.

'Where is Warwick?' she demanded.

'Put safely out to sea, commanding the channel fleet.'

'And Clarence? Where is Clarence?'

'With his grace of York and . . .' he began, and stopped when she stood up in great agitation. 'Madam,' he continued, trying to calm her. 'The king does not consider the threat serious. Why, he has made a large detour to the shrines of St Edmund and Our Lady of Walsingham and not taken the direct road north.'

Cecily clapped her hands . . . a servant came into the solar. She told him to send her a scrivener with writing materials, and have a courier, no two, wait below. 'And instantly!' she commanded.

He bowed and ran from the room. At once a physician appeared through the doorway. 'Your grace is over-wrought,' he said, rebuking Miles with a frown.

Then Cecily made it plain she was entirely mistress of her will, her home, and everyone in it. 'I did not send for you Master Physician,' she said coldly. 'But as you are here you may give instructions for the drapes and shutters to be removed.'

'Your grace!' he said, aghast. 'My duty compels me to say . . .'

'I wish for light and air.'

He opened his mouth to object but one look from his patient sent him scuttling through the door.

Miles grinned. He was delighted by her resolution, and, being Miles, would have risked the impertinence of saying so, but she gave him no opportunity.

Immediately she asked for details of the king's plans to crush the Lancastrian rebellion.

'It is hardly a rebellion, your grace,' he reassured her, adding with a smile: 'Merely, as you aptly call it, a pop-Robin.'

'Yet I would know each detail . . .'

He told her all he himself knew, and calculated: 'By now they will be close to Stamford. I received a dispatch last night from Lord Richard and it was sent from Fotheringhay.'

'And after Stamford?'

'Grantham.'

She sat down. 'Then I shall send a courier to the king at Stamford, another to Fotheringhay should he still be there. A third to Grantham.'

'Your grace,' began Miles, feeling for words. He wondered how best to tell her that a sudden communication from his mother after so long might convince the king she had lost her wits.

She read his thoughts, understood the problem, and surmounted it.

'The dispatches will be for the Duke of Gloucester from his loyal servant, Master Metcalfe – to inform him that Robin of Redesdale is Warwick's cousin by marriage.'

Miles gaped.

'And that it is imperative the king treat seriously this revolt, and send at once for Warwick, for the Archbishop, and for my feckless son of Clarence. If they do not answer the summons . . .' She left the rest unsaid.

XI

Richard read Miles's letter and his heart turned. So it had come. The proof of Warwick's treacherous intentions, and the final threat to his own love for Warwick's daughter.

He carried the letter to Edward who read it in silence then tossed it to Thomas Montgomery, his Knight of the Body. 'Command a *Te Deum*, Tom, and a Mass of Thanks for the recovery of my lady mother.'

He waved his hand to dismiss them.

'Stay, Dick,' he said – as Richard turned to leave. And when they were alone he asked. 'Your Metcalfe is reliable?'

'As my life!' said Richard, adding: 'He was at Middleham.'

'That,' said his brother smiling, 'is not at present the strongest recommendation.'

Richard flared. 'Our lady mother will vouch for him . . .' he began. But Edward stopped him.

'I but teased you, Dick,' he said. 'I know of your love for your friends at Middleham. And I accept that Metcalfe is reliable.'

'As my life,' repeated Richard.

Edward nodded. He stood up and strode to the window. 'So! This is more than we thought.'

'Do we send for the Nevilles?' asked Richard.

'Aye. Though they will not come. Neither Warwick, nor the Archbishop, nor our brother. Aye, Dick. Send for them.'

'And we move north to Newark?'

Edward nodded. Then suddenly he said: 'Dick, I value your loyalty . . . which, I know, is costly. If I could have given you your Anne . . .' He broke off.

Richard made no reply.

At Newark the pattern settled further, and it was more alarming. Intelligence came that Robin of Redesdale was moving south with a far larger army than the king's. Agents distributed copies of his proclamation in advance and one was taken to the king. 'Sweet reasoning,' was his only comment but not for one minute did he underestimate the danger. In the proclamation he himself was ominously compared with the deposed kings Edward II, Richard II and Henry VI, justice was demanded for the true nobility, and the Woodvilles were damned as avaricious parasites. Within an hour he had sent to the Earls of Pembroke and Devon for reinforcements, ordered the Woodvilles to leave him and escape to safety as well as they could, and commanded his little force to head for the safety of Nottingham Castle.

There he waited.

Couriers reached Nottingham with news from the continent. The Nevilles had met in Warwick's town of Calais, and with a papal dispensation the Archbishop of York had married Clarence to his Isabel. Already they had issued manifestoes supporting the proclamation of Robin of Redesdale.

Still Edward waited.

Richard was distraught. To the king and the garrison he appeared to be the same as ever: calm and patient and entirely dependable; but a few close friends knew what was passing beneath that iron exterior; the agony he felt because Anne Neville was lost to him for ever. It was neither loyal nor reasonable to regret at this late stage that he had not fallen in with Warwick. But Richard regretted it with all his heart. He could not bring himself to look at Edward, though the king, sitting hunched and withdrawn in the great chamber, barely noticed it.

Dom Edmund did; and the priest cared enough for Richard to be sharp with him, accuse him of gorging on self-pity and tell him to pull himself together.

Richard heard half the lecture. No more. And then he turned away saying there were matters no priest could understand. Dom Edmund had a special place in his affections but he would allow no one, no one he repeated, to meddle in his most private affairs. And immediately he regretted it. The priest showed his distress. It was in his face and voice, his whole demeanour, as he bowed politely and requested permission to retire. Richard, crimsoning, asked his pardon, and afterwards heard the lecture out.

There was a cool, refreshing deal of sense in what Dom Edmund said. But the void was still inside him.

He told Robert Percy what had happened and Robert tried to help by leading him into a drinking bout which seemed to last for days.

The king looked on, amused to see young Dick and his chamberlain in their cups, and then irked by boredom, he joined them. But only he had the Plantagenet granite head for drink, and only he enjoyed himself. Richard and Robert took little pleasure from it; passing from euphoria and abandonment to querulousness and tearfulness. But the release and oblivion Richard sought eluded him. When maudlin drunk he begged his brother to send to Middleham for Francis Lovell, Warwick or no Warwick; and Edward, liking the mischief of it, gave the order at once. Then Richard became sentimental, thought of his old hound Bat, and had men scour Nottingham for a brachet bitch until they found one. 'Does this have all your love, lad?' shouted the king as Richard slobbered a kiss on the brachet's muzzle. 'You need more than a bitch!' And not many cups later Richard found himself pawing and panting in the king's bed with a buxom, willing girl, not caring who she was, though he called her Anne.

She answered to the name, and he sat up and hit her full in the face. When she cried, he cried as well; tangling her hair about his fingers and begging her forgiveness: while beyond the curtains Edward laughed, and Robert vomited, and the frightened brachet changed her whimper to a howl.

XII

She was the daughter of the castle seneschal, a young childless widow aged seventeen, and her name was Eleanor.

This was all his squire told him when Richard opened red-rimmed eyes to face reality again. The boy was gently wiping his face with a cool wet cloth. Through the confused details of his drinking bout he could remember very little save her oval face and the straw colour of her hair. And her tears. Yes: there had been tears . . . slow-falling and strangely opalescent, not watery-clear. He had felt their warmth on his cheek and tasted their saltiness.

'How came she to my bed?' he asked abruptly.

John Parr, the squire, was a friendly boy and franker than most. 'Not your bed, my lord, his grace's.'

Richard closed his eyes. He remembered now. 'How came she to my brother's bed? By his order?'

'I do not know, my lord.'

Nor, in fact, did anyone save Eleanor herself.

The garrison would believe she had pleasured the Duke of Gloucester by royal command. Edward himself, accustomed to discover willing ladies in the most improbable places, would set down her presence as a happy coincidence. His closest household officials would say it was a case of the lady finding the wrong brother in the dark. Her father, an ambitious man, would guess that she shared his ambitiousness and so had made herself available. Robert Percy, shaking off his headache, would prove himself a practical chamberlain by adjusting the household accounts to include expenditure on a royal whore.

The truth of the matter was simple – only known to Eleanor: that like many other women she was attracted by the sallow young prince, but, unlike them, she happened to be by when he was vulnerable. He found in her everything he most needed: an unjealous confidante, a skilful mistress, an opiate to calm his fretting; and to her he was an adorable enigma – half-child, half-ancient.

125

Francis Lovell, arriving post-haste from the north to answer the king's summons and bring assurances of the continued loyalty of John Neville of Northumberland, was met by Robert Percy in the bailey-ward.

'Dear Lovell,' he cried, embracing him. 'Our Dick is hooked clean by the seneschal's daughter, and all else is forgotten.'

'That,' said Francis, 'is impossible.'

And he knew he was right when, directly after Richard had welcomed him to the household, he took him to one side and asked: 'What of Anne?'

Francis told him she was not at Middleham, nor had he seen or even heard of her for the greater part of three months.

Richard's deep disappointment told Francis that his love for Anne was unchanged, and quite different in character from the devotion he felt for the seneschal's daughter. 'My lord,' he said. 'I wish I had tidings for you of the Lady Anne.'

Richard shrugged. 'I am not starry-eyed, Francis. And were we not both taught to take a fall without breaking bones?' He clasped his friend's shoulder. 'But what of you? Self-centred Gloucester talking only of his loss – while you are now a married man. How does your Anne?'

Lovell's face clouded. 'I envy you your love,' he said briefly – and then, seeing the concern on Richard's face, he told him frankly what he had never told anyone before.

At the end Richard squeezed his shoulder. 'It sometimes happens . . .' he murmured slowly. 'But I grieve it should be so with you.'

'Do not,' said Francis quickly. 'You said yourself we were both taught to take a fall without breaking bones. And I am rich in friends which I have learnt is more precious than anything under the whole wide sky.' He smiled at Richard. 'Now, Dick. Will you take me to the king? I have messages from the Earl of Northumberland.'

Edward received him graciously and heard John Neville's assurances. Then he asked: 'Would you serve us, Lovell?'

'Aye, your grace, willingly.'

'With my royal brother?'

The question was answered by Lovell's bow and radiant smile.

Sovereigns who could command such devoted service were

sometimes disinclined to share it, and had Edward Plantagenet been a less generous brother he might have envied Lovell's loyalty to his brother. But he was generous in all things. 'A good plan,' he said chuckling, 'for you and he with Percy and Metcalfe are all from the same stable.' He turned to his brother. 'I believe you would compound a fellowship of Gloucester's White Boar. Is that so, lad?'

Richard grinned. 'Aye, brother,' he replied.

✻

The waiting ended abruptly. Activity began.

The Nevilles and Clarence were in Kent . . . in London. Robin of Redesdale had skirted Nottingham – to cut off the king. Instantly Edward and Richard moved to slip his net. Eleanor watched them go, waving from the curtain wall to the little figure in black armour who turned once to look back. The tiny army felt its way south, snapping up enemy pickets and scouting parties but avoiding any main engagement until reinforcements came from the south and west. Pembroke and Devon led their separate powers until they met at Banbury. And there these two loyal lords quarrelled with each other, separated again, and Robin's rebel host fell on Pembroke and defeated him.

Edward heard the news at Olney, from fugitives who cried that Warwick as well as Robin were at their heels.

He smiled grimly. 'Our kingmaker is industrious,' he remarked, taking a cup of wine. 'And we are obliged to meet his strength with guile.'

Of the councillors in attendance only Richard and Lord Hastings had sufficient confidence in Edward's resourcefulness to share his smile. But even they were surprised when he gave the order to disband the army.

Hastings protested. 'Your grace will be utterly defenceless.'

'No, Will. There are greater forces than our little army, so let us disband it before the ranks melt away.'

He stood up. 'Yet you may serve me by taking word of this to Burgundy,' he said to John Howard. 'Bid my sister's husband threaten with his voice and purse-strings, but *not* with cannon. Mark it, all sanctions on these rebel lords save arms . . .'

Then the king made orders that as an insurance, a second party should ride independently for the Low Countries, and his treasure must be securely hidden.

'I shall remain here with my body servants. The rest of you will make your escape as well as you can.' And he warned them: 'Move far and fast.'

Many of them paid him the tribute of begging his permission to remain. But he was adamant. Only he and his personal household should stay in Olney. Even Hastings the chamberlain and the Duke of Gloucester must leave.

Both began to object. Their place was with the king.

He smiled. 'Your place is to obey the king. And Will, I would have you gallop north and ferret out a power. Then keep fast. Do not move until I send this ring.' He held out his hand. Hastings kissed the ring and left.

Richard's face betrayed his eagerness to be of service. 'And I, brother?'

'Take yourself off to a bolt-hole. When I send word you may call in the local levies . . .'

'But, my lord . . .'

'I mean it, lad. I must be alone. Go where you will – to the Low Countries, Norfolk's stout fortress at Framlingham, Pleshey, or Orford. But be certain you are not taken. It would be an ace in Warwick's hand and unbalance my position.'

Richard kissed him and turned to go.

'Or Dick,' said Edward as though in an afterthought, 'Nottingham is stout and safe at all times.'

'Aye, your grace.'

So Edward the king waited calmly to be taken captive by his rebel subjects and Richard returned to Eleanor.

In the security of Nottingham they watched the king fox his way back into power. The Nevilles were disconcerted to find they had a model prisoner. Instead of raging at them and defying them, he was charming, ever polite, never impatient, even amenable to their plans. He appeared unmoved when they beheaded some of his chief supporters, including the queen's father and one of her five brothers; merely remarking that now he would have to appoint another Constable of England in the place of Rivers. Clarence was so relieved by Edward's bland acceptance of his marriage to Isabel that he began to wonder if his brother might make him constable. Edward heard his request, and immediately promised to consider George's claim. He summoned a parliament when Warwick bade him, agreed that the country would be quieter if George of Clarence and the Archbishop of York were to govern as his councillors from London, and in all respects behaved impeccably.

His patience and his wise decision to leave his cause in the hands of the people, quickly bore fruit. For years the country had suffered under the factious government of Royal Councils dominated by a few great magnates, and it enraged the people, especially the rising menalty of townsmen and merchants, that Edward should be captured and intimidated by a handful of great lords. Put shortly, after the trade depression of mad Henry's reign they wanted a strong king, not a kingmaker; and the country was soon ablaze. Edward was hurriedly taken north, to Middleham, then south again to Pomfret. And there he heard that Hastings had obeyed his orders and raised a power in Lancashire. Still soft as peppermint Edward requested to see his jailers, and bewildered them by announcing he considered it was time to send for his councillors. Did they not agree? The Nevilles bowed themselves out from the presence of their own prisoner and consulted with each other. They were stupefied by the turn of events and talked of witchcraft – for how else could Edward have outgeneralled them without so much as drawing an eating knife? But talking was no use. They realized that the only way to snatch something from the hollow victory was to acquiesce.

Richard laughed out loud when he heard of his brother's adroitness, and the royal summons came for him to go to Pomfret.

'Nell!' he told his mistress. 'Edward is the wonder of the age. To manœuvre so shrewdly! He could catch a greased pig with one hand! You'll see, within a month he'll make a royal progress to the capital and be fêted like a hero.'

She put her hand in his, and tried hard to control her tears – because she knew it would always be like this. She would lose her Dick again and again to Edward and England, and nothing could prevent it.

He was already giving orders . . . to make all ready for an immediate departure . . . to call out the Nottingham levies . . . to send couriers to the king and to Baynard's Castle . . . special instructions to the seneschal on the keeping of the castle.

Then he saw her tears. 'Come!' he said. 'There's no help for it. I have to go. But we shall be together again. Soon, my love. Yes, soon.'

XIII

In the months that followed Eleanor of Nottingham persuaded herself that he had meant to keep his promise. He would have returned if he could. Sometimes when she was alone, but only then, she would give way to depression and wonder how much he belonged to her or she to him, if his affections could be measured, or were they immeasurable like her own. Then she would feel her swelling belly and assure herself he would have kept his promise if it had been possible. But Richard of Gloucester was the king's strongest bulwark and seldom free to please himself in anything.

Affecting to placate the Nevilles, but in reality to escape a dominance he was at last beginning to find irksome, Edward had taken the opportunity to slip from the grip of the Woodvilles and advance his young brother to a place of immense power. Richard was now Constable of England and Chief Justice and Chamberlain of both North and South Wales, and he worked from dawn to dusk, and often far into the night, because England was at war with herself.

Eleanor could not know how little Richard's heart was in his task, that each move against Anne Neville's family was a splinter in his own contentment. All she heard was of his impartiality and judgement, his skill in strategy, his enormous powers of endurance. Shrewdly she discounted at least half of what she heard – but even so, from the remainder, it was clear that her little lord had an enviable reputation and she was proud of his achievements. She was grateful too, because he sent her messages and small tokens to prove he had not forgotten her although he lived mostly in the saddle. She passed the news on to her father: of the Lincolnshire rebellions, the outlawing of Warwick and Clarence and their flight from England, John Neville's advancement to the Marquessate of Montagu, the plotting and the riots – and the news was passed on by the seneschal to the garrison, the garrison to the town. Richard of Gloucester became, as it were, a special favourite of everyone at Nottingham.

He was their duke, their own man. And when, on an April day in 1470, his first child, a tiny dark girl, was born at the castle, they lighted bonfires and made a public feast. Richard sent gifts from Wells in Somerset with instructions that his daughter must be named Katherine, and promises that soon he would visit her. But when? He did not come and the news worsened.

Warwick was being treated like a prince in France. He plotted with that master of guile King Louis. Unbelievably he was to be reconciled with Queen Margaret. He had turned his coat and the colour of his rose, would support her son's rights as Prince of Wales, would prove to Edward and the world his own right to the title Kingmaker. Mad Henry should have his throne again.

Still Richard did not come. Eleanor was open with her father and confessed her fears.

'He will come,' said that wise and ugly man. 'Twice he has used this castle as a refuge and the house of York is now windswept by the news from France.' He did not add the real reason for his conviction. News had come from France that Anne Neville was betrothed to Edward of Wales. This more than anything would drive Lord Richard to his daughter Eleanor. 'He will come,' he repeated firmly. 'He will come.'

And Richard did, dirty and dishevelled from a long, long ride, accompanied only by Lovell, Percy, Dom Edmund, and his lean brachet Bat.

They brought bad news. Warwick and Clarence had landed in the West Country. But Richard would not talk of it. He was of a mind to see his daughter, then eat and rest.

His manner had altered in the past few months. His responsibilities as Constable and the weight of his own affairs seemed to have shaped him like beaten silver in repoussé work. At one time he would have leapt to obey his brother without much questioning. Yet now, for some unaccountable reason, when Edward commanded him to meet him at Lincoln and join in the race for London against Warwick and Clarence, he sent no reply and stayed where he was.

Eleanor allowed herself to believe it was for her sake he remained in Nottingham, and dreamed giddily, ambitiously, of becoming his wife.

Dom Edmund knew better and guessed that Richard was so exhausted that he had lost all subtlety of mind. Quite simply he was using his brother's misfortunes to assert his independence and prove his own individuality. But it was an appallingly dangerous time to do it, and Dom Edmund said so. Francis and Robert supported him.

Richard regarded them, his small oval face drained of all blood. Then he spoke to his brachet, scratching her muzzle as he talked. 'Good Bat! Good bitch! Your silence is more loving than the tongues of my friends. You see the truths they are blind to. You understand that when a sunburst wastes to a moonbeam he forfeits all respect . . .'

'My lord!' expostulated Dom Edmund. 'The king, your brother —'

'Is a sot, Bat!' continued Richard softly. 'Did they not tell you, Bat? I tell you now. He is a sottish monarch, reduced by his odious queen to less than what he could have been.'

The priest and Francis eyed each other uneasily. Robert was already at the door to see if anyone was nearby. The bitch licked her master's wrist.

Francis Lovell laid a hand on his arm. 'Some of this, my lord, is true. Yet I beg you not to speak of it.'

'A man's heart should be kept close,' said Dom Edmund severely.

'Save in the confessional, Bat,' continued Richard. 'But sometimes a wider confidence is necessary.' He looked directly at his friends. 'Had I followed Richard of Warwick, Anne would be my bride.'

'Aye,' said Francis softly, 'she would.'

'But she is not,' said the priest bluntly. 'And if you do not serve the king you will have neither the Lady Anne nor your honour, nor anything at all.'

Robert had returned from the door. 'Obey the king,' he urged. 'Ride to meet him as he has commanded.'

'No! He leans too heavily upon me. Hastings is there, John Neville with his power. And the new Earl Rivers. Yes,' he cried, not troubling to keep the scorn from his voice. 'There is yet a sprinkling of Woodvilles close to the throne.'

They could not persuade him. He left them to walk off his humours. Bat followed at his heels.

'Dom Edmund,' pleaded Robert. 'What can be done?'

For a moment the priest did not reply. Then, slowly, he spread his hands in a gesture of resignation. 'Nothing. We should do nothing and let him be.'

'He is not himself,' muttered Francis.

'Are any of us?' asked Dom Edmund. 'We are all jaded. After such a year it is not to be wondered at. And Richard has borne the heaviest weight of care.' He hesitated and would have continued but he was cut short by a noise from the courtyard below; a sudden ringing of hooves on the cobblestones, then a yelp and a scream, and curses and shouts.

Robert moved swiftly to the window embrasure. It was close to dark but he could make out a horse, a group of men, a dog.

'Poor Dick,' he said dully. 'His brachet is killed by a horseman . . . a courier by the look of his trappings.'

Dom Edmund and Francis joined him at the window. Through the twilight they saw a man-at-arms draw his falchion, kneel by squirming, squealing Bat, and silence her for ever. And they saw Richard, a small figure on the step. He, too, watched it done and threw the man-at-arms a word of thanks. Then he took a message wallet from the courier whose horse had trodden Bat, and went inside.

The three men left the window.

'This,' said Robert shortly, 'will further blacken his mood.'

'With reason,' added Francis.

'Aye.' Dom Edmund sighed, and he sighed again. 'Load upon load. After such a year! It is no wonder he takes refuge in petulance. But his scruples are not dead. Not dead,' he repeated. 'They are merely sleeping.'

'Yet I could wish —' began Robert, and stopped abruptly.

For a second time there was shouting from below. They ran to the window. Burning sconces lighted the courtyard. Richard stood on a mounting block, his face grey with anger. He was calling for his armourer and the castle seneschal.

Robert cupped his hands. 'My lord,' he roared. 'My lord Richard.'

Richard looked up. Immediately he beckoned to them.

'What has happened?' shouted Francis Lovell. A string of horses clattered through the yard and drowned his voice. 'What has happened?' he repeated.

Richard shouted through cupped hands. 'We ride east. Our brand-new marquess has turned his coat.'

'John Neville?'

Richard spat on to the cobbles and nodded. 'Aye, he,' he shouted. 'The loyal, dependable, trustworthy Neville.' He spat again. 'May

133

God curse him for his treachery.' The seneschal appeared at the doorway. Richard said something to him, then turned back to the window. 'Edward my brother has need of us. Come below. We ride for Lynn, and thence to Burgundy to raise a force.'

Dom Edmund smiled at all the activity below the window. 'Did I not say his scruples were but sleeping?'

XIV

It was done.

Edward Plantagenet, setting out with a tiny fleet from the shores of Burgundy to thrust mad Henry from the throne had named it his Enterprise of England. Others described it as a heaven-sent miracle, for how else could he have won the north country, then the midlands and finally London? how else weaned Clarence from his father-in-law and crushed the mighty kingmaker and the main force of Queen Margaret on a fog-enveloped Easter Sunday at Barnet Field? For it was done. Proof of the miracle lay in the Tower chamber where Henry, unwashed and happy with his birds, was being held for the third time in his life; and near him in a similar cell the slippery Archbishop Neville.

Proof of it also lay on the pavement in St Paul's: two hacked bodies, naked but for breech clouts, all that remained of Richard, Earl of Warwick, and his brother John, Marquess of Montagu.

For two days they lay there to be gaped at and prayed over, reviled and honoured, until a slight figure dressed in black led a cortège to remove them for honourable burial. He had a slight limp from a wound taken at Barnet three days before. As brother to the king and Constable it was neither his duty nor necessary to be there. Earl Rivers held the king's warrant. But it was fitting.

When the bodies had been wrapped and placed on biers, eight friars, appointed for the purpose, came forward to bear them from St Paul's. The Constable murmured to Earl Rivers, then took his place with three companions behind the bier which carried Warwick's body. Two were recognized by the crowd of onlookers as Robert Percy, the Duke of Gloucester's chamberlain, and his great friend Master Francis Lovell. The third, wearing a lawyer's gown, was unknown.

❊

Clarence was vexed. 'Admit it was ill-advised, Dick. Inopportune.'

Richard merely bowed and indicated that his brother should precede him into the council chamber.

But Clarence hung back and persisted. 'To wear black . . . make a display!'

'I seldom wear other colours. The ceremony was simple.'

Clarence still had not finished. 'I cannot think why . . . unless it was done to disadvantage me!'

'No one,' said Richard coldly, 'considered you.'

'Exactly! He was Isabel's father, Dick, the grandfather of my children . . .'

'You were at liberty to keep us company.'

'Keep you company! God's teeth! He was the king's prime enemy!'

'Enemy or no, Neville, Percy, Metcalfe and I owed him much.'

George sneered. 'Four loyal donzels . . . the Fellowship of the White Boar.'

'Aye!' cut in Richard, his temper rising. 'But, of course, loyalty is a virtue you do not over-value!'

Richard's jibe had smarted. 'Men,' Clarence said loftily, 'care not a pie for nursery chivalry. I tell you Dick, you embarrassed me.'

Richard shrugged his shoulders.

George coloured. 'By my honour!'

'A thin oath indeed!' returned his brother with contempt, walking away.

The king saw at once that his brothers had quarrelled. 'I care not a straw for the cause,' he told them sharply. 'But resolve your differences. There is work to do.'

'Your grace —' began Clarence, but Edward cut him short with an impatient gesture.

'My arse, brother, will not sit warm to the throne until our enemies are scattered.' He nodded to the Secretary of the Signet who rapidly gave the council the latest intelligence: that on the day of Barnet Queen Margaret had landed in the west country with her son and his betrothed wife and a large force under the command of Edmund of Somerset.

Richard looked down at his feet when he heard this. In the pit of his stomach there was a hard, hard knot, and he barely listened to Lord Howard's plea that the campaign be taken west without delay, nor to Will Hastings's estimate of the forces at their disposal.

XV

During Richard's long absence from London Duchess Cecily had retired from public life to live simply as a widow under vows. She could do no more, she said, for any of them save pray. But indirectly she served them handsomely because, by a device of property held in trust for the benefit of her children, Miles Metcalfe now had control of her affairs, and he had used part of her fortune to establish a secret and elaborate intelligence system all over the southern counties. Their rewards being great, his agents were alert and quick to report events, and the system proved invaluable to the king and his brothers as they progressed into the west country on Margaret's tail.

At Windsor they heard that her move east had been a feint. Hearing of the disaster at Barnet, she was rushing to meet Jasper Tudor, Earl of Pembroke, in the safety of Wales.

The trumpets were sounded and at top speed the king's new army moved to Malmesbury. Miles's agents reported the Lancastrians' track – through Wells, Bath, Bristol – and now they were sharpening their swords for a pitched battle at Sodbury Hill.

'Sodbury, let it be,' said the king. 'Though I like not the name for the great victory God will send us there.'

But Sodbury Hill was bare of Lancastrians. They were already force-marching north to Gloucester and the footbridge over Severn.

'Keep her from that bridge,' ordered the king. 'Dick, double speed messengers to your city.'

The Governor of Gloucester obeyed his Duke. The gates were shut and the walls manned. But Edward was dumbfounded to learn the Lancastrians had made no assault. They had taken one look at the barred city and marched on. 'It was her *one* chance of slipping us into Wales . . . She cannot have turned craven, not Margaret of Anjou!'

'She carried her most precious possession,' Hastings reminded him. 'Prince Edward is untried in battle.'

'Bedevilled by love!' exclaimed the king. A smile broke across

137

his face. 'She will not risk his pretty skin! And so he is our largest asset. We will scotch them at the next crossing over Severn.' He looked inquiringly at his scouts.

'At Tewkesbury, your grace.'

'Her route from Gloucester?'

'Through wooded slopes, deep lanes. Evil country for a worn army, your grace.'

'Fodder?'

'None – or little.'

Edward nodded. 'Excellent. But we are late in starting on the race.'

Again the trumpets sounded and the king's men force-marched north, choosing the upland rock-strewn route to the east of Margaret's.

Richard of Gloucester was in command of the van, a position of honour which he had held and well earned three weeks before in the approach to Barnet Field, and it was scouts from his force who reported that the Lancastrians had turned at bay on a ridge of high ground before the gates of Tewkesbury. He halted the army and with Robert Percy and a squire rode forward to inspect the enemy's positions for himself. At first sight they looked formidable for the sloping approach to their main battle line was cut into irregular and dangerous patches by lanes and high hedges and thick coverts. But the River Avon was behind their right wing, running deeply and broadly to meet Severn not far away.

He and Robert grinned at one another. Both were remembering their lessons in strategy at Middleham.

'Lines of retreat,' squeaked Robert in a fair imitation of the bald Agincourt veteran who had been their instructor.

'Aye,' replied Richard. 'Lines of retreat.'

He reported to the king, taking with him a rough sketch to show what he and his scouts had discovered.

'Good lad,' said Edward eagerly, studying it. 'Somerset on the right. The Prince and Wenlock at centre. Devonshire to the left.' He looked up. 'Will, my old friend, I'd have you match yourself against the rebel Devonshire.'

Hastings bowed.

'And I shall take the centre. York truly against Lancaster. Though,' he added, 'I would gladly drive Somerset into this river here.' He jabbed at the paper with his forefinger. 'This is where the greatest dangers lie, for Somerset is a wolf in battle. The greatest danger . . . or the greatest honour. Lose or win.'

Clarence coloured when the king suddenly said: 'And you shall have it, Dick.'

'And I, your grace?' he asked peevishly before Richard could even thank the king for the honour done him.

'Why, George. You shall command the reserve and pursuit. You sit a horse better than anyone here, and your intimate knowledge of our enemies will help you track them down.'

Clarence's colour deepened. He would have protested but the king had already begun directing Hastings and Richard on formations and tactics. When all were agreed, he dismissed the company. 'Take what sleep you can, my lords, and break your fast with meat.'

XVI

The Constable of England sat on a dais with the Earl Marshal, John Mowbray, Duke of Norfolk, at his right hand. Before them stood the defeated Duke of Somerset and a dozen other Lancastrian captains. He leant on the arm of his chair and covered his eyes with one hand as he heard their plea for justice.

One objected that they had been plucked from sanctuary in Tewkesbury Abbey and the king had offered open pardon.

Norfolk broke in impatiently to say such pardon was never extended to commanders but only to the common soldiers, and the objector said no more when he saw Somerset's contemptuous eyes fixed on him.

This duke was single-minded in his devotion to the house of Lancaster. He would beg no Yorkist's mercy, plead no defence, and it enraged him to be associated with men who deigned to do so. His father and his elder brother had died for the House of Lancaster, and he dearly wished that he himself had been slain in the battle before Tewkesbury. He neither expected nor wanted mercy, and would not let it pass when in the examination Norfolk sneered at Henry of Lancaster as an heirless lunatic.

'My king is but heirless through the malice of a foresworn coward,' he shouted, and he pushed one of his companions forward, ordering him to tell everyone there how Prince Edward had died.

Richard took his hand from his eyes and looked steadily at the Lancastrian captain who cried out in a loud voice that Edward Prince of Wales had died beside the Avon, beaten to his knees, while crying to the Duke of Clarence for aid.

There was a moment's silence, afterwards pandemonium.

George jumped up from his seat beside the dais to declare his honour was impugned, but Somerset's clear voice rang out and drowned his protestations. He accused Clarence openly, calling him turncoat and treacherous, feckless, craven and merciless.

Clarence cried hysterically that he was maligned, insulted. He demanded justice.

Richard made no answer until the uproar spent itself when he rebuked Somerset for introducing a matter which fell outside the competence of the Constable's Court. It was too gentle a rebuke for George who began to storm again. Richard let him finish, then without looking at his brother, he repeated firmly that his court had no concern with the circumstances of the death of Edward of Lancaster, nor was it a court of honour.

He consulted briefly with the canon jurists who stood at his left hand and gave his judgement that because of the legal distinction between general and particular protection and the fact that Tewkesbury Abbey had neither bull nor charter, the king had been free to seize the rebels. By their own actions they were condemned, for none would deny his part in the battle before Tewkesbury.

The Lancastrian captains were silent. Somerset actually nodded his head in agreement. None of them moved or gave any sign when the young Constable slowly, and rather quietly, sentenced them to be shriven and beheaded without delay.

Just before they were taken from the hall Richard stood up, removed his cap of estate and bowed to them, saluting them as men of honour.

Somerset smiled gratefully and returned the courtesy. Then he led his commanders out to execution.

XVII

King Edward and the Duke of Clarence rode north to Coventry. But Richard of Gloucester remained at Tewkesbury for a day longer. Only his intimate friends knew the reason. Then Robert Percy brought the news he waited for.

'She has been found, your grace.'

'Where?'

'With Henry's queen. In a house of religion across Severn.'

Richard's smile was taut. 'She is . . . How does she?'

'I . . . we do not know, my lord.' He explained that Sir William Stanley had found the ladies and had already taken them to the king. 'Where your brother Clarence is, my lord,' he finished.

'So?'

Robert did not mince his words. 'He is the Lady Anne's brother-in-law . . . her father's estates are forfeit to the crown, but her mother's . . . They are vast, and she is co-heiress with my lady of Clarence. You would be wise to gallop north, my lord.'

Robert's warning had been justified. Richard arrived too late. By the time he reached Coventry the king had given the Lady Anne Neville into George's care.

Richard received the news in silent dismay and went directly to the privacy of his apartment. There he railed against the king. Did faithless George deserve such trust, such open-handedness? Had Edward forgotten his own claim to protect Anne? his constant love for her? Did he not understand that George would try to keep her shut away, a lifelong maid, just so long as he could enjoy her revenues?

He saw her once at Coventry, but only for a moment, and she did not look at him. She kept her eyes down and looked at no one, and her pale face told him nothing, nothing at all. She was attentive to Queen Margaret, but, again, this told him nothing, for the queen's grief would have touched the heart of her worst enemy. She was utterly broken, no longer a proud and powerful queen, simply a pathetic husk. Anne's compassion, the gentle hand on Margaret's arm, was a natural sympathy for someone who already lived in hell.

After an hour's irresolution he sent his condolences on the death of her father, but the message was quickly returned – and by his brother George in person.

George made it clear that his sister-in-law should be left undisturbed. For the moment Richard acquiesced, but he was determined to see Anne at the earliest opportunity and learn her mind. Diamond cut diamond. Somehow he would outmanœuvre his brother.

But George moved first, sending his sister-in-law secretly to Isabel in London, and just at a time when Richard was at his busiest with affairs of state. He had missed his opportunity in Coventry and, because of his plethora of duties as Constable, he would have small chance to see her yet in London.

There was a last flicker of Lancastrian rebellion in the south-east. Fauconberg, the admiral of Queen Margaret's channel fleet, had landed at Sandwich, raised a mob of Kentishmen and marched on London. But it was not a serious threat and meant little, and when the king reached the capital with his brothers the rebellion broke and Fauconberg slipped back to Sandwich.

Edward made his return an occasion to remember. His troops marched through Ludgate with banners flying, the golden sunburst of the king highest of all.

In the place of honour at the head rode Richard of Gloucester – a small black figure on a large white charger who shyly acknowledged the citizens' cheers. They cheered spontaneously and affectionately, not simply because he was the brother of their adored King Ned. Perhaps never in his life was he to know the real reason: that they cheered because at last he had found a way to their hearts, and not as his brothers did with their good looks and magnificence and exuberant charm, but quite simply with his courage. The Londoners knew of his bravery at Barnet Field, and now they had heard of his outstanding bravery at Tewkesbury. It was this they cheered. And Richard, moved by their affection, was touched and puzzled at the same time and did not in the least mind that behind him, where Edward rode with Hastings, the cheers grew louder still.

Far to the rear came George of Clarence, collecting his tributes of affection and making sure of it by scattering largesse, and at the end a stooping, tragic figure with her eyes fast closed, seated in a chariot.

Men were silent as she passed by and crossed themselves as though she were already dead.

For so she was in the eyes of England, and Edward was to claim fifty thousand golden crowns as her ransom from King Louis and without a scruple of anxiety let her leave the kingdom to live in broken-hearted isolation for eleven more years.

Margaret of Anjou was no longer of any account, but Edward knew, and his council knew, that the last vestiges of poison would be drawn from her, and the last threat to peace in the realm destroyed, if she was widowed.

That same evening the council met at Westminster.

The king was frank. 'None of us have cause to hate Henry of Lancaster. We may love his many virtues: his learning, his gentleness, his piety. But we must love England more.'

One by one they gave their counsel. They were in agreement with the king. When it was the Duke of Gloucester's turn he shrugged his shoulders and said nothing. Edward accepted this as general consent, but Richard found himself wiping his sticky hands on a handkerchief below the Council board. Then, horror-struck, he shuddered. It was Pilate's hand-washing, no less. Furtively he crossed himself, remembering the kindness of poor Henry years before when he and George and Peter had visited the Tower.

A grim smile played at Edward's mouth as he said: 'You are in accord, that something must be done . . . to show our love for England. Yet not one of you has been precise. Is it left to me?'

Hastings replied for them all. 'You are our king, your grace.'

'Very well,' said Edward, 'the final responsibility is mine.' He drummed on the table with his fingers, stopped, stroked his chin, then looked at his advisers in turn. None of them met his gaze. Once more he drummed the table, stopped and said abruptly:

'My lord of Gloucester.'

Richard looked up.

'I would have you leave for Sandwich at daybreak. Admiral Fauconberg must be caught and clipped so that he can cause no more ferment in my kingdom.'

Richard stood up and bowed.

'I shall myself follow in a day with reinforcements.'

Richard bowed again. He turned to leave and make preparations, but Edward had not finished.

'But first, you have a duty as Constable of England.' His eyes

144

travelled round the council board. 'Take with you Hastings, Rivers, Essex and Howard.'

Richard looked at him blankly, though he knew what was coming.

'And carry my order to Lord Dudley, Constable of the Tower . . . that Henry of Lancaster,' he hesitated. 'That Henry of Lancaster is to be helped to heaven.'

There was silence as a clerk penned the order and affixed the king's privy-seal.

Edward examined it, nodded, and handed it to his brother. 'For the love of England, my lord of Gloucester,' he said quietly.

Richard bowed a third time, and followed by the four peers he left the council chamber.

XVIII

Once or twice on the route to Sandwich Richard found himself
wiping his hands again.

By now Henry's body would be lying in St Paul's for all citizens
to see he had died 'naturally' and without pain. His son's body,
hacked and gashed and hurriedly entombed, would already be
corrupting under the flagstones in Tewkesbury Abbey. It was the end
of the house of Lancaster, for the sole pretenders now were base
Welsh mountebanks; the sons – no less – of a royal wardrobe clerk
and the grandsons of a bishop's butler, and though Henry in an
hour of lunacy had legitimized his half-brothers, the Tudors' lineage
was obscure and curious, flawed everywhere with the bar-sinister,
and no Englishman would tolerate their insolent claims.

The last petals of the Red Rose were down, yet Richard of
Gloucester took no joy in it. Worn with the unceasing activity of
many months, his heart was revolting at all his mind had learnt to
accept. He was caught up in violence, had been part of it all his life.
Everywhere, all the time, there was blood and death and pain and
anguish, intrigue and treachery. It clung about him like a spider's
web – and he wondered if he would ever in his life be freed from the
spider's constant spinning, if anyone could free him. And the spider
spun one more skein even before he reached Sandwich.

A following courier brought a message folded in a leather wallet.
It was given to Robert as Chamberlain. He quickly read it, and rode
up the line to Richard.

'My lord!'

Richard's melancholy was so deep that Robert had to repeat
himself.

'My lord, I have tidings.'

Richard started.

'From Nottingham, my lord.'

Robert took Richard's bridle and led his horse away from the line.

'Well?'

'You have a son, Dick.'

146

It was seldom now that anyone addressed him directly by name and Richard instinctively knew what it signified.

'And —'

'Eleanor of Nottingham is dead.'

Richard looked at his horse's head, at the scurriers who rode on each flank of the line of soldiers, at the line, at the wood which then lay to the right, at the sun, at Robert, at his horse's head again.

'God rest her soul,' he muttered softly and crossed himself.

And that was all. He said no more. Robert told him that Eleanor had named the child John; that as she lay dying she had spoken often and lovingly of her lord; that the seneschal awaited instructions as to the care of the Lady Katherine and Lord John Plantagenet. But Richard said nothing. He pricked his horse and rode back to his place in the line.

On his own responsibility Robert Percy sent the courier back to Nottingham with expressions of Duke Richard's grief, and instructions that for the time being his children's nurse was charged with their care.

Richard rode on in silence and no one knew his thoughts. Nor did he speak in public of his children for many months to come. What grief he felt for Nell was private even from his most intimate friends. But they could see he bore his burdens sadly – even when, without a battle, Fauconberg obliged him by submitting and accepting the royal pardon.

Richard returned to London to receive fresh honours as Great Chamberlain of England, Steward of the Duchy of Lancaster beyond Trent, and such authority over Earl Percy of Northumberland that he was virtually Lord and Viceroy of the North. To maintain the new dignities the king gave him the rich prize of all Warwick's lands in Cumberland and Yorkshire, which included Middlcham, the castle he had always accounted home – but even this failed to raise his spirits. Anne, who was Middlcham's proper châtelaine, still remained fast shut in the inner parts of George's London house.

He would not have admitted it to anyone but in degree this was a relief. In his dejection he had begun to wonder about his love for Anne. Was it genuine or grounded in his pity for her present helpless and hopeless state, in his antipathy to George, in his impossible longing to return to the happiest period of his life which had been in her company at Middleham.

One day on an impulse he found courage to ask the king for Anne, but Edward, though he sympathized and made vague promises, was then most concerned with the Scottish raids on the northern frontier.

'Trounce the King of Scots, Dick,' he commanded. 'Teach him a sharp lesson. And we will talk of the Lady Anne when you return.'

Half angry, half relieved, Richard obeyed.

He left his chamberlain Robert Percy to negotiate the lease of a house in Bishopsgate, and rode with his household up the length of England. Suddenly he was overjoyed to be free of the backbiting and intrigue and lush opulence of his brother's court. On the moors and meeting the sharp, cold winds he found he could relax. His mind sharpened. He smiled. He was himself again as he rode on to trounce the King of Scots.

XIX

Richard's campaign against the Scots gave him time to work out his private problems. He was helped to see the true nature of his love for Anne. On his return, he went to Westminster to ask for her hand a second time.

'Your grace made promises,' he reminded the king.

Edward smiled at him. 'Aye, dear Dick, aye!' he said, and turning to George of Clarence, asked: 'Could we now refuse him anything?'

Clarence frowned. 'The affairs of the Nevilles are entirely in my hands by your grace's commission.'

'Aye, George,' said the king. He sighed. 'But would you have your sister-in-law a maid for ever?'

'She is no maid,' said George, 'but the widow of your grace's enemy, Edward of Lancaster.'

'By God's teeth . . .' began Richard colouring: but the king silenced him with a gesture, and looked curiously at Clarence.

'His widow?'

'They were wedded last December by the Grand Vicar of Bayeux, by a dispensation from the Patriarch of Jerusalem.'

The king burst out laughing. 'George, I'll not believe you were duped by such hole-and-corner tactics. Wedded! Then why not a dispensation from his holiness in Rome? Why were they not bedded before witnesses? Why has the girl never been proclaimed Princess of Wales?' He prodded George's chest. 'You're not so naïve, brother. Margaret hated Warwick and if she agreed to a betrothal it was simply to suck gold and troops from the French fox Louis. Wedded! You know as well as I that, later, if it had suited her, Margaret would have disavowed the ceremony altogether.'

George shrugged his shoulders angrily. 'Widow or maid, she is my concern,' he cried. 'And I, too, am surprised that your grace should be deceived by Dick.' His voice grew louder. 'He may want Anne, but he wants her fortune more. And she is mine.'

Edward frowned. 'I happen to believe him when he says he loves the girl and, with my permission, would make her his wife.'

'You have always favoured him,' shrilled George.

'With reason,' said the king smoothly. 'For while you were keeping company with England's enemies, Dick was at my side.'

George reddened but with indignation not shame. 'He has been rewarded – and richly.'

'Would you have been less generous in my place?' demanded the king. 'You have all Warwick's southern estates and are reappointed my Lieutenant in Ireland. Though you are eloquent, Dick's constant service to the crown is a more cogent argument to gain my support.'

George tried to cut in, but Edward held up his hand. 'While you have been fully occupied in London guarding your sister-in-law and country estates, Dick has been guarding the Scottish border and trouncing our royal cousin James.'

There was a short silence. Then George insisted stubbornly: 'You gave her to me.'

'Aye, so I did.' The king turned to Richard. 'How does she answer, Dick?'

'I have not . . . I cannot see her,' complained Richard. 'The Duke of Clarence has barred my admission to his house.'

'I had the right!' insisted George.

'Are you her protector or her jailer?' inquired the king.

He said it flatly, keeping the contempt from his voice because though he wanted to show his affection and gratitude to Richard, he knew that somehow his two brothers must be reconciled for the sake of peace. They stood before him, Gloucester white-faced and trembling, Clarence sulky and thunderous. Between them they could do great harm to the realm. Edward sighed. Then he noticed Richard's chaplain standing a little to the rear, a priest whose opinions he had learnt to valuehighly.

'Dom Edmund of Walsingham,' he called.

The priest stepped forward.

'How,' asked the king, 'shall we reconcile these pert princes?'

Richard looked down at his shoes, but George glowered at the priest.

Dom Edmund considered. 'Your grace would wish, I am sure, that the Duke of Clarence should continue for the present to have the governance of the Lady Anne's welfare, and that my lord of Gloucester should be at liberty to pursue his suit.'

'You read my thoughts well, sir priest,' said the king. He stood up. 'George, Dick, let this advice content you both.'

·   ·   ·   ·   ·

As a matter of tact Richard waited twenty-four hours before calling formally at Clarence's town house, and, at first it seemed to have been wise. His brother received him genially and courteously, but when he reached the point of his visit and asked to see the Lady Anne, George affected wide-eyed surprise.

'Surely, brother, the king made it clear that I have small rights of wardship over my sister-in-law.'

Richard frowned.

'And therefore,' continued George blandly, 'I do not consider myself responsible for her whereabouts.'

'The Lady Anne is not here?'

'I neither know, nor care where she is, brother,' said George sweetly.

The courtiers beside him grinned at Gloucester's discomfiture.

'The king,' said Richard hotly, 'gave me liberty to press my suit.'

For the first time George's eyes darkened. 'Aye, on the word of your lick-spittle priest.'

'Edward asked his advice.'

'He should keep his place; not meddle in my affairs.'

Richard's lip trembled as he said: 'I demand the right to see the Lady Anne.'

George composed himself. 'You will demand nothing in my house, brother of Gloucester, for here neither your fawning nor your hypocrisy carries the slightest weight.' Deliberately he turned his back on Richard, linked arms with his cronies, and began to talk of other matters.

Because the king had admired and openly coveted Miles Metcalfe's highly successful intelligence system Richard had felt obliged to hand it over, and the Gloucester couriers and agents in the south were now the king's. But, though Miles had given his secret lists to the Secretary of the Privy Seal, it was not difficult for him to find the right men in London to make discreet inquiries as to the whereabouts of the Lady Anne Neville.

While they searched Richard remained at Crosby's Place, the fine house in Bishopsgate which Robert Percy had taken for him as a London residence. He sat sometimes alone on the dais in the great hall, half-listening to the musicians and singing-boys who entertained him from the gallery, and at others walked in the garden with one or other of his household. He would interview no one, nor transact any business, and, while he waited impatiently for Miles's agents, the place-hunters and Gloucester dependants who had brought suits and grievances to their lord were forced to kick their heels and wait as well.

After four restless days, during which Richard grew more and more cantankerous, he sent for Miles and soundly rated him for selecting a pack of dunderheads.

Miles hastily defended them, pointing out that they had not only scoured London and Westminster but every great house within twenty-five miles of the city.

'Then, as I said, they are dunderheads!' said Richard testily. He paced up and down. 'Someone must know where she is, and servants are bribable if they are offered enough.'

Miles did not miss the inference. 'I have told my men that if it is necessary there are sufficient funds available to bribe the Lord Mayor himself.'

'Then why have they not found her?' demanded Richard. 'She is no common chit but Warwick's daughter. As such she is recognizable.'

Miles said nothing. Something Richard had said made Miles very thoughtful. Possibly his agents were failing merely because they were looking for Warwick's daughter; an obvious, too obvious, target. If, quite simply, they were to look for what Richard had called a common chit . . .

'She *must* be found,' insisted Richard.

'She will be,' Miles promised.

Within twenty-four hours one of his agents had found her: disguised as a cook-maid in the kitchens of an inn in Cripplegate. Miles took the news to Crosby's Place where Richard was in the garden with Francis and Dom Edmund.

The excitement in Richard's eyes died as he heard it. His face was drained of all colour. 'A cook-maid!' he cried passionately. 'By the splendour of God! I shall be revenged on Clarence for this humiliation.' He lashed with his cane at a clump of late-flowering marigolds. Orange petals were scattered over the path.

'Yet she is found,' urged Dom Edmund attempting to soothe him.

But Richard was so angry that it seemed for one moment as if he would go directly to Clarence's house and challenge him.

'And tell him you know of her whereabouts?' asked Francis. 'No, Dick. Stopper your fury. We have to play this game shrewdly if it is to be won.'

Richard eyed him, and then suddenly, to their relief, he managed to smile.

'Forgive me,' he said. 'I hook myself too easily on George's bait . . .' Momentarily his face clouded. 'Later, in some way, I shall be revenged on him,' he promised.

'Aye,' said Miles. 'But first we must fetch out the Lady Anne.'

He was of the opinion it could be best done by a small show of strength. Only the innkeeper and his pot-boys stood in their way, and they would be unlikely to show much resistance to three or four armed men.

'Just so!' said the priest. 'Much depends on the extent of the innkeeper's loyalty to my lord of Clarence, or his greed —' He rubbed his hands. 'Though as to the latter, we could buy his blind eyes with a purse.'

'Dom Edmund,' said Richard wryly, 'you would appear to be expert at abducting kitchen-maids from taverns.'

Dom Edmund looked so thunderstruck that the others shouted with laughter, but then he joined in it himself. 'I have a taste for plots,' he confessed, wiping his eyes. 'And this situation has all the ingredients of high romance. There will be ballads sung of it.'

'Which no doubt you will write,' said Richard taking his arm. 'Then let us find Robert and go to act out the plot.'

The priest's levity died instantly at the suggestion that Richard himself should take any part in the enterprise. His place was to wait at Crosby's Place until the Lady Anne had been suitably accommodated in sanctuary.

'Which is the correct place for her,' he insisted. 'Quite out of your brother's reach.'

'And mine as well,' said Richard grimly.

'Surely, Richard, you understand that she could not come here! The king has given leave for you to press your suit, but it would be ungenerous to place her under an obligation to yourself. She must have the liberty to choose; and in sanctuary she will have that liberty.'

'The freedom to accept me or reject me?' murmured Richard.

'Yes.' And having been candid the priest turned to the others. 'Now, gentlemen,' he said. 'Will you take Robert Percy with you to the Cripplegate inn? The Lady Anne knows all of you from Middleham and will trust you, and take with you a chaperone. A lady who may accompany her to sanctuary.'

'I can provide a chaperone,' said Miles quickly, his face pinker than usual. 'There is a certain knight's daughter in the Chepe who would gladly accompany us – bringing her tiring-maid.'

'A certain knight's daughter!' echoed Francis, and turned triumphantly to Richard. 'Did I not tell you, my lord, that he was prinking himself out like a bullfinch in spring?'

Richard clapped Miles on the shoulder. 'So! Our grave advocate has turned suitor in a sweeter court!'

'It's Ribbet's daughter, I'll be bound,' cried Francis. 'The blue-eyed Alice.'

Miles nodded. 'Aye. With my lord's permission we shall marry.'

'But why did you not tell us of your love?' asked Richard.

Miles looked down at his shoes. 'It would have been . . . ungracious to speak of my own happiness in love when you, Dick, were so sad in yours.'

'But sad no longer,' said Dom Edmund. 'All, I am sure, will now be well. Go fast to the Chepe, Miles, and beg your lady's attendance; then to the inn – while I approach the priest at St Martin-le-Grand.'

Richard quipped him again. 'Will you affect a disguise for this stealthy work, Dom Edmund, and walk out as a footsoldier, or, possibly, a Venetian merchant?'

But it was simply a veneer of light-heartedness. As he watched his friends leave the garden he was still uneasy, not because he believed they would fail but on account of the unanswered question which had pressed upon him since Tewkesbury and before. He walked up and down on the shingle path; sure now of his own love for Anne, but fretting all the same because he was so unsure of her feelings for him.

XX

The singing-boy paused and looked over his shoulder. 'It is this way, your grace.'

'Aye,' replied Richard, slowly following.

He stopped once more, pretending to examine the painted frescoes on the south wall. Dom Edmund pressed his arm. 'Come, Dick,' he urged. 'You cannot hesitate now. The Lady Anne awaits you.'

'Let me be . . . for a minute . . . but a minute.'

'The Great Chamber is this way, your grace,' called the singing-boy impatiently.

'One moment, lad,' said Dom Edmund loudly. 'My lord admires your frescoes.' Then quietly he chided Richard. 'You have come this far with confidence. What keeps you from her now?' He knew quite well why Richard was holding back, but he was determined to drive him on.

'What . . .' Richard could hardly say it. 'What if after everything she should be unwilling?'

This, decided the priest, was no time for honeyed words. 'You mean, of course, what if she should find you repugnant and prefer another; or wish to remain maid in honour of Edward of Lancaster?'

Richard nodded.

'Why, then you will know precisely where you are. Which,' added the priest, 'is better than enduring uncertainty in this draughty garth.' He took Richard's arm and physically forced him onwards.

Richard found his knees and hands trembling when they entered the Great Chamber. It was a sparsely furnished room, and ill-lighted because the tall unglazed window had been sealed against the weather. There was a single charcoal brazier, and close to it sat Anne Neville on a cushioned bench. She wore a thick winter gown of purple velvet with a head-dress of the same colour, and looked sombre beside her blue-eyed attendant who Richard guessed was Alice Ribbett, Miles's lady.

It smote Richard's heart to see how she had changed. He hid his distress, bowed deeply and then would have moved forward to give her a cousinly kiss but she was already on her feet and greeting him with a low wide curtsy.

He remained still, embarrassed by the way she so obviously treated him as her patron and protector, and not as her childhood friend Richard Plantagenet. To his dismay she remained in her low curtsy while she formally welcomed him and thanked him for everything he had done for her, addressing him continually as 'my lord prince' or 'your grace' and speaking French in the stiff fashion of court, not the homely north England dialect so well known to them both.

He replied in the same fashion, raising her to her feet, asking to be presented to her companion. Then, Dom Edmund and Alice Ribbett moved away to allow them a measure of privacy, and he sat beside Anne on the cushioned bench, accepting the heavy fact that she wished this to be a formal interview, an exchange of uninteresting pleasantries, and nothing more.

And it might have been if he had not caught the scent of costmary. There was a small bowl of dried costmary on the floor, and near him on the bench was a half-finished sachet-bag which Anne must have been sewing to pass away the time. The scent instantly carried him two hundred miles away and more, to Middleham and the herb garden where he and Anne had so often been together.

'Costmary,' he said softly, taking a pinch of the dried herb and crushing it between his fingers. It was a plant he had never forgotten because once she had plucked some costmary leaves to soothe a bee-sting on his wrist.

'Anne,' he said and then spoke in the dialect of the north. 'Do you recall the herbs at Middleham?'

For answer, she touched the very place on his wrist where six, no seven, years before the bee had stung him.

'You remember?' he asked, amazed. 'You truly remember?'

'Of course, Dick,' – and she, too, now spoke in the language they had used as children. 'How should I forget?'

He caught her hand, and for a moment they were silent. Then simultaneously they broke the silence; smiled, waited for each other, and as so often happens – both started off again at the same moment.

This made them laugh out loud, and so happily and naturally that Dom Edmund nodded his head in satisfaction and whispered to Mistress Alice that all was well.

Richard wisely led her away from dreams to reality and he turned deliberately to matters which had to be mentioned because so much depended on them. At first she was reserved to the point of hostility, or so it seemed to Richard until he realized she was now much shyer than he remembered. He wondered if it was this which prevented her from mentioning Edward of Lancaster, for she said nothing of their betrothal or of his violent death at Tewkesbury. Nor did she speak of her long stay in France and all that had happened to her since – except to thank him for the honour he and his friends had done to her dead father.

Richard avoiding asking direct questions, guessing rightly that the sorest of her wounds would have to scar over before she spoke of them to anyone. Instead he told her of all that had happened in his own life since their last meeting.

Anne had no dainty convent sensibilities. She was still very young and her upbringing had been strict, but she had known exile and life in military camps, and she accepted the fact that young noblemen pleasured themselves and proved their manhood by begetting bastards. It neither surprised nor shocked her that Richard acknowledged his two children, Katherine and John; and, though she cast her eyes down when he spoke well of their mother, she felt no jealousy, simply admiration for his candour and his loyalty to a woman who had given him love and comfort when most he needed it. She knew from his manner that he was remorseful because he had not remained entirely faithful to her during their long years of separation, but she was grateful that he did not try to make things easier for himself by adding yet another betrayal. He would not dishonour Eleanor's memory by pretending she had meant no more to him than a garrison whore. Anne understood his feelings, and he sensed that she understood. Far from dividing them, by some miracle Eleanor had brought them closer together.

'Anne,' he said very quietly. 'I would take you home to Middleham.'

She looked away. 'Your brothers would consent?'

'I have the king's word.'

She still looked away from him. 'And George?'

He made no reply.

'I have learnt much of my brother-in-law's love and protection,' she said, and could not keep the bitterness from her voice. She faced Richard squarely. 'And as his concern is with my mother's estates and revenue I make no doubt you could buy his consent.'

'Anne,' he murmured, much distressed by her bitterness.

But then, once more, she touched his wrist where the bee had stung him.

'And I would go with you, Dick,' she said. 'Home again to Middleham.'

PART THREE

Prince of the Northern Marches

I

Slowly and carefully Dom Edmund sat down on the ground, and, once settled, he used his hands to pull his legs into the most comfortable position. At forty-five he looked much older, and felt much older, too. True, there were a few people older than he at Middleham; one, indeed, having almost reached the unheard age of seventy-nine, though this ancient was hardly to be envied, being toothless, deaf, and given to fits of drooling lunacy; but none of Dom Edmund's seniors had to endure the cramps and screws and clamps of rheumatism which had lined and furrowed his face and frosted his hair to a silvery grey. Did he suffer in this way simply because of what he wryly called his 'stretching'? or had the trouble been started forty-five years before when he was born in a mill over water at Walsingham?

Dear Walsingham! A luxury of age was the way a man's mind wandered, helter-skelter, up and down, backwards and forwards, from this to that. And, truly, it was more comfortable to think of Middleham and not of Walsingham – for no one there was left, and all his affection rested with the Lord Richard and his family.

He wondered why the children were late. By this time they ought to have been there with him. Should he punish them with lessons indoors, or keep them out in the sunshine? In the herb garden perhaps? sniffing the scents and making posies as they rehearsed their catechism?

They were always late, but today later than usual. Perhaps Richard Metcalfe and the young Prince Edward might have kept more to time if it had not been for Katherine and John . . . two scatterbrains who shared none of their father's strict punctuality, none at all.

He rested against the donjon wall until he heard a footfall and opened his eyes. A donzel was passing on his way to the hall.

'Boy!'

'Sir?'

'I wonder, have you seen my pupils?'

161

'They are with her grace in the outer bailey, Dom Edmund. A tinker has come from the Scottish border.'

'So. I thank you.'

The boy bent to kiss his hands – because though they were wrinkled and twisted, the priest had hands that blessed and made God at Mass. Then he went on his way.

Dom Edmund closed his eyes. A tinker's visit – his wallet stuffed with fal-lals and ribbons, hawk jesses and humbling knives – would keep the children occupied for half an hour more. No matter. Tinkers themselves were educators, as newsmen, entertainers and travellers – and if the Lady Anne were with the children . . .

A tender smile spread across his face as he thought of his dear lady . . . surely the wisest, happiest and most loving châtelaine, wife, mother and foster mother in the whole kingdom? Still quiet and reserved, as Dom Edmund believed a great lady should be, but always so concerned for other people. When Robert Percy had married his heart's desire and brought her north from the queen's household, Anne had put everything aside to make sure Joyce was properly welcomed and made to feel a member of the Middleham family. No one could have been more concerned for Miles when his blue-eyed Alice died in childbirth, and she had mothered little Richard Metcalfe with exactly the same devotion she showered on her lord's bastards, and her own young son, Prince Edward. Aye, she was a lady full of love.

It was at this point in his reverie that he heard more footfalls and even before he looked up he recognized Richard's light tread. Behind his lord was Francis Lovell, now knighted and Captain of Middleham, and a tall saturnine man who wore a travelling cloak.

'Dom Edmund, you remember this gentleman?' said Richard as the priest slowly climbed to his feet.

The priest peered at the tall stranger, and a memory stirred at the back of his mind.

'Short memory, weak eyesight,' he began, but Richard gave him no time to finish.

'Sir James Tyrell.'

Now he recognized him. 'Of course.' He bowed. 'I have much to thank you for.'

'He has ridden with hardly a pause from London,' said Richard. His voice was clipped. 'To bring me word from my lady mother.' He took the priest's elbow in a firm grasp and walked him away from the others. 'I would have no one hear either my question or your answer, for you are free, entirely free to deny my request.'

Dom Edmund blinked. Behind them he heard Tyrell and Lovell talking together. 'A request, my lord?'

'Aye.' Richard hesitated; then he walked him rapidly across the uneven cobbles.

The priest, stumbling, asked him to stop. 'You forget, my son. Since they were . . . stretched, my legs have been rebellious individuals.'

Richard stopped instantly and was all concern. 'I should have remembered . . . Here, we will rest against this wall . . . How could I ever forget . . . No, there is moss on the stonework . . . Truly, I did not forget . . . Yet Tyrell's news . . . Tyrell has brought such news . . .'

That a man generally so concise in all he said should ramble in such a way both puzzled and alarmed Dom Edmund. He begged him to be calm, and compose himself, and he underlined his claim to be heard by calling him Dickon – the affectionate name used by only two others besides himself, Richard's wife and mother.

Richard did as he was bidden.

'And ease out those deep lines of care,' urged the priest. 'Frowns are for bad-tempered men, my Dickon. Now,' he continued, when Richard found a smile: 'what is your request?'

The forced smile died. 'Edward will have George's head.'

Dom Edmund said nothing.

'He has tired at last of his dangerous follies. My mother sends word George is to be tried for his life.' Richard looked away while he said this. Then he tried to meet Dom Edmund's eyes. 'Tyrell will tell you everything, but it all amounts to this: that George's lunacy has driven him to stir up rebellion in the Fen country.'

Still the priest was silent.

'A pathetic affair . . . dangerous to no one at all, save George . . . and it flickered out, but Edward will have his head for it.'

Dom Edmund spoke at last, to say quietly: 'Since your brother Clarence lost his wife, he has been . . . over-reckless.' He paused, then asked: 'He has been imprisoned?'

Richard nodded. 'Committed to the Tower. My mother knows there is no love lost between George and me – yet she asks that I ride south at once in an attempt to save him from Edward's wrath.'

163

'He is not worth it.' The coldness in the priest's tone was unmistakable.

'He is my brother,' urged Richard.

'As is King Edward,' said the priest. 'What is your request?'

The question – now repeated for the second time – fused the same incoherence from Richard as before. 'Dom Edmund . . . No one . . . I have not forgotten . . . Your racking and imprisonment . . . No one . . . Brutal and unnecessary . . . Clarence was ever vengeful . . . No one. My mother remembers . . .'

Embarrassed and concerned the priest cut him short. 'Come to the point, Dickon.'

'My mother would have you accompany me —'

'To plead for Clarence?'

'Yes.'

The priest crossed himself. It was the only way to ward off those devils who urged him to shout at the top of his voice what they had immediately put into his mind: that to plead for Clarence would be hypocrisy. Try as he might, he could not still or even ease his terrible hatred for the man who had wreaked a petty revenge on him simply because he stood high in Richard's love and high in the king's regard.

The mossy stones behind him, the cobbles beneath his feet, and the blue sky above were less real at that moment than the memory of being plucked from Crosby's Place when Richard was far away on the king's affairs and unable to protect him; of being taken into the street and then so knocked about that he failed to recognize the court where, before a bench of puzzled magistrates, he had to answer a trumped-up charge of sorcery. Claiming the right to be judged only by the Church or by the Duke of Gloucester, he had been given back to Clarence's men for holding and questioning pending his removal to a Church court – and then, dear God; stripped naked before them all in a cellar as cold as death itself, humiliated by men with no respect for God or his priests; then stretched and tugged two ways, wedded to that wooden-rack until he would have confessed, and did, to anything they demanded. Afterwards, imprisonment – pitch-dark imprisonment – wearing one drab piece of sackcloth, barely fed, and kept close to his cell, fouling each part of it, until a tall saturnine man named Tyrell had come to release him.

Tyrell had worked secretly for weeks to find him and then with a King's Commission, freed him into a world he neither loved nor trusted any longer.

The Duke of Gloucester's rage had been terrible – but though some were punished, Clarence shrugged off all blame by showing the priest's confession made under questioning. And a grimed, desolate, wronged man had taken his torn sinews and despair back to the quiet of Crosby's Place and afterwards to Middleham. Very slowly he had healed, in body and in mind, but his soul was still endangered by his deep hatred for George Plantagenet. He crossed himself a second time.

'You would have me plead for Clarence?'

'Yes.'

'I cannot.' The words came from deep inside the priest.

'Very well. I understand.' For a minute, two, Richard was silent and thoughtful. Then he said. 'Give me your arm. Come, we will return to the others.'

II

Dom Edmund struggled with his conscience while his lord rode southwards to save one brother from the other. In one sense it was a wasted journey, for Clarence was neither examined nor brought to trial all summer, but the time was not mis-spent. Richard began to appreciate how powerful the queen's family had become during his long absence from the court; how small his own influence was with Edward compared with theirs.

He returned when the leaves began to fall and there was a great slaughtering of cattle and pickling of meat and storing of provender against the approaching winter. With him was his Council of the North – and they would stay for a short time, no more, before returning to London for Christmas and a royal wedding which would follow: the marriage of the king's young son, Prince Richard of York to Anne Mowbray, sole heiress of all the Norfolk family's wealth and land.

Richard, generally so happy to be home again with his beloved wife and son, was this time withdrawn and grey-faced, and Dom Edmund, seeing it, felt his heart turn in sympathy. His lord's face told him what he had been going through at court, and it moved him to go to Richard and say without any preamble: 'When you return, Dickon, I would go with you.'

'No, Dom Edmund. I have no right to ask it. Not now.'

The priest was adamant. 'It is seldom that a man with regrets has a second chance. Please, I beg you.' He smiled. 'Besides I would prefer to keep Christmas in your company.'

Richard put an arm about his shoulder. 'Thank you my old friend . . . ' He fumbled for words. 'Ned has always admired your wisdom. He often speaks of you. Your voice, with mine and my mother's, might tilt the scales.'

III

When the Duke of Gloucester rode south for the second time he left most of his northern councillors behind. Francis, as Captain of Middleham, had the charge of his family. Of his closest friends only Robert Percy and Dom Edmund travelled with him.

He did not care to be separated at Christmastime from Anne and the children but it was important to show Edward and the Wood-villes that his single-minded purpose in travelling so far was *not* to keep Christmas, nor witness his nephew's wedding, but to continue pleading for George's life. And, after five years of governing the north country, and serving the king to the best of his ability, he now considered he had the right to separate his public from his private life. He would go to court as Viceroy and Captain of the North with just claims upon the king in return for services done, and not simply as brother Richard. And if the Woodville faction should see him as sombre Gloucester, and frown amongst themselves because he haunted the revels as a living ghost, then so much the better.

His first meeting with the king, soon after their arrival in London, was not a happy one.

Judging it best to leave Dom Edmund for the time being at Crosby's Place, Richard went alone to court to seek out his brother. There, indifferent to the presence of the Woodvilles, and in the same breath as he greeted Edward, he began to plead once more for Clarence.

A frown crossed the king's face. Having suffered barely an hour before from the nagging of his queen, he now found it intolerable to be nagged in the opposite direction by his brother. It was unlike him to be discourteous, but he was short to the point of rudeness and, when Richard stubbornly persevered, bluntly bade him hold his tongue.

Richard coloured at this public rebuke. He stepped back a yard, bowed stiffly, and had begun to walk away before the king, relenting, called him back.

'Come, Dick,' he said. 'I meant not to be sour and sharp with you. Forgive me.' And then, with a wide glance at all who stood near by, and raising his voice, he continued: 'I know your worth, and love your loyalty. But I would have no one, no one at all speak of our brother George at this holy season.'

There was no mistaking that he included his queen as well as his brother in this command. She judged it best to hide her vexation. 'Of course, my lord. We would not spoil our revels with talk of traitors!' She smiled agreeably . . .

A smile, Richard told himself, as false and meaningless as brother Clarence. He left the room, but not before he had been surprised by a smile of sympathy, as true as the queen's was false, from a most unlikely source, from her brother Anthony, Earl Rivers, who stood a little to the left of her chair.

At supper in a private chamber at Crosby's Place he confessed his puzzlement to Robert and Dom Edmund. 'Why should Rivers encourage me? Why? Would he urge me to be rash, so impatient in goading the king that I destroy all chance of saving Clarence,' he paused.

Robert, far more matter-of-fact, thought this oversubtle. To him Earl Rivers was simply a Woodville, and therefore greedy and two-faced.

But Dom Edmund disagreed. He had come to know Rivers in their Burgundian exile and much admired his intellect and piety. Not one of the queen's family was a fool, but Rivers stood out amongst them as a talented man of contrasts: the champion of Europe in jousting and one of the most gorgeous peacocks in all Edward's luxurious court, and yet at the same time he was a scholar, a poet, a pilgrim to far distant holy shrines. The priest was full of his praise: 'Had there been more men like Rivers by the throne in these past twenty years, our civil wars would have left less mark on England. Truly, my lord, he would be a valued ally.'

Richard took this in. 'You really believe I may trust this enigmatic earl?'

'I do. He is a man of honour.'

'Honour?' repeated Robert, genuinely amazed. 'And he a Woodville!'

'You will see,' said Dom Edmund calmly, drinking from the horn
of wine before him. 'You will see!'

✳

On the Vigil of Christmas Anthony Rivers called at Crosby's Place.
He carried with him the very first book ever to be printed in England, *the Dictes and Sayings of the Philosophers*. He knew that it would
be of particular interest to the Duke of Gloucester because it had been
printed by his old mentor in exile, William Caxton.

He was right, Richard was interested and inquired kindly after
the mercer turned inventor who had brought his press from Bruges
to Westminster. But Richard was even more interested in the fact
that Rivers was accompanied by Henry Stafford, Duke of Buckingham.

He wondered if it was significant – if Rivers had brought him to
Crosby's Place to prevent any possibility of a frank discussion, or
had he brought him as a sympathetic ally?

Being unable to decide, and Rivers not making a move to help
him decide, Richard chose to forget Clarence for the moment.

He offered refreshment – spiced wine, baked carp, cheese comfits,
and sweet cakes – watched the earl's man replace the thick volume in
a specially constructed wooden box, and listened to Rivers expound-
ing on the marvels of Caxton's invention and its social consequences.
And no one mentioned Clarence until the time came for them to
leave. Then, it was Buckingham, not Rivers, who remarked, almost
as an aside, that Richard's hall, lighted by sconces and tapers, warmed
with many braziers, and strewn with rushes and fragrant herbs, and
with a trestle laden with vigil fish, was much more homely than the
draughty palace of Westminster.

'And both,' he finished dryly, 'are more comfortable than the
Tower.'

Richard might have followed the lead, but Miles Metcalfe, newly
come that day from York and tired after his journey, stumbled
clumsily against a bench and sent it crashing on its side. The noise,
Miles's mumbled apologies, and the fact that Rivers and Buckingham
were bowing their farewells, made Richard change his mind.

He gave them his hand to kiss, offered the hospitality of his home

169

whenever they cared to visit him, and sat back in his chair while Robert Percy led them away through the buttery to the great doors.

'My lord,' said Miles. 'You will forgive me for saying that I know more than you of your cousin Buckingham. He has been at court since he was twelve years old. He is much influenced by the queen . . .'

Richard broke in. 'But it is common knowledge that he dislikes her for marrying him off to her sister Katherine.'

'She has indulged him for thirteen years,' continued Miles doggedly. 'Giving him play-things to keep him happy like a pet. She has of course kept him out of state affairs which he resents, but it is she who has moulded him, and made him what he is.' He looked directly at Richard. 'You know her power, my lord, her flair for aggravating weaknesses and softening virtues.'

Richard nodded.

Miles hesitated. 'I do not . . . No, I do not think at this stage you may consider him as anything but a Woodville, nor overtrust him.'

Richard looked at his chaplain. 'And you agree?'

'I believe so,' said Dom Edmund. 'Because Buckingham . . .' He hesitated. 'You will think me fanciful, perhaps, but Buckingham to me is a reminder of your brother, Clarence.'

'My brother Clarence?'

'There are – similarities.' Quickly the priest went on: 'I should trust Rivers as you know, but no, not Buckingham . . . I must join Miles's counsel.'

'And you, Robert?'

'The king will hear you or not hear you as his loyal brother. I do not think you need the aid of his relations by marriage.'

'So!' Richard considered. His attorney, his chamberlain and his confessor were in agreement. 'Very well. I shall do as you advise.'

IV

Christmas passed, and Richard of Gloucester began to plead once more for his brother's life. This time he took Dom Edmund with him, and the sight of one of George's victims begging for him affected all who saw it. The king was deeply moved. He stepped down from his chair and, with his own hands, raised the priest from his kneeling position, and, had he been alone, might then have granted what Dom Edmund asked. But the omnipresent Woodvilles prevented this; and, afterwards, the queen played skilfully upon Edward's sympathies in a way neither Richard nor his chaplain had anticipated, by suggesting that such a bent and tortured priest ought rightly to be avenged by his king and protector, the sole fountain of justice in all England. In this way she contrived to appeal both to Edward's pity and to his pride as father of the English people, but still he temporized, refusing to make a decision until parliament should meet after the wedding of his son.

On January 15th the marriage was solemnized: Richard of Gloucester and Harry of Buckingham escorting the little bride to the royal chamber for her nuptial banquet.

'A task, cousin,' murmured Buckingham as they rode their stately way, 'which devolves upon me in the absence of your brother.'

Richard nodded, but said nothing.

Afterwards, tired of the feasting, he slipped away to Baynard's Castle where his mother kept to one small cell, living austerely under rule. She had refused to attend the wedding to mark her displeasure at Edward's treatment of her second son.

'God knows, Dickon, George deserves death; but not at the hands of his own brother and certainly not because that low-born widow wishes for it.'

Richard sat on a low stool and hugged his knees. 'Yet I doubt, madam, if he can be saved.'

She crossed herself. Her face was too white to whiten any more, but from the increased trembling of her hands, Richard could

171

measure her distress. Gently he took those trembling hands in his. 'I wish . . .' he began and stopped.

It was impossible to comfort her, though that had been his intention; to warn her and to comfort her.

'I know, Dickon,' she spoke softly. 'I know.'

For some time they remained silent. Then she said distantly, as if he were not there. 'For Gloucester I would use this knowledge. Yes, I would use it. But I cannot for Clarence.'

He regarded her curiously.

'It would be too costly to England . . . too costly. And George is contemptible.'

Her voice altered. 'But should Edward proceed . . .' She stood up, her whole body now rigid and still as though she was possessed. 'Tell him from me, my son, that the mark of Cain will devastate our house. All his father's work, his own, and yours; all that has been done to give England peace and order will be destroyed. His royal sun in splendour will be blackened, and his children, you and yours, and George's too, cursed and damned.'

Richard shuddered, seized her hand, begged her to take back her words and, in the name of God and his Saints, to bless away her curses. He did not realize it but he was shouting.

It took a huge effort of will to compose himself, and then he signed her with the Cross from the crown of her black coif to her breast, from shoulder to shoulder.

She looked up at him and there was sadness in her eyes as she said: 'Tell him from me, I would he was merciful to my son.'

Panic caught hold of Richard. It seemed as if she did not know that anything had happened. He could not prevent himself from blurting out: 'You will bless us, madam. You will bless us.'

'Bless you? Why, Dickon, I have done so all your lives.'

'Yet . . .' he began: and stopped.

'Help both George and Edward for my sake,' she asked.

He kissed her hand and then her cheek. 'I will, mother,' he promised.

Beyond her door he stood clenching and unclenching his hands. He must get to Edward without delay and warn him.

He ran down into the courtyard, and sent a servant to bid Dom Edmund meet him at Westminster palace as quickly as he could. He made the man repeat the message and then smacked his horse's rump with the flat of his hand. The beast reared and sprang away through the gatehouse. Richard mounted his own courser and galloped out into Thames Street. He outdistanced all his men in his haste to reach the palace.

Sounds of merrymaking came from the Great Hall but the Duke of Gloucester would not enter the palace. He strode up and down outside the great gate waiting for his chaplain. Up and down. Up and down. Up and down.

After what seemed a long time Dom Edmund arrived in a horse litter. When he saw the priest's features twisted with pain, Richard's own face blanched with concern.

'Dom Edmund,' he said. 'It was a cruelty to bring you from your bed.' Tenderly he lifted him out of the litter. 'And nothing but such a matter would have made me do it.'

'Set me down!' gasped the priest. 'No. Do not carry me. I am better on my feet. My staff! – thank you, Dickon.' He swallowed hard, ran trembling fingers down the side of his face. 'At night – after lying still in bed – my joints – my bones are fixed. But in a moment I shall be myself. Tell me, while I rest, what is the matter?'

Richard told him, and the priest crossed himself. 'Mother of God!' he murmured. 'Pray for us all.'

'Bid Lord Hastings I would see the king,' ordered Richard over his shoulder.

But by the time Dom Edmund declared he was ready to walk with him into the hall, and they were slowly making their way up the flight of steps, Hastings himself came out to meet them. He bowed, low, but Richard could not catch what he said because of the music and shouts and the noise of the feasting from the Great Hall. Hastings began to repeat himself, then changed his mind and led them through a side gallery. As they walked he spoke softly to Richard, spreading his hands in a gesture of regret.

Richard stopped for a moment. 'Gone from his own son's wedding feast?' he said incredulously.

Hastings smiled. 'Be just, my lord. The young prince was returned to his nursery before you left the feast yourself.'

Richard nodded: 'Yes. Yet . . .' He walked on. 'I would see him.'

Hastings made the same gesture of regret.

'Will, this is an urgent matter. Or I should not be here at all.'

Hastings shrugged. As chamberlain he had rule of the king's

household, and could deny even the king's brother: but a great deal of wine was singing in his head and so he smiled and shrugged, and led them along the gallery towards the king's private apartments. If Gloucester needed urgently to see the king . . .

He stumbled, tripping over the enormous length of his shoe-toes – so enormous that they had to be cord-looped to his knees, and difficult enough to manage even when sober.

Richard prevented him from falling, and even while he thanked him Hastings was telling himself that of course Gloucester's shoe-toes were not in the mode, being short and without cords, and of course, Gloucester was sober. Gloucester was always different – the odd Plantagenet out. So unlike Ned. So unlike George.

'I would see the king, Will,' Richard reminded him.

'Yes, yes.'

On they went, Dom Edmund's staff tapping on the flags and Hastings plopping down his shoes like a goose, and smiling because with Ned he could and did share everything from a state secret to a whore, then frowning because with Gloucester he could share nothing – except their love for Ned. Love and jealousy: adoration and scorn.

'You are quite sure, my lord, that you wish to disturb the king?'

'I do,' said Richard coldly.

Hastings bowed, and on they went. Ned would be angry: Gloucester too. Gloucester down in the king's affection – Hastings up maybe. The wine in his head sang a new and different song. Gloucester's self-control and high standards were simply self-righteousness and prudery. So – to smart that prudery . . .

Before the door of the king's bedchamber stood two men-at-arms with lances crossed. Hastings made a sign. They gaped in dismay, but at a word from him they obeyed, and stood back from the door.

'Your grace,' said Hastings, bowing low.

'Thank you, Hastings.' Richard returned the bow. Then he pulled aside the curtain and led his chaplain into the room.

Years of hearing confessions, a million words at least about innumerable sins, had blunted Dom Edmund's disapproval, and with some cause he believed he was unshockable. He learnt his mistake in that opulent, heavily-scented chamber. Not that he was shocked by the sight of his anointed king sprawling drink-sodden and mother-naked on a day-bed, nor even that he continued to caress and fondle his companion while his brother, frozen with embarrassment, stood not two yards from him. Modesty made the priest lower his eyes, but he was not shocked. Yet he was truly shocked when Edward jeered at Richard's tale, calling his brother loon, and their mother a God-crazed lunatic – or, he added, wearing a lop-sided smile, more likely possessed by the devil as she was a Neville. In which case she was better locked up . . . like Clarence.

Richard began to shake with fury at this outrageous affront both to his wife and to his mother, and Dom Edmund risked a great deal then by seizing his arm to prevent him striking the king.

Edward saw this through tiny pig-eyes, grinned, and drove in more pins by declaring that the way certain people attempted to save traitors from just punishment approached close to treason itself, but they need trouble themselves no further: George of Clarence would be tried before his peers and parliament in the morning.

Richard cut in, but his protest tailed off when Edward deliberately turned to whisper to the whore in his arms, then give a mighty belch.

Dom Edmund pressed his lord's arm, trying to guide him towards the door; but when Richard would have turned, Edward quickly spoke again, saying plaintively that no one could imagine the dilemmas of a hard-pressed sovereign – and how disheartening it was to be obliged to charge a brother with treason and proclaim a mother imbecile all in one morning.

Richard, not trusting himself to speak, turned and walked away, whereupon the king called him a knave and insolent and hurled a cup of silver at his brother's back. Thick malmsey sprayed in an arc across the chamber. Some spotted the priest's habit, a little marked the velvet of Richard's doublet. Then, as drunkards will, the king abruptly changed his humour, giggled at what he had done, and laughingly bade his brother and the good canon sit with him and drink, or, he added generously, they could use his Jane, his dear, dear Jane Shore, if they wished.

Richard bowed, and taking the priest's arm, led him from the room.

Behind them Edward shouted to his guards.

Obedient to his command they seized the Duke of Gloucester and his chaplain.

Richard looked in fury at Hastings who stood leaning against the wall. It was a look which rebuked the chamberlain. Quickly he stood up straight, and walked into the chamber – to reason with the king. When he emerged again, he signed to the guards to return to their posts.

'Your grace,' said Hastings, 'I attempted to warn you.'

'You did,' he said. 'And I shall remember it. I shall remember much of tonight.'

He and Dom Edmund walked away along the gallery.

Hastings watched them with misgivings: the duke whom he loved and envied, admired and scorned, and the bent old priest. He cursed himself for a fool. He had been rash – too hasty with Richard of Gloucester. One day Richard of Gloucester might be rash and hasty with him.

V

Edward the king still had incredible powers of recovery. Within four hours of his debauch he was sober, clear-headed, and penitent. He sent Hastings to Crosby's Place with a personal message for his brother. Richard heard it, his face devoid of expression, and when Hastings went on in an attempt to justify his own actions, he found himself dismissed peremptorily; and later that morning, in the great hall of Westminster where Parliament had assembled, Richard refused to meet his eyes or give any sign that he was forgiven.

In fact the Duke of Gloucester looked at no one as he stood beside the throne hearing his brothers rend each other: the king himself accusing Clarence, and Clarence, with nothing to lose, meeting each charge with insolence.

Six months' imprisonment had told on Clarence. His hair, once thick and golden and the envy of many courtiers, hung lifelessly to frame a face now pallid and blemished with angry pimples. His eyes had lost some of their sea-blueness, and he seemed to have shrunk a little so that his gorgeous clothes ill-fitted him. But he had lost none of his fluency, and to begin with his eloquence was so brilliant that he almost seemed to be persuading the court that he, not Edward, was the wronged party, and that he stood there at the bar of the Lords simply because he was a victim of the Woodvilles' malice.

But, though his brother's pertness and insolence stung Edward's pride, he lost neither his dignity nor his temper and proved the quality of his kingship. Even those who loathed and mistrusted the queen's party, and were delighted to hear it execrated publicly before all England, knew the real worth of their king, and they respected the way in which, despite all provocation, he continued inexorably with the indictment.

The charges were formidable: that the Duke of Clarence had schemed privately to marry his niece, the young heiress of Burgundy, evidence being sworn by Louis, King of France, that his intention was to use the resources of the Duchy against the English crown; that he had broken the king's peace by the false arrest of numerous persons, amongst them a servant of the late Duchess Isabel; that he had perverted the king's justice by falsely charging this servant with poisoning the Duchess Isabel; that he had defamed the king and assailed his dignity by spreading false reports that this servant had been suborned to her art by the queen; that he had taken the king's justice into his own hands in that, at the trial of this servant, he had intimidated or bribed the royal magistrates and appointed jurors; that he had published or had caused to be published treasonable writings; that he had caused to be spread throughout the kingdom a treasonable accusation the king practised witchcraft and eliminated his enemies with poison; that he had impugned the royal honour by publicly refusing to eat or drink at court, putting it out that he feared poisoning at the king's hands; that he had further impugned the royal honour, and the honour of Cecily, Dowager Duchess of York, by declaring the king was the bastard of a low-born archer of Rouen and not the first son and heir of Richard Plantagenet, late Duke of York; that he had committed treason in attempting to disprove the validity of the king's marriage to the Lady Elizabeth now Queen of England . . .

It was a horrifying sequence of crimes, and as each was presented, examined and proved in turn, Clarence began to lose his wits. In the light of conclusive evidence as to his guilt he still made hysterical assertions of innocence. His denials became absurd. Then, panicking, he made mortally dangerous admissions. At last, when Edward finally charged him with breaking the king's peace and levying war against his sovereign in Cambridgeshire and Huntingdonshire, he made the most ludicrous defence of all.

'For I am rightful King of England,' he screeched.

His peers, dumbfounded, gazed at him in dismay as he went on to justify his crazy claim.

'It was here in this hall seven years ago,' at the re-adeption of King Henry that parliament proclaimed me heir next in succession after Edward, Prince of Wales.'

Richard at last looked up and bent to whisper in the king's ear: 'Brother, he is demented, bereft of reason. Have done with this. He is no more responsible than a mad dog.'

But Edward was inflexible. 'Mad dogs,' he said out of the corner of his mouth, 'must be put down.' Then, raising his voice, he calmly answered Clarence: 'All attainders of King Henry's parliament at that time were reversed, and all enactments rescinded by the Law

178

of England.' His voice grew louder. 'It is also law that no man may profit through the result of his own crime, and you yourself slew Edward, so-called Prince of Wales, in defence of your true liege lord, Edward the Fourth of England.'

Clarence's last vestige of control snapped at this. He screamed and raved with rage and tore at the points on his doublet, denouncing the king, denouncing the queen and all her family; railing then at Gloucester for his subtle tricks to cheat him of Warwick's lands, railing at Hastings on the king's left hand for blinding his sovereign to the malicious knavery of the Woodvilles.

A tense parliament saw him removed, dragged through the ranks of peers and away through the doors until he was out of earshot.

Edward clutched the arms of his throne, his knuckles white. 'My lords,' he cried. 'Not once, but many times I have forgiven the Duke of Clarence all his treacheries, but his follies and his treasons have grown beyond my pardon. For the safety of the realm, he is indicted before you.' He stood up. 'I charge you as his peers to declare his innocence or guilt.'

There was a flourish of trumpets as he stepped down from the throne and walked with his attendants from the hall. And behind, quite alone, walked Richard Plantagenet, not staying to cast a vote on his own brother's fate, and carrying, not wearing, his cap of maintenance to signify he left parliament as a private gentleman without state, and not as the Lord Richard, Duke of Gloucester, Constable of England, and Prince of the Northern Marches.

Two wharves were being re-made between Billingsgate and the Tower and a pile-driver pounded up and down through all the short daylight hours, and sometimes, by the light of lanterns, into the nights as well. Metal head met seasoned oak with thuds which echoed from St Katherine's hospital to London Stone, and from Bishopsgate to Bermondsey. It was like a great funeral drum proclaiming the doom of kings and those who would be kings.

Edward still temporized. He would not or could not sentence Clarence.

The pounding by the Tower went on and on. At last the king

acted, appointing the Duke of Buckingham High Seneschal, ordering him with this authority to sentence Clarence in the Lords.

The barge that had taken Clarence to Westminster returned. Clarence seemed the same, a little more bowed perhaps, and he would not look up at the citizens who gaped at him from the wharves and jetties, but otherwise he was the same.

The pile-driver still thumped. Its constant pounding had begun to wear the nerves of those who lived by East Chepe. Richard of Gloucester, who must have heard it, too, at Crosby's Place, came regularly to the Tower; sometimes alone but more often with his lawyer and a spare, gaunt Austin canon. As regularly Gloucester rode to court: some said to press his brother to action, others said to restrain him and plead with him – for the king went on being indecisive. Clarence, tried, attainted and sentenced to death, was yet alive. The king would not make the order.

Rumours grew: that the Duchess Cecily, adjusting her mind to think of her son as dead already, had ordered Requiems to be said at Baynard's Castle – and the chaplains had hardly been able to dissuade her; that the city's darling prophet Hogan had been unofficially consulted by Lord Hastings on the king's behalf; that the queen's eldest son by her first marriage, the Marquess of Dorset, had been seen paying a secret visit to the Speaker of the Commons.

The last might have had some substance because on the morning of February 18th the Speaker himself went to the bar of the Lords to request that the sentence on Clarence should be carried out. And this, said the citizens, gratified that the commons should have so strong a finger in the pie, had decided the matter.

They were not to know that the speaker's demands simply coincided with the king's wishes. He had already decided on his brother's fate, convinced at last that Clarence was too unintelligent and unreliable, too unstable and far too dangerous altogether to be spared.

The pile-driver stopped that afternoon, its work well done.

In the unaccustomed silence knots of Londoners gathered on Tower Hill. They heard the proclamation: The high and mighty prince, George Plantagenet, Duke of Clarence, had made his testament, been shriven and executed privately within the Tower.

VI

The return journey to Wensleydale through that bitter winter of 1478 was long and arduous and sometimes extremely dangerous. At the end of a week they had yet to reach Bedford Castle and by far the worst of the journey lay ahead – but none of the party complained. After that interminable waiting from January 16th to February 18th – thirty-one days of brittle suspense made worse by the regular pounding from Tower quay, none of them were of a mind to stay any longer at Crosby's Place. They had all longed to get away.

On the rare occasions when the wind was not in their faces and they could unmuffle their heads, Robert and Miles would talk to each other. The priest was too thickly cocooned to speak, and Richard travelled for days in silence. He was lip-fastened by misery, vowing never to return to London unless his mother needed him or he was summoned by royal command to assist in urgent affairs of state. He would delegate all his judicial work as Constable and Admiral of England, appoint a proctor to look after his affairs at Crosby's Place, and keep to the north.

Only in the north could he remember Edward the King as he once had been and so continue to love and serve him. Only in the north might he forget the Woodvilles who had wreaked such havoc on the house of York: corrupting Edward, debasing his honour and alienating him from his mother; and, though George had always been the chief cause of his own downfall, it was the Woodvilles who had pushed him that last inch to final ruin. The queen and her family and no one else could have persuaded Edward to deny George's right to public execution by the axe and with the time-honoured privilege of speaking from the scaffold. Instead he had died in their low Woodville way, privately, through strangulation, his corpse finally humiliated by being stuffed callously into a malmsey barrel.

As Richard bent his head to avoid the wind, and guided his horse along the stone-hard ruts on the highway or simply allowed the beast to carry him forward, he told himself that the memories of his brother's trial and death would swell up again and again to harrow him even in the north. And one in particular was a condemnation of himself – of that abominable thrill of pleasure which had run through him when they told him George was dead. It had horrified him, proving that everyone who, like the Woodvilles, tried to defame him were right and that his pleas for Clarence had been hypocritical for all he had really wanted in his heart was to see George suffer.

No one now could persuade him otherwise.

He was too ashamed to listen when at Nottingham Dom Edmund attempted to convince him that his reaction had in fact been prompted by the suddenness of the announcement joined with relief that the matter was over and done with.

'No! No!' murmured Richard. 'It hangs yet like a blemish on my soul.'

For half a minute the priest was silent and thoughtful, aware that after those days of tight suspense at Crosby's Place Richard could best be helped through being forced to think of other matters. And Dom Edmund knew of a matter large and grave enough to do just this; something he had judged it prudent to keep to himself until such a time as Richard had to be told.

It was a risk to tell him now, but he could think of no other way of driving the guilt fantasies from his mind.

'My lord,' he said. 'When we were in London, Miles Metcalfe brought me a message from the registrar of Bishop Stillington.'

'Stillington?' said Richard. He was perplexed. What had this to do with his own deep shame?

'The Bishop of Bath and Wells and late Chancellor,' Dom Edmund hesitated, trying to decide on the best way of putting the matter. 'He asked me to visit him. I did. He was gracious, very hospitable, but his talk was discursive, so rambling that at the end of half an hour I felt obliged to remind him I had duties in your household and asked to be excused. It was only then he admitted that he had certain high confidences which in your interests, my lord, he wished to reveal to me.'

Still bewildered, Richard touched his left temple and repeated dully: 'High confidences?'

'Yes.' The priest took a breath, and told his story.

As he did so he noticed a change overtake his lord. Barely perceptible at first, it became more apparent as the tale unfolded. He was losing sight of himself, forgetting his remorse. He sharpened visibly, interrupting once or twice to question the bishop's reliability and integrity; and when the priest had done he sat drumming the arm of his chair with agitated fingers.

'You are convinced there is truth in this?'

'I am, Dickon. Utterly convinced.' He looked away while he explained why. 'The king pardoned your brother Clarence many times for follies almost as large as his latest treason. Yet this time, though he temporized, he would not forgive. He dared not.'

Richard gasped. 'You cannot mean that George was aware of this secret?'

'Both aware of it and rash enough to let the king know he was aware of it.'

Richard put his head in his hands. For as long as two minutes he neither moved nor made a sound. Eventually he looked up and said: 'My mother also knows.'

'Surely not?' muttered the startled priest.

'I believe she does. It was something she said to me . . . No matter. Who else knows of this?'

'The bishop, his registrar – and I suppose other confidants. In your household only Miles.'

'Why Miles?' the question came sharply.

'Because someone had to know in case . . . in case anything happened to me, and I judged it wiser not to tell you while Clarence was alive. The knowledge might have carried you to the same end – and I love you very dearly.'

Richard shook his head. 'Had I known I could perhaps have saved my brother.'

'Which brother?' asked Dom Edmund; his eyes on Richard were steady, unflinching. 'Which brother?' he repeated. 'To save one you would have destroyed the other, and maybe yourself as well.'

Richard saw the point at once. 'Yes,' he said briefly. He put his hands on the priest's shoulders. 'You took much upon yourself to keep this from me. It was my responsibility to decide. And yet,' he paused. 'And yet I am glad that you did, and I thank you for it.' After a moment he added: 'Will you bid Miles, and remember always yourself, that the bishop's arcanum must be kept close. Never, ever uttered. I shall, for the same reason that made you confide in Miles,

183

tell the Lady Anne of this. She should know, in case any accident should overtake me.'

'Very well, my lord.' Dom Edmund uttered a silent prayer of thanksgiving. He looked down at his feet. Here was the old Richard again: the fantasy driven from his mind by something so substantial and momentous that he would have no inclination to dwell on fancies. As if to prove his thoughts were right Richard gently pulled the priest to his feet.

'Come,' he said. 'We will see the seneschal and tell him that his grandchildren make progress at their books and in all things else as well.'

184

VII

It seemed as if Richard's vow to remain in the north country would be impossibly difficult to keep.

No sooner was he established again at Middleham and preparing to summon the Council of the North than Hastings sent a private courier with letters from the king.

One was a formal declaration that although the dignities, officers, lordships and estates of the attainted Duke of Clarence were forfeit to the crown, sufficient had been set aside for the maintenance of his heir Edward, now created Earl of Warwick, and his daughter Margaret. This was clearly intended to reassure Richard and Anne that the welfare of their niece and nephew was not being overlooked. At the same time, and as a token of the king's high regard for their brother, the Neville earldom of Salisbury was bestowed on their young son Edward.

The other letter was less formal. Because he was sensitive to Gloucester's dignity, Edward ordinarily expressed his written commands in the form of polite requests; but here he begged, as man to man, that Richard should be at court as often as his duties north of the Trent would permit. There was a hint of peevishness in the letter as though he had been affronted by Richard's abrupt departure, but this only underlined the main burden of the letter, that Edward wanted the company as well as the counsel of his sole remaining brother.

Richard read through the letter twice. Could Edward ever be really lonely in his packed and glittering court? It was the nearest he had ever come to admitting that he preferred his own family to his wife's. Richard was moved. Edward's half admission solidified his love for him but he was no longer a hero-worshipping boy and prudence told him to stay away from his brother. Only with two hundred miles between them could his love for Edward and the quality of his service to the crown remain constant.

He attempted to express this as painlessly as possible in his reply, but he had never found it easy to be informal with the king and the letter was beyond him. Sensibly he left it to Miles who wrote a masterly letter guaranteed to comfort the king, yet, at the same time, make Richard's position clear: that duty would keep him mostly in the north.

Richard smiled when he read it. 'My devious attorney. It is no wonder York elected you Recorder.'

Miles flushed with pleasure, both because of his lord's praise and at the thought of the honour done to him by the second city in the kingdom. 'It needs your signature, my lord.'

Richard wrote his neat signature at the foot of the letter.

✳

So Richard kept to his resolve to have done with the court, and was in London only twice in the next four years. But he kept himself informed of the main work of the king's council, appointing one of his own northern councillors, a lean man called Ratcliffe, to be his eyes and ears at Crosby's Place. James Tyrell posted backwards and forwards between them, and Richard was thus able to see the first signs of collapse in the king's policy of keeping England in the front ranks of European nations by balancing the power of Burgundy and France.

Louis was already nibbling at Burgundian territory and, unless something were done, he would soon swallow it entirely. This put Edward in a quandary because he had an annual tribute of eighty thousand crowns from France which made him independent of parliamentary grants. Five years before he had been the sort of man who would have thrown the tribute aside and made a mighty demonstration of armed strength in defence of his ally Burgundy, but now he had changed. He was irresolute. He used words not swords in an attempt to check Louis's appetite and though still a shrewd negotiator, he was no metal for that bland old fox of France.

It was significant that Richard suddenly found his hands full with troubles on the Scottish border. He met them resourcefully and successfully although despite his fame as a military commander, he did not relish campaigning. But the troubles had one advantage in that they bound Percy of Northumberland closer to him. Busy as second-in-command in the border forays Percy forgot his disgruntled envying and grew to admire Richard for his endurance and courage as a warrior, and for his strategy as a military commander. He shared with Richard, too, the knowledge that France was behind the Scottish troubles.

It was evident that Louis was stirring up the Scots for his own benefit, and never more so than in the spring of 1480 when James III violated his truce with England and what had been a series of isolated troubles threatened to develop into an invasion of England.

Richard and Northumberland beat back the Scots, but their agents reported the whole of Scotland was being roused and a great army made ready for a campaign in the following year.

The threat was sufficiently serious for Richard himself to go to London, and persuade the Council that an army must be prepared to meet the Scots. Edward agreed. How pleased he was to see his brother. He would have granted him anything. But then he was vexed because Richard left almost as quickly as he had come.

Richard could not bear to stay because already the king was so altered that it sickened him. It frightened him as well, and he crossed himself remembering their mother's wild prophecy: '*His royal sun in splendour will be blackened.*' And so he left, taking his heartaches and anxieties to Anne and his closest friends at Middleham, warning Northumberland and the chief northern captains that they must do the best they could with their own followers and as many indentured men as could be levied.

He was not surprised when neither Edward nor his army appeared at the promised time. They had reached Nottingham where, only half-way to the battlefield, Edward settled down to feast and hold court. It was left to Richard's generalship and his small northern army to check the Scottish advance. Afterwards he rode with Northumberland down to Nottingham to spur on the king. It was no use. Edward's eyes were looking south not north. He was immersed in his diplomacy, or what was left of it. While the Scots harried England, Louis had calmly bitten further into Burgundy. Now all Edward could think of was to conclude as soon as possible the negotiations for the marriage of his eldest daughter Elizabeth to the Dauphin of France. He had every confidence, he said, in his brother of Gloucester, and in the Earl of Northumberland. Let them prepare an offensive for the next season, and he would carry his own sword in the campaign.

They toiled back north again – to invest Berwick, that toothsome citadel Edward had never ruled and longed to possess, and make ready for a full-scale war against the Scots. The next year the king broke his word to them for a second time but the lack of a few southern levies did not deter Richard from waging a campaign that was to be the talk of the border country for three hundred years. He penetrated to the heart of Scotland, temporarily seizing Edinburgh itself, and with so firm a grip upon his men that the capital escaped looting and firing. If, in the year following, these advantages were pressed home, James he knew would be at England's mercy, compelled to concede all territorial gains and agree to the most stringent conditions of peace.

And Richard achieved something else which set all the bells of England ringing – he forced Berwick to surrender. Once more it was under the rule of the English sovereign.

Edward's command that his royal brother should come south for the Christmas season and receive the honours of parliament was not to be denied. Yet again he left his family at home and travelled only with his chamberlain, Robert Percy, and James Tyrell. They were attended by servants and a troop of men-at-arms.

Edward wept with joy to see him, putting an arm about his shoulders and walking him up and down the great hall asking question after question and barely waiting for a reply. He poured out his gratitude and promised great rewards, suddenly raising his voice and commending to all the service and loyalty and devotion of his brother.

Richard knew this was not fulsomeness. Edward meant what he said, but by nature he was too reserved, and far too shy to accept compliments with the grace of a courtier. All he could do was murmur a word or two and keep his eyes cast down. His abashed silence seemed surly to some of those who watched the royal brothers walk up and down; the elder, though huge and richly gowned in cloth of gold, actually leaning physically upon the younger who was so much his opposite, being lithe and small and dressed in a sombre tunic of near black.

It was only a few days later that Richard was summoned peremptorily from Crosby's Place. It was dinner time. The horn had sounded. But the king's command was urgent.

Richard rode at once to Westminster and found it unnaturally silent. There was no music or singing – such as the king loved – and though there was a fine smell from the kitchens, servants and waiting-men fidgeted in idleness beside the buttery. Their master, the king's butler, wore the anxious air of a man aware good food was going to ruin. The courtiers stood back and bowed when Hastings led the king's brother into the great hall.

Richard quickened his pace and passed Hastings when he saw John Howard, the king's chief envoy to France, standing behind the throne. Edward himself was scarlet in the face, and even before his brother could walk the length of the hall, he was shouting the news in a voice shrill with indignation: Burgundy had made peace with France, and Duke Maximilian's daughter was to marry the French Dauphin.

In the bitterest terms he bewailed his fallen fortunes. His policies were smashed to fragments. His annual stipend was lost. His daughter was jilted in the eyes of Europe.

'And England's diplomacy is simplified,' he added with a hard laugh which had no humour in it, 'to the mere hope that the King of France might soon succumb to apoplexy.'

Richard tried to comfort him, but he lacked Edward's grand manner, his indifference to the presence of other people, and he could not easily express what was essentially a private sentiment in such a public place. He was glad when Edward cut short his murmur of sympathy with an abrupt demand for advice. 'What may I do, Dick? What shall be done?'

Richard barely hesitated. It would be no comfort to urge patience on a proud man smarting for retaliation. 'In the spring, my lord, you may hammer home all your advantages against the Scots and force peace on James who is Louis's accomplice. You may compel him even to enlist against his old ally. And in this time, Burgundy will have the breathing space to recover his energies and his good sense. A trade pact with feeble France can never match what he has gained from commerce with England.'

The king looked up – there was a flicker of the old Edward in his eyes. He held out a hand to Richard, and all he said was: 'Good lad. Good lad.'

It was left to Hastings to break the difficult silence – and in his own inimitable way. 'If, your grace, we are to discuss pounding the Scots into dust as a preliminary to doing the same to Louis of France, it would be better done on a full belly. May we have dinner?'

As reward for his service to the king in the border campaigns the Duke of Gloucester and his heirs were given for ever the Wardenship of the West Marches with permanent lordship of the lands he had seized from the Scots, the city of Carlisle and all the royal estates in Cumberland. It was a dazzling, unprecedented reward for though he and his heirs would owe perpetual obedience to the English crown, their enormous appanage was a principality within a kingdom, to be governed as autonomously as the Duchies of Brittany and Burgundy.

Attending the parliament that gave him this award, and planning with Edward and his captains the next campaign against the Scots, kept Richard in London for far longer than he had intended.

When he left to take possession of his new estates and raise levies in the north, he carried a patent of nobility. To please him further – and it had truly pleased him – Edward had created his old friend Francis, Viscount Lovell.

VIII

Easter was early in 1483 and Middleham was only thinly decorated with spring flowers. But the household made merry in the great hall with music and entertainment provided by a lewd but very pert Jack Pudding and two tumblers sent especially by the Lord Mayor and Twenty-Four of York to please their lord at Easter. And the feasting was sauced by everyone's memory of the tedium of salted herrings and dried ling and fish from the castle moat and stew ponds in the forty-day fast. Though the beef was also salted and the geese and poultry thin and ill-flavoured after the rigours of winter, to eat flesh again both roast and boiled – with extra Easter viands of cheese dumplings and butter cakes and violet-and-butter cakes and primrose pie and pasties and hashes and spoon-meats of stewed mutton, beans and greens – was a banquet after the boring Lenten diet.

Yet the lord of Middleham himself barely touched any food. He was equally sparing with wine, sipping occasionally at the silver cup before him, refusing to have it refilled.

When the eating was done he watched the tumblers and wore a smile, but Anne knew that the smile was simply a politeness and that his eyes were seeing other things. He was preoccupied with preparing for the campaign against the Scots, deciding against the day where lay the best terrain for forcing pitched battles in the Border country, how supplies could be maintained with baggage trains, how to the best advantage he could employ the levies, detachments of moss-troopers, bowmen and cavalry, and the pieces of ordnance at his disposal.

Two or three times he shook his head as if to clear it of military matters, and turned to smile at Anne and press her hand, or speak to his son. And young Edward would tear his eyes from the entrancing performance of these men who curvetted and leapt in the air like long-legged frogs, to give his father that serious smile which was so peculiarly his own. How solemn was her little Earl of Salisbury, thought his mother; how solemn, too, her little Duke of Gloucester

191

– both as alike as peas except that Edward was so delicate, his father so hardy.

For all his ten years the boy looked barely seven, and was like a candle to the sun compared with his half-brother John of Gloucester, now a scatter-brained energetic lad of twelve sitting down in the hall at the donzels' table. Anne dearly loved her foster son because he was a part of Richard but the contrast between him and Edward was very cruelly marked. Even Richard's daughter Katherine, a beautiful and bobbish lass sitting not far from her, and little Richard Metcalfe, permitted to be at table with his father because this was the feast of Easter, looked more robust than her own Edward.

A gust of laughter fixed her attention on the tumblers. One was standing stork-like on the other's head and at the same time pulling hideous faces and juggling with five plates.

She turned away – looked at John – at Katherine – at little Metcalfe – at her own boy, and grieved in her heart because she knew he had inherited his sickliness from her. Richard occasionally tried to soothe her anxieties for Edward by reminding her that as a boy he himself had been a weakling, and now, at thirty, though small and still slighter than most men, he was as vigorous and hale as anyone in the kingdom. But it was no consolation, for she knew the truth and he did not: that it was she who was flawed.

It had not been apparent until long after Edward's birth. At first she had taken the vomiting and pains and swelling of her ankles as signs of pregnancy, and this had delighted her for she longed to bear Richard many children. But then had come the distressing realization that she could not be pregnant after all, and yet the same pains and swellings and attacks of vomiting continued. She had managed to keep the disease a secret from her beloved Richard, and only her physician, Joyce Percy and her maid knew how she often felt giddy and limp after the smallest exertion and that parts of her skin were yellowing. Sometimes for months on end she regained her old vitality, and suddenly, for no reason her physician could understand, the old pains and troubles and feeling of lassitude returned, and she failed to respond even to his most drastic treatments. The discoloration of her skin was growing worse, and it could only be a question of time before Richard noticed it. When he did, and found out about her disease, he would know that she alone bore all responsibility for little Edward's sickliness. It was this that she dreaded.

Further roars of laughter, with cheers and handclapping, and the tumblers were bowing to the high table. The entertainment was over.

The musicians struck up in their gallery, and porters began to move tables and benches and clear a large space down the centre of the hall.

Anne clasped Richard's hand. 'Bring back your mind to our dear Middleham, my lord,' she said. 'There will be dancing.'

He smiled. 'Aye,' he said. 'But first we will go to my chamber. I have there your Easter gift . . .'

Francis Lovell leant over to remind him of something else.

Richard nodded. 'And we should hear Ratcliffe's report, my love,' he said to Anne. 'So that he may ride on for his well-earned rest.'

His London proctor, Richard Ratcliffe, had called that morning to deliver his latest intelligence in person. He was on his way home for leave.

Richard beckoned to the Middleham comptroller, who swiftly replaced the page behind her chair and listened attentively.

'They will be summoned directly, your grace,' he said, when Richard had given his instructions.

Anne's spirits were high as they walked from the hall together. For the sake of both his work and his family life Richard generally kept them in two separate compartments, but she sometimes longed to be present at his councils, simply because it would give her an opportunity to be with him. He was so seldom at Middleham.

She tried to tell him this as he fussed about her in the tall, dark room that had been her father's, finding her a quilted seat, carrying cushions himself, and bidding his secretary, John Kendall, blaze up the fire for the afternoon was chilly.

'I too,' he said simply, 'would have you with me every second of my life. But, Anne, you would find our councils tedious – just as I should find it tedious to accompany you on your daily tasks about the castle.'

She laughed outright at the thought of Richard being involved in her duties as châtelaine of Middleham. 'Yet,' she pointed out, 'you have invited me to be with you today.'

'Not for a meeting of the Council of the North.' He cupped

her chin. 'And so, madam, you will not be bored to madness by long-winded talk of fiats and punitions, commissions of array, of the peace, of oyer and terminer, the structure of financial credit, pledges for loans, repayments by charter, enrolling demesne leases, the supervision of liberties and franchises, and all the mysteries of frankpledge.'

He stopped abruptly, and Anne, believing he had finished, began shyly: 'I did not know . . .'

But he closed his eyes and went on. 'And then there are other matters we must dispatch with equal regularity; such as the removal of fishgarths . . .' He stopped again, opened his eyes and kissed her cheek. 'No, Anne, I will not tease you further. Truly, you would in general find our meetings tedious. But today ours is a family council.'

He went to fetch his Easter gift for her: a Venetian brooch of pearls and precious stones. And she was kissing it and kissing him and declaring her own gift for him was nothing in comparison when Secretary Kendall put his head through the doorway curtains to announce the household council: Dom Edmund, Lord Lovell, Sir Robert Percy and Sir James Tyrell, Master Metcalfe and Master Ratcliffe.

Anne greeted them with great excitement. 'See what my lord has given me,' she cried.

They admired the brooch in turn. Miles declared with a lawyer's tact that never before had he seen so beautiful a jewel, although he himself had bought the gift for Richard and carried it safely from York only the day before. But he and all of them were silent when Anne sent a page for her gift to Richard and the boy returned carrying a young brachet hound.

He set it on the floor and Ratcliffe, who did not know of his lord's resolve never to possess another brachet, began to coax the puppy and admire her points. He liked to think he had an eye for a good hound, he said, and this one . . . His voice trailed off when at last he noticed what Anne had seen at once.

She begged to know what was wrong – how she had offended her dearest lord.

'I remembered,' she said breathlessly, and close to tears. 'I remembered you told me . . . you once told me that you had such a brachet when you were little . . . at Fotheringhay . . . I thought . . . I believed it would be acceptable.'

Only Anne's distress could have made Richard bend down to coax the half-grown bitch, and call her Bat quite naturally and without thought. 'Acceptable?' he replied. 'Of course she is acceptable.' And still managing to keep his voice light he added: 'I have had two such hounds before and this is so identical to the others I was startled.'

'You are not angry, Dickon?'

He kissed her cheek. 'Angry! To receive such an Easter gift!'

The other men quickly helped by admiring the third Bat, and commenting favourably on her points.

'When she is grown,' said Robert. 'She will make a fine guard for Lady Anne.'

'For me? Oh, no, Robert.' Anne turned to Richard. 'I had hoped my lord, that you would keep her with you – both to protect you and be always a reminder of your most loving wife.'

'And that she shall be,' declared Richard. 'Won't you, Bat, eh? eh? eh?' He lifted the pup and let her lick his nose. Her eyes were uncannily like those of his first Bat.

Ratcliffe had no idea what all this signified, but he sensed the tension and he felt uncomfortable. It was a relief to him when Richard put down the puppy, ordered the squire to serve wine, and then sat by his lady on the quilted bench to begin their council.

'We ought to return directly to the dancing,' he reminded them. 'And Ratcliffe, I make no doubt, would wish to be on his way well before night fall.'

'I thank you, your grace, yes,' said Ratcliffe.

He bowed and made his report of the latest open and covert feuds and alliances in the council and at court. His written reports, regularly passed on to Richard by way of Tyrell, had by necessity to be abbreviated and discreet. In the safety of Middleham he could be frank and he described the smouldering, almost Byzantine atmosphere which surrounded the king and in which situations could alter from day to day.

Little that he said surprised Richard or his friends but Anne became more and more incredulous. She was Warwick's daughter and not naïve about ambitiousness, yet it was difficult for her to understand why highly-placed courtiers should plot and counterplot, and why, of all people, the queen should scheme. Her amazement gave place to anxiety, and, when Ratcliffe talked of wise precautions and the urgent necessity of establishing the Gloucester power, a dreadful fear stole over her.

Richard sensed it, and broke off the discussion. 'Why, Anne,' he said. 'You need not be frightened.'

'No?' she cried. 'When you speak of guarding yourselves against the malice of the queen?'

He tried to reassure her. 'It is natural, Anne, for her to seek control of her son the Prince of Wales. She is an ambitious woman, older than the king but still likely to outlive him, and well she knows it is not the English custom to give dowagers a share in government. It is natural that she protect her interests.'

'Yet Master Ratcliffe spoke of her malice reaching you' – protested Anne – 'of certain dangers you face as brother to the king.'

'Only,' said Miles gravely, 'if the king should die, my lady, and there is nothing in all we have heard that suggests such a probability.'

She looked quickly away from Miles. 'He lives wantonly, Dick. It is known. You have told me so yourself that he is altered.'

Ratcliffe tried to reassure her that despite the king's habitual debauchery, his energies remained almost unflagged. 'I saw him less than a week ago, my lady,' he said.

Richard pressed her hand. 'You must not be frightened, Anne. We have loyal friends and wise councillors.' He smiled. 'In Ratcliffe here we have as sharp a ferret as any in London, and he will keep us informed through James. Meanwhile we shall build up our power in Cumberland.'

'It will be done directly,' added Francis Lovell. 'Now that my lord has such an appanage we shall be safe through strength.'

Richard stood up. 'There let it rest for the present,' he said. 'For we should return to our larger family in the hall.'

The movement stirred the brachet pup who had been sleeping in the rushes at his feet. She woke up ready for play and seeing a loose floating piece of coloured cloth hanging from Anne's arm, leapt in the air to catch it.

There was a rending sound and a yelp as Richard seized Bat. But he did not beat her as he might have done. He simply held her in the air and gazed steadily at Anne. Then he said to the others: 'Go you to the hall. The Lady Anne and I will follow directly.'

When they had gone he set down the puppy and put an arm

round Anne's shoulder. With his free hand he tilted her chin and turned her face towards him so that she had to look into his eyes. 'What is it, my love?' he asked tenderly.

She looked away, her eyes swimming with tears. She had so quickly covered it with her torn sleeve, but he had seen the small yellow discoloration above her wrist.

'What is it, Anne?' he asked again.

Bat, for no reason, began to howl.

IX

A cloaked rider whipped his horse up the steep hill from Middleham village to the castle, clubbered over the wooden bridge, through the gatehouse and beyond into the inner bailey.

'Praise God you are here,' cried the porter running to take his bridle. 'My lord has been on a knife-edge these past two days.'

The tired man slid to the ground. 'I am expected?'

'Are you not from London? The master-physician for her grace?'

'From London, yes. But I am no physician.' He opened his cloak to show he wore livery beneath. 'Take me to your lord.'

For Wensleydale in the early spring it was an unusually mild day, and Richard was with Anne walking slowly up and down the paths in the herb garden.

Since he had found out about her illness he had scarcely left her side – although her physician and two more from York and a third from his estate at Sheriff Hutton had done their utmost to convince him she was not mortally sick.

'Do not dissuade him,' Dom Edmund had advised her privately when Richard determined to send for physicians from the south. 'It is his way of showing his love and care for you, and this is precious. Later, when he can convince himself that he is in no immediate danger of losing you, he will return to his work. For the present, let him do as he wishes, my lady. Let him be busy.' And the old priest added with a chuckle: 'I know well that he would send to the Turkish Sultan for a Saracen doctor if he thought it would do you good.'

So Anne had accepted the advice and she gloried in the luxury of being close to Richard, yet she was not a little dismayed by his hunt through the north for more and better physicians, and by his self-recriminations because he had only just given Ratcliffe leave and so had no one in London to whom he could turn for expert advice. Then he had had the idea of appealing to the king for his own physician Master William Hobbes. Tyrell had galloped off to London at noon on April 2nd to make the necessary arrangements. Counting, at the most, a six-day journey each way Hobbes should have arrived by the 14th. But the 14th passed – the 15th – and it was on the 16th that Richard fretted and fumed as he walked with Anne in the herb garden – to break off when he saw the comptroller leading a man in livery through the wicket-gate. He recognized the livery.

'A messenger, your grace,' said the comptroller, bowing. 'With ill tidings.'

'Hobbes cannot come?' said Richard, then seeing the man was perplexed, he explained: 'Master Hobbes, the king's physician. I sent for him to attend her grace. Come,' he rasped out impatiently. 'I see by your livery you are my Lord Hastings's man. Tell me of Master Hobbes.'

'I know nothing of this, your grace,' said the messenger. 'But the king's physician has been much occupied of late.'

'Occupied!' Richard, tense and anxious, was suddenly angry. 'How occupied? How? I need Hobbes here. Such urgent —' He broke off. Anne had taken his hand.

'Your grace,' said the messenger. 'My lord Hastings bids me tell you that our sovereign lord the king is dead.'

Richard stared hard at him for a moment. The man would not meet his eyes. 'Edward,' he said, no more; and freeing himself from Anne's hand, he turned and walked several paces to a raised herb bed. There he poked at the earth with his fingers, picked a sprouting piece of chervil, and held it to his nose. Afterwards, look- ing up at the sky and with his back to the messenger, he said: 'How?'

'His grace went angling two days after Easter. He collapsed. Master Hobbes gave out that he had a stroke of apoplexy.'

Richard picked another piece of chervil. Almost as if he was there beside him he could hear his brother say: *And England's diplomacy is simplified to the hope that Louis of France might soon succumb to apoplexy.*

'And so he died?' he asked over his shoulder.

'Not at once, your grace. He lingered, growing weaker each day. And on the ninth he died.'

Anne and the comptroller crossed themselves, likewise the mes- senger; but Richard continued poking in the raised bed of herbs.

Anne eyed the comptroller. Evidently he expected orders and was nonplussed by his lord's strange silence. She decided to take command herself. Rather softly she said: 'Have Dom Edmund and the castle chaplain say Masses for his grace's soul. Let the bell be tolled – and send word to the village priest that he do the same.'

'I will, your grace,' said the comptroller.

'And bid my lord's servants, Lady Percy and my maids attend me in the chapel.'

Briefly, she thanked the messenger.

'I have a letter, your grace,' he said. 'From my Lord Hastings.'

He gave it to her, bowed and followed the comptroller from the garden.

After the wicket gate had clicked and she knew no one could observe them, she went up to Richard, intending to comfort him, but without warning he burst into a passion of sobbing. It alarmed her terribly because it was so unlike him, and almost as if a stranger shook and heaved within his skin.

She laid a hand on his arm, simply to show she was there, and again he frightened her by reacting abnormally to her touch. He spun round and tore back her sleeve to show the ugly yellow mark above her wrist. Then he lifted her arm so that the blemish touched his raised shoulder.

'See!' he whispered. 'Your sickness touching my deformity!'

She shrank away from him as he let go her arm, and then, like a hurt animal, threw back his head and cried: 'I thank you, God! Tom slaughtered. Peter taken by the sea. My father's head chopped like a turnip. Rutland murdered. Clarence strangled. Edward dead before his time. My mother crazed. My only son a weakling. My wife diseased. I thank you, God.'

Anne was not strong, but with all the strength she had she struck him hard across the face.

And when he whimpered, she did it again.

Then she put her arm about him, murmuring: 'Dickon, Dickon. My love, my love,' while he wept and washed away the picture in his mind of Tom and Peter, York and Rutland, Clarence, and Edward the Sun in Splendour, the noblest, finest, most handsome paragon of knighthood in the world.

Richard was paler than usual but had full control of himself as he let his body-squire dress him for Mass. He kept his mind empty. The letter from Hastings, still unread, lay on a chest.

Down in the village a bell tolled like an echo to Paul, the great castle bell, which boomed out over Wensleydale for Edward the king. In the Chapel the boys and singing-men were chanting, and the household officers, men-at-arms, servants, wives and children laid Mass pennies on the pavement and knelt to pray for their dead king.

Racked with anxiety Anne had not waited to make the accepted formal entry with her lord, and had shoved her ladies ahead of her into the Chapel, sending a page to fetch Dom Edmund from the vestry. Now they were standing by one of the massive pillars close to the priest's door, Anne speaking so softly that no one, not even her waiting ladies, could overhear what she said. Dom Edmund listened without interrupting until she had finished. Then he tried to re-assure her.

'He has more strength than most men. When he shows weakness it is the more unbearable.'

'It was horrible, frightening,' she repeated. 'He was half-beast, half-babe.'

'But not the Richard we both know and love,' he insisted. 'Believe me, my lady. In an hour, even less, he will be over it and himself again.'

Anne crossed herself. 'He mocked God,' she whispered.

'God,' said Dom Edmund quite seriously, 'is quite strong enough not to mind.'

She looked at him aghast.

'If you doubt it, ask God yourself.' A noise from the courtyard told him that Richard was coming. 'Now I must go and vest.' He pressed Anne's hand. 'Do not be anxious. He will be over it by the end of Mass.'

Only two were sitting in the private apartments; the Duke of Gloucester and his lady.

Dom Edmund stood beside Anne's chair. He bent a little to

murmur in her ear. She glanced up at him to nod and smile her thanks, then turned back to listen to Richard interrogate Hastings's messenger.

The distortion she remembered in the herb garden was totally gone. In fact, his manner was so ordinary and so in character that she found herself faced with a fresh anxiety – wondering if it was she and not he who had been so altered by the news of Edward's death. She shook her head as if to clear it. Whoever had changed, whatever had happened, these things were best forgotten.

Richard was searching in his questions and asked them so rapidly that he flustered the messenger and was obliged to slow down his pace. They were pertinent questions, too. When he had finished and inquired if anyone had anything else to ask the messenger, neither Robert nor Francis nor his secretary, Kendall, had a word to add. The messenger was dismissed.

'Well, Francis?' said Richard when he had gone.

Francis began to pace up and down the room, kicking the rushes aside with his toes. At length he said: 'The king's seizure was fourteen days ago and no one saw fit to send you word. He died a week ago and still no one sent word until my lord Hastings, not the council, orders a messenger to ride here. The new king, your nephew, is at Ludlow with his Woodville uncle, Rivers . . .' Francis paused. 'I do not care for this. I do not care for it.'

'Nor I, my lord,' said Robert. 'And we are ill-prepared to meet the queen's malice.'

There was a silence. Richard broke it himself: 'May we trust Hastings?'

No one answered. He picked up Hastings's letter from the chest and read it for the eighth or ninth time. It was terse, urgent, but it hid as much as it revealed. He read it aloud:

'*The king has left all to your protection – goods, heir, realm. Secure the person of our sovereign Lord Edward the Fifth and get you to London.*'

Once more he asked: 'May we trust Hastings?'

'That what he writes is true, yes,' said Francis slowly. 'But, for the rest . . .' He broke off and shrugged his shoulders.

John Kendall was equally doubtful. 'The messenger has told us the king's executors include your grace's friend, Lord Stanley, and the queen is excluded. Yet it seems she has taken the reins of power. Why did not Lord Hastings inform you sooner, your grace?'

'And as Will Hastings is on the council,' added Robert Percy, 'it is strange he has not insisted that the king's codicil appointing you Protector be proved publicly.'

It was Francis who summed up all they were thinking by saying: 'It is dangerous to trust Hastings, and yet we *must*. Otherwise the danger will be greater still.'

Richard looked at them in turn. They seemed to be in agreement. 'Then what must be done?'

There was a silence.

'Come, gentlemen. Tell me. Dom Edmund you have not spoken once. Advise me. What shall be done?'

Without hesitating the priest replied. 'Wait. Simply wait. The courier from Hastings is but the first swallow of a flight winging north.'

X

It was difficult to accept Dom Edmund's advice in the uncertainties of the moment, but Richard accepted it.

He ordered Francis to call in the local levies; sent word to Richard Ratcliffe that he should return with all speed to Crosby's Place; and, feeling the need of Miles Metcalfe's judgement at this critical time, he sent to fetch him from York. Only an hour afterwards he changed his mind. Miles should be at the centre of affairs, and the centre was not Middleham. A second messenger followed the first with a counter-order instructing Miles to ride instead to London, and with it was a warrant signed formally by the Lord Protector of the Realm authorizing the Recorder of York to command and use the royal courier service which he himself had invented.

On the 18th came another liveried messenger from Hastings to say that the council, top-heavy with Woodvilles, had ordered Earl Rivers to bring the young king from Ludlow to London with an escort of two thousand men-at-arms, and the coronation was already fixed for May 4th. Hastings begged the Duke of Gloucester to remember that by custom a protector's authority ceased as soon as the king was crowned, no matter how young he was. The message concluded with an urgent plea that he ride south with a strong following and seize the king before he reached London.

Richard heard all this in silence, his face impassive; and afterwards, John Kendall wrote two dispatches at his dictation. One was to his sister-in-law the queen to commiserate with her. The other was to the Council in which, without prolixity, he made his position as protector very plain indeed. Hastings's messenger was followed within the hour by James Tyrell. He was spattered with mud from head to foot, his face lined and grey with exhaustion. He knelt to kiss Richard's hand and beg his forgiveness for having remained in London.

Richard cut him short, lifted him to his feet, and called for a chair and wine.

'Nothing, James, in the whole world is so precious that it cannot wait for one or two minutes more. Catch your breath. Drink some wine.'

As he took the cup, Tyrell's hand trembled. 'I made London to find the king close to death.'

'Aye,' said Richard. 'Drink some wine, man. Take your time.'

Tyrell sat down. 'When they gave out that he had died I thought it prudent to stay . . . Ratcliffe not being there.'

'Sir James,' said Richard. 'Drink your wine. Rest for a moment.' He smiled. 'We'll be no wiser if you blether.'

Tyrell sipped at the wine, then, in a voice that grew stronger as he talked, he told them of the king's last days, of the long lying in state, of the burying at Windsor, of the rumour which circulated that the Council was divided, yet its policies shaped willy-nilly by the Woodvilles. Hastings led a small opposition, supported by Stanley, Howard and Arundel, but the queen had the chancellor, Rotherham, in her pocket – and had gulled the remaining bishops with promise of enlarged privileges for the clergy. She felt confident. Her son the Marquess of Dorset had boasted openly before a crowded court that the queen could make and enforce decisions without the king's uncle of Gloucester.

There was a ripple of protest round the room.

Richard leant forward and asked Tyrell to repeat what he had said.

Tyrell did so, and capped it by saying the queen had already made certain of the Tower. Her brother Edward was raising a fleet – ostensibly to use against French privateers. Her son Dorset held the treasury. Her brother Earl Rivers held the king.

To most of Richard's following in that room, all that Tyrell said was simply a southern affair, and the men he spoke of simply names. But they sensed the magnitude of the threat to their beloved lord. His closest counsellors were dismayed. Francis Lovell's eyes blazed with indignation. Robert Percy angrily clenched and unclenched his fists. The Lady Anne was pale with fear.

Only Richard was composed, apparently unaffected, and he astounded them all by asking, when Tyrell had finished: 'What of Master Hobbes?'

Tyrell blinked because the question had thrown him, but quickly he recovered himself. 'You will understand, my lord, he counts the king's death a personal failure. Disgrace keeps him to his house. He would not come.'

'Then we,' said Richard lightly, 'shall have to go to him.' He stood up and made a sign to his secretary. 'John, I would have you add a caveat to my letter for the Council. Warn all councillors that nothing, nothing which is contrary to the customs of this kingdom or contrary to my royal brother's will may be decreed without harm.'

Anne instinctively gathered little Edward in her arms and hugged him protectively. She knew that Richard had made up his mind; that he had decided to do as Hastings asked, and once committed he would keep to his purpose. And she was right.

It became noticeable that from that time he rarely asked advice from anyone and acted on his own initiative.

✳

Final preparations were in hand for the departure of the Lord Protector for the seat of government in London. Meanwhile the pattern of allegiances settled into a clearer, far more recognizable shape.

A courier arrived at Middleham wearing the distinctive livery of the Duke of Buckingham. The message was brief and plainly showed Buckingham's hatred of the queen. He was entirely at the disposal of the Lord Protector and was even now moving east to Brecon with a following of one thousand men.

'So!' Richard was thoughtful. At length he said to the courier: 'Take two of my fellows to keep you company and find your lord. Tell him I thank him for his courtesy, and we shall meet at Northampton. But,' he added, 'I would have him dismiss seven hundred of his thousand. Three hundred men will be ample.'

Before the man was out of the room Richard was calling for John Kendall. He dictated a courteous letter to Earl Rivers to say he looked forward to greeting his new sovereign and nephew at Northampton on the 29th.

At the same time he gave instructions that three hundred men-at-arms should be hand-picked from the levies at York, and this detachment, with a flying squadron of horsemen from Wensleydale would be the limit of his escort.

The restriction both puzzled and worried Francis Lovell. He went to Richard and reminded him of Hastings's urgent advice that his following should outnumber the king's.

'I have not forgotten, Francis, but Edward left England to my protection not to my sword.'

'Dick, I beg of you. Rivers will have two thousand men-at-arms. We shall have a little over six hundred – and that includes Buckingham's Welshmen.'

'Put two thousand against two thousand – two dogs of equal strength with a bone between them – and what, by nature, happens? They fight. But if the dogs are ill-matched, the larger will be disarmed, so confident the bone is his that he fails to observe the cunning of his smaller rival.'

'The risk is fearful . . .' began Francis.

'Be sure I do not underestimate Anthony Rivers, but I have an instinctive feeling that he underestimates me. Which is to our advantage.'

Francis made one last attempt to persuade him to change his mind but Richard was adamant.

'Understand me, Francis,' he said. 'I will not throw England into civil war simply because Hastings and Buckingham, yes, and you and I and two-thirds of the nobility do not care for the naked greed of Edward's widow. Without risking civil war I shall do all that lies in my power to prevent her milking England by ruling through her son. But if my schemes fail, and she in turn decides that I must be destroyed, only *then* shall I be justified in returning north to fight for my family and my appanage.'

Francis shook his head. As a soldier he was appalled by the risks Richard was taking. As a realist he would not himself have been so over-scrupulous with an enemy so palpably unscrupulous. And as a man of his time he saw small sense in a head-in-air interpretation of a protector's duties which could, quite literally, cost Richard his head. But he dearly loved his old friend, and it was this which prompted him to say: 'Dick, I would go with you.'

'The thought lay in my mind,' said Richard, 'for I shall need your counsel. Make over your command to the comptroller and leave the best of your veterans to keep Anne and my son secure. Dom Edmund shall stay to keep them company.'

'And John?'

'Kendall? Why, he comes with us. As my secretary he is essential.'

'I meant your son John.'

'He?'

Francis nodded. 'I promised him I would ask you, Dick. It is time he rode out.'

'Why so it is. He shall be one of my squires. I wonder, Francis, if you recall how you and Robert and I rode out from this same castle when we were lads?'

'Could I forget such a day? And you as sad then, though it was nineteen years ago, as you are sad now at the need to leave behind your heart's love.' After a moment he added: 'Few men in the kingdom could claim such constancy.'

'Or such true happiness in his love,' said Richard quietly. He took his friend's arm. 'So tomorrow the three of us shall leave again in the king's affairs – though I believe you only go to see a small dog trick a big one.'

XI

'You would oust your wife's people, cousin?'

'I would.' Buckingham's face puckered. 'They forced me to marry her. I would force them a little, too.'

Richard looked at him through narrowed eyes, trying to size him up, wondering how far Dom Edmund had been correct in saying that Harry Buckingham was too like Clarence to be comfortable.

'You have no higher motive?' he said at length.

Buckingham flushed. 'My motives, your grace . . .' He broke off and controlled himself. 'They are of small account.'

'I question that,' said Richard evenly. 'Motives are invariably important.'

'Then tell me, cousin, what are your motives for questioning my integrity?'

Richard admired this shrewd riposte put without a trace of asperity because he liked plain-speaking. He did not answer the question but he smiled at Buckingham, and Buckingham returned the smile although he was far from easy in his mind.

Accustomed to luxury he did not care for the discomfort of this draughty and smoky inn, although, outside the castle it was the best lodging Northampton could provide. He did not care either for the idea of having little more than six hundred men at their back, while Rivers's force, only fourteen miles away to the south at Stony Stratford, outnumbered them by more than two to one. And, having made a forced journey of over one hundred and thirty miles from Wales merely to offer his name and his sword to the Lord Protector, he did not relish the coldness of his reception. But he was a realist. If Gloucester liked candour then he should have it.

'I think,' he said slowly, 'that if I were in your place, cousin, I should be as cautious as you. I should eye with suspicion anyone who had been bound so tightly and for so long to the Woodvilles. Perhaps you are right to question the integrity of someone as close to the queen as her brother-in-law – being her brother-in-law yourself.'

Richard laughed out loud, and pushed the ale jug across the table. 'Francis, sit with us,' he said to Lovell who was standing by the door. 'And, cousin, have your captain join us at the table. We shall be more comfortable.'

Buckingham responded to Richard's change of manner, warming to him, making it clear that he put himself entirely at the protector's service. And Richard who, once he had trusted a man, found any offer of friendship irresistible, took Buckingham into his confidence. He outlined his first plan.

'But Rivers, surely, will not come?' cried Buckingham.

'Not come, cousin? Apparently he has every advantage on his side. He is closer to London than we are. He has a far greater following than we have. His ward is safe in the keeping of Richard Grey and old Vaughan. Why should he not come?.

It was Francis Lovell who replied. 'Because, as you said, he has all the advantages.'

'The apparent advantages,' corrected Richard. 'And you seem to pre-suppose he is entirely committed to his sister's cause.'

'Why he is!' Buckingham interjected.

Richard raised an eyebrow. 'Hastings tells us that Dorset sends out the Council's orders; that Dorset has been urging his uncle Rivers to quicken his pace, reminding him that at all costs the young king must reach London before the protector. And Rivers has never cared for Dorset.' Richard grinned boyishly. 'I imagine he will resent his nephew's constant pestering.'

Buckingham regarded him with astonishment. 'You really think this will bring him here?'

'Partly, yes. But there are other reasons, too. Rivers once made me a discreet overture of friendship, since when I have found him worthy of study. For all his sharp wit and scholarship he is known to be unimaginative even ponderous in anticipating what might lie more than a day ahead, and though he is the greatest jouster of this or any age, he remains curiously ignorant of military strategy. Now this is to *our* advantage. He will be lulled into over-confidence by the strength of his present position, and he is quite resourceful enough to claim that the king lies at Stony Stratford simply because this town cannot contain his escort as well as ours. And then I am sure he will come because he undertook to do so and he is a man of honour. Moreover, being a man of exquisite politeness, he will regard it as incumbent upon him to pay his respects to the Lord Protector.'

Richard refilled his horn and drank, while the others gaped at him.

'God's head! Cousin!' cried Buckingham in admiration. 'It is small wonder the king made you protector of this realm.'

Richard grinned again. 'I should have added that Rivers is a very curious gentleman. Yes, he will come, if only to satisfy that curiosity. So, Francis, perhaps you would order supper for three – the best they can provide – for six o'clock? I judge he should be here by then.'

✻

The king's half-brother Lord Richard Grey stood at his right hand and the chamberlain Sir Thomas Vaughan at his left. Both men were tense, and Sir Thomas visibly shaking. The twelve-year old Edward was bewildered because his uncle Rivers was not there, and not a little frightened by the unexpected appearance of his uncle Buckingham and yet another uncle whom he hardly knew.

They knelt to kiss his hand and express their sympathy on the loss of his father.

'Thank you, my lords,' he murmured, and corrected himself. 'I thank you, cousins and uncles.'

Richard of Gloucester stood up and smiled at him. 'Lords, cousins or uncles, we are of your family,' he said. 'And so would serve you.'

Edward knew how dearly his father had loved the Duke of Gloucester, and he responded instinctively to the appeal Richard always had for children, but a gentle pressure – so gentle that it was barely perceptible – against the right arm of his chair prompted him to say: 'Where is my uncle Rivers?'

Richard was struck by the boy's similarity to his mother. Indeed from the tone of his question it might have been the queen speaking. 'Last night he supped with us at Northampton,' he replied. 'To discuss the weightier affairs of the kingdom.'

Edward frowned. 'Why?' he asked petulantly.

'It was necessary, your grace,' replied Buckingham. 'For as your advisers and servants will have told you, the Duke of Gloucester has special responsibility to the whole kingdom as Protector and Defender appointed by your father's will.'

The boy looked immediately at his half-brother.

'Is that not so, Lord Richard?' added Buckingham in a honeyed voice, guessing that this was the first the young king had heard of it.

Grey was not certain how he ought to answer; whether to admit it but in guarded tones, or bluster a denial. The young king took his perplexed silence as assent and turned to Vaughan for confirmation.

'Yes, your grace,' said the old chamberlain. 'It was decreed by the king, your father.'

'In order to keep you from unwise counsellors, your grace,' added Buckingham. 'Such as those who have already deceived you by attempting to break your father's last wish and deprive his grace of Gloucester of the protectorship.' Without giving the boy a chance to interrupt he went on to say why the last king had such a high regard for the Duke of Gloucester. 'Which fits him to guide your government,' he concluded. 'While you are young.'

It was all done in Buckingham's sweetest, most persuasive manner, and goaded Grey to point out that the government could well be managed by the queen, the Marquess of Dorset, Lord Rivers . . .

'The ruling of the land is men's work,' replied Buckingham. Then, in the same honeyed voice he went on: 'His grace's mother has no authority to rule by law or custom, and nor will she have the time or opportunity because she will be caring for her other children and praying for her dead lord's soul.'

'But what of my uncle Rivers?' shrilled Edward.

'Your royal father wished that England's government should be managed by princes of the blood. Earl Rivers, the Marquess of Dorset, and Lord Richard here have attempted to deprive your uncle of Gloucester of his protectorship.'

The boy looked at his uncle who said bluntly: 'You accept my protectorship? You are content with your father's decree?'

There was a long silence. Everyone looked at the young king who, at length, with his eyes still on his uncle, nodded his assent.

'Then I must arrest Lord Richard Grey for his part in the conspiracy.'

'Edward,' shouted Grey. 'Come lad, speak to him.'

'A disrespectful lord as well as treacherous, your grace,' added Richard smiling.

He signed to two men-at-arms who pushed and pulled Lord

Richard from the room. When the noise had died down, Richard said: 'Sir Thomas Vaughan will wish to resign his office as chamberlain to your court in Wales, your grace.'

'Aye, yes indeed,' said the old man. Quickly he put his white wand of office at the king's feet.

'And ride with my lord Lovell to Northampton?' suggested Richard. The old man bowed. He tripped over his feet in his haste to get away.

'My uncle Rivers?' quavered the boy.

'Nephew,' said Richard quietly, 'I was obliged to arrest him in Northampton. He was part of this conspiracy which might have cost England dear in civil war.' He put a hand on the boy's shoulder. 'I know you loved him well and I could love his many qualities, but for you and for me, nephew, the needs of England's peace must always come first.'

Buckingham knelt for the second time. 'Now that your grace is in the safe keeping of the Lord Protector, with your permission I shall disperse your Ludlow escort. The men will be pleased to return home.'

The young boy looked from one uncle to the other, then to his captains who stood about the room. 'Yes,' he said, and added primly: 'Bid them be orderly in their dispersal.'

⁂

Miles Metcalfe was already operating the king's courier service. He sent men to meet Richard at every tenth mile on his route with news from London: that the Woodville fleet had weighed anchor and sailed with part of King Edward's treasure; that Dorset and the queen with all her children had fled into sanctuary at Westminster, taking the remainder of the treasure and as much as they could of the palace plate and furnishings. That Archbishop Rotherham, the Chancellor, in a dither of fright, had taken the Great Seal of England to the queen and left it with her.

Hastings sent other messengers including the lawyer William Catesby who was commissioned to open his master's policies to the Lord Protector. It was an expression which fetched a frown to Richard's face, but he listened to Catesby's thorough digest, and then, without comment, ordered him to join John Kendall's secretariat in the rear.

Miles himself met the royal entourage at Barnet to kiss the young king's hand as a councillor of the north and tell him Lord Mayor Shaa and the aldermen of London were waiting at Barnet Hill to lead him into his capital. This done he spoke privately with the Protector.

'The lords have forced Archbishop Rotherham to fetch the Great Seal again and he is deprived of his chancellorship. All is secure. The conspiracy is dead. England lies at your feet, Dick.'

XII

Richard had inherited his father's indifference to the trappings of greatness, and the courtiers who now waited on him as the Lord Protector and Defender of the Realm found him incomprehensible. He appeared to regard his enviable powers as added responsibilities. He was a prince who took no pleasure in being at the centre of events, the pin to which every web of government was attached. In fact he gave only one sign of enjoying the exercise of power and this was in the opportunities it gave him to reward loyalty and service. Amongst the many useful appointments, he continued Edward's admirable practice of admitting fresh blood into the Council, and appointed Catesby to please Hastings, and Lovell, Percy, Ratcliffe and Tyrell to please himself.

May 1483. Richard had found the government of England in a state of collapse, his brother's treasury sucked dry like an egg, the law courts temporarily suspended, the Council depleted. Now, with a full Council, loans from the city and the goodwill of all who knew his capabilities, he began his rule as Protector.

❋

John Kendall's pen raced over the paper as he made notes at his lord's dictation. His head was confused, his hand ached, and he dearly wished that he had ordered the French scrivener, Pelot, to do the work. Thinking of Pelot broke his concentration. He lost the thread and was forced to stop and beg his lord's pardon.

'I should beg yours, John,' said Richard. 'Forgive me. My thoughts tumble when I write to the Lady Anne. What is your last note?'

The secretary read it out: that the coronation was fixed for St John Baptist's day, and that the Council, publicly proclaiming him Protector and Defender of the Realm, Regent of the kingdom and

215

Governor of the king, proposed to put it to Parliament that for the good of England, the protectorship be continued until the king came of age.

Richard considered. 'You have not written that parliament is already summoned.' Kendall quickly made a note. 'Now, for the rest . . . Tell her how my son John does here as body-squire. You know more of this than I. I rely on you. Paint her a picture. She loves him well and will wish to know.'

'Aye, my lord,' said the secretary, scribbling hard.

'And bid her bring with her my daughter Katherine, and, as it will make his father jolly as a thrush, young Metcalfe may come too. He shall be page to the king.' He smiled. 'So many children! . . . Say I look to her to mother the nursery we are establishing in the Tower. The king is there against his crowning, and our nephew, Warwick has been summoned to keep him company. There will be little York, as well, when the Archbishop can prise him from his mother at Westminster.' He waited until Kendall's pen stopped scratching. 'Explain why I believe our dear son Edward should be kept from the stinks and ills of this city in early summer. He lacks robustness and is better in the clear air of Wensleydale – or, if my lady wills it, at Sherrif Hutton. In either case he shall be in Dom Edmund's charge for the present – and command that priest to guide him well.' He chuckled. 'Warn him that if he fails in this I shall have him made bishop.' Kendall smiled. No stronger threat could be levelled at such a man as Dom Edmund.

'That is all, my lord?'

'Yes – except to bid my lady come with all speed. I shall pen a note in my own hand at the end of your letter.' He turned to leave, then, remembering something that would give her great pleasure, he added: 'One other matter. Ask my lady to bring my brachet from Middleham – so that she may protect the protector.'

'Very well, my lord.' Kendall scribbled 'Bat' and pushed his notes to one side. 'The letter shall be written and brought to your grace directly . . . but, as we are alone, may I ask for your guidance?'

Richard was in a hurry to visit his mother at Baynard's Castle and already half through the door, but the question made him return and close the door behind him. He valued Kendall's shrewdness, and knew from experience that he would not trouble him with anything within his own competence. 'Well, John?' he said.

'Is it your wish that Master William Catesby should be familiar with your affairs?'

Richard answered the question by asking another: 'Is he not a member of the king's council and my lord Hastings's attorney?'

'A councillor yes, but as to the other . . .' The secretary spread his hands.

Richard leant his weight against the table-edge. 'What is in your mind, John?'

'I find it curious that he visits me so frequently, for, as a councillor and chancellor of the earldom of March, besides being a noted pleader of causes, he is a rising man of affairs.'

'You think he is out to change masters?'

'Possibly. No one knows better than Catesby that, as your grace's secretary, I am bound to pass on to you all that I hear. Yet he has told me frankly that Lord Hastings is a disappointed man.'

'How disappointed?'

'Because although he wished to honour the will of the late king by supporting the protectorship, he also hoped for an increase of his own influence when the young king was separated from his mother's family.'

'In a word, he and his friends hoped to rule through me,' said Richard.

Kendall nodded. 'And he is somewhat soured by the Duke of Buckingham's high place in the affairs of state.'

'Soured?'

'Aye, the word is Catesby's, your grace.'

'Are they grown men or nursery lads?' Richard burst out, 'to itch like ugly virgins at a marriage, avid for the one thing they cannot have!' He began to crack the joints of his fingers. 'There are two possible reasons for Catesby's candour. Either Will Hastings is sending me a backside complaint through his attorney – the sort he could deny all knowledge of, or Catesby is an opportunist and sees it would be advantageous to shift his allegiance.'

'Yes, your grace. And I would know how you would have me react to his confidences.'

Richard considered for a moment. 'Accept them,' he said abruptly. 'Test him with small confidences of your own. And I think you will find him reliable.' He made an exclamation of disgust. 'In all the kingdom I trust only one lawyer – and him I love. But because lawyers are trained in the slippery skills of deviousness and deceit,

217

honest men must use them. I leave this to your judgement, John. Give him a pension if he proves worth our confidence and a place in the household.'

❋

The Protector's known affection for Thomas, Lord Stanley assured him the entrée to Crosby's Place at all times, and it was natural that when the Duchess of Gloucester arrived from Middleham, Stanley should be there to welcome her to London.

It was a happy event, a meeting of neighbours with mutual interests in a household where the servants spoke the distinctive language of the north country and all the courtesies and laws of northern hospitality were followed.

Stanley was a spry little man, known affectionately in his own Lancashire as 'our canty Lord Tom', and he had all the uninhibited gaiety of small and portly men. He picked up Bat by the scruff – let her lick his crimson nose; quipped Miles Metcalfe that his son Richard outdistanced him in beauty as far as the sun outshone the moon; was very merry and gracious with the Lady Anne; and fussed politely over Richard's daughter, the Lady Katherine.

But when they had gone to their apartments, Stanley did not take his leave. Instead he took Richard's arm to steer him into the garden to blether a little, as he put it, and enjoy the sunshine.

He'd a racy way of blethering, darting from topic to topic – some of them grave, others humorous – some important, others quite insignificant; and in exactly the same breath as he told Bat to stop running round his feet he chided Richard for his treatment of Hastings. He conceded it had been necessary to issue a protector's proclamation to justify the overthrow of the Woodvilles, but in publicly stigmatizing the late king's ministers for ruining his health by encouraging his dissipation and excesses, though it was evidently aimed at the Marquess of Dorset, it could also be interpreted to include Lord Hastings.

'Unfortunate. Bad policy. You've poor advisers, your grace . . . Now that's a fine bank of marigolds!'

Richard was not put off by this diversion. Nor had he missed the significance of Stanley's expression *'your advisers'*. It conveyed a

218

subtle rebuke for excluding Hastings, even Stanley himself, from his most intimate circle.

'I respect your advice, my lord,' he said politely. 'For I have owed you much for many years. But you know as well as I that the proclamation was essentially against the queen's party, and my targets Grey and Dorset.'

'Aye. This we guessed, your grace.' Another significant pronoun. Stanley was either threatening to align himself with Hastings or he was already committed. 'Yet it was not made plain, and all England knows that Hastings was your royal brother's boon companion.'

'Yes,' said Richard tartly. 'I understand he and Dorset shared Shaw's wife with the king, to make a triumvirate of lechery. But,' he added quickly before Stanley could interject, 'you may be sure that had I believed Will Hastings to be as worthless as Dorset I should not have permitted him to keep his offices, nor assist at our councils.'

For the first time Stanley was at a loss for words, not knowing whether to show anger or pain at this demonstration of hard authority, and Richard, having made his point, softened the hurt of it by saying: 'Tell Will of this, my lord . . . You are right. These are fine marigolds!'

XIII

The Duchess Cecily had sent for Miles Metcalfe to ask a favour of him, but treated herself first to an adventure into the past.

For ten minutes and more she questioned him about Durham, Redesdale and Tynedale, and the great castles she had known as a girl, Raby, Brancepeth, Wark, Tynemouth and Bedlington and Morpeth.

Then, with a sigh, she put the north country and the past from her mind and returned to London in the present. She bade Miles sit beside her on a bench.

'In theory,' she told him, 'I am a holy widow sealed solely to the things of God. But, in practice, I remain a Neville, an old woman who fills the time with prayers but who likes as well to keep a finger in the world's pie.'

He smiled at her candour, as she smiled in return.

Then with great seriousness she asked him to use his influence to impress Richard with the need for caution.

He eyed her in surprise. 'Caution, madam? His position is strong.'

'Maybe,' she said. 'But will you promise to feed him with the idea that he must buttress his position? And will you do this regularly and gradually that he might digest it more willingly?'

Miles hesitated. As an answer he repeated his conviction that Richard's position was particularly strong.

Cecily sniffed. 'What of the king of France?' she asked.

'Why, he is sick.' Miles was puzzled by her sudden question. 'There are reports he will die.'

'Of course he will,' she said in a satisfied tone. 'Even that fox cannot slip the net of death, although he has asked the Pope's permission to have the Chrism of France beside him, and he has there, too, the Cross of Victory and the Staff of Moses.' She sniffed again. 'He was ever bloodless, and none of his trickery will save him from dying badly.'

'Dead,' said Miles, 'he can do no further harm to England.'

'But in dying, he will harm her.' She clutched Miles's hand. 'I am grown very old and have learnt to study death. Bid Richard consider what a candle does at the time it dies. There is one last gust of light before the darkness. And Louis, despite all these efforts to buy his way through purgatory, will be true to his mean self towards the end. His cunning will be concentrated in a last effort to discomfort England.' She let go Miles's hand. 'He may best do this through his pensioner, Tydder.'

'Is he not called Tudor?' said Miles gently.

'Tydder or Tudor, it is all one,' she said loftily, inferring that the names of the low-born were of no account. With all the Neville arrogance she flayed this upstart of base and obscure ancestry, saying she had it from her daughter Margaret that Tydder was as ill-favoured in appearance as he was in character, being ferret-faced, sly and parsi-monious. But the King of France would use him, she warned, because, though a proscribed traitor, Tydder insolently claimed the earldom of Richmond and pretended to the English throne. Given the opportunity Louis would plot with Duke Francis of Brittany and launch this unwholesome replica of himself on England as a final act of spite before he died.

'So bid my son keep his eyes on this Tydder or Tudor who plots in Brittany.'

Miles stood up, believing she had finished, but she held up her hand. 'And urge him to tread carefully in his own Council. This is even more important.'

Miles tried to reassure her by repeating what he had said before: that Richard's position was strong.

'Conspiracies breed fast where children are kings,' she said severely. 'Use your wits, Master Metcalfe.'

He was astonished at her knowledge and her lucidity as she asked if it was not true that Hastings was envious of Buckingham, that Hastings was suspicious because Thomas Howard now gave whole-hearted support to the protector, that Hastings was humiliated because he had moved from the centre of affairs to the outside of the circle. He admitted that in some degree all this was true.

'And you say Richard is strong?' she cried. 'I have known Will Hastings since he was a lad. I have watched him mature into a generous, warm-hearted – but spineless man. He lacks the character to accept a low place in the Council.' And that lack of character, she continued, would make him vindictive and drive him to form a party as dangerous in opposition to the protector as the Woodvilles had ever been; gathering together malcontents, like Rotherham of York, who should have been punished not taken back into the Council, and Morton, Bishop of Ely, who was Lancastrian at heart and would enjoy driving wedges into the house of York. Stanley was also suspect in her eyes because he came from the wrong side of the Pennines, and because he was Tydder's step-father – for Margaret Beaufort had passed hotly through the beds of two husbands before reaching Stanley's.

'Madam,' said Miles, daring to interrupt. 'Your son is aware of this.'

'But has he realized that it would be true to Hastings's character to go full circle and enlarge his little party by asking for the support of the Woodvilles?'

Miles's face told her that even he had not thought of this.

She continued: 'Has he realized that his chief motive for advancing Buckingham is his likeness to George of Clarence?'

'I do not think so,' replied Miles slowly. 'Though it had occurred to me.'

'A dangerous, foolish way to lay a brother's ghost,' declared the old lady. 'And if I know Richard, he will already have forgotten George's thousand faults and remember only his dozen virtues. It is his weakness to be like a moth to a candle-flame with such men as George and Harry Buckingham. He finds their good-looks, eloquence and charm irresistible.' She noticed Miles's worried frown. 'What do you know of Buckingham?'

'Very little,' he confessed. 'No one does. He is . . . altogether new to us.'

'Then, should he resemble George too clearly, and prove to be as shiftless a breed-bate, this could spell great danger to Richard?'

'It could,' agreed Miles.

She seized his hand again in her dry snake-skin fingers. 'Louis – Buckingham – Hastings! Miles, I beg of you to feed him with these ideas and show him the danger in which he lies. Bid him watch Harry Buckingham. Make him look to Brittany and Louis of France. Make him move to kill this conspiracy before it swells up and swallows him.'

He looked away from her. 'Kill?' he said.

'Yes, Miles,' she said quietly. 'If he pretends not to understand you, and refuses your advice, then you must speak directly to him. Tell him from his mother that he may no longer enjoy the ease of governing mercifully at second hand. Now that he rules England he must be ruthless for England's sake.'

'And if he will not be ruthless?'

'Advise him from me to accept the counsel of Bishop Stillington.'

The start he gave told her that Miles already knew what this counsel would be, and if he knew, then Richard knew as well.

'Yes, Miles,' she said gravely. 'As his mother I send him this advice.' Then she smiled. 'Will you come again to see me?' she asked. 'To talk of Northumberland and Durham?'

He stood up and kissed her hand, promising to do so.

'And bring your boy with you. I should like to see him.'

Miles coloured with pleasure. 'He would be honoured, madam.'

'To see an old woman shrouded in black? Nonsense, Miles! But it would please me . . . and I should try not to frighten him.'

'He would be honoured, madam,' insisted Miles.

'And what do you call him? No. I shall guess. It is Richard.'

'Yes, your grace.'

'Of course. To name him after your greatest friend is just and loyal.' She spoilt the pleasure of that moment for Miles by continuing in the same steady voice. 'Prove your friendship for him. Have him chop off Hastings' head.'

XIV

Anne was talking behind him.

She talked rapidly about many things: of Bat's escapade in the buttery . . . of the young captain who was casting sheep's eyes at her new waiting lady . . . of Middleham, and the brewing day there, the trust she had in her stillroom women . . . of their lack-wit nephew Edward Warwick who hated meat but had a strange passion for cherries and syllabub, and what in the end could be done for him . . . of little Metcalfe's new crimson jacket given him after his visit to Baynard's Castle . . . of William Herbert's request for the hand of the Lady Katherine . . .

Though her chatter was pointed with questions, she neither expected nor required any answers for her purpose in talking was simply to free Richard from the need to talk until he wanted to. It meant she could talk without so much concentration and so keep her attention on Richard as he stood with his back to her examining the angry lump on his cheek in a small Italian looking-glass.

It had been a pimple but now, he decided, was become a boil. It shone, was red, blue at the edges, a day or two distant from ripeness. It hurt already. It would hurt more. Yet it was not this that had started the icy sweat in his crutch and his armpits, but a memory of Will Hastings in Burgundy, Will Hastings at Olney, Will Hastings at Tewkesbury, jovial brave Will, as loyal as a stick to his king. Only another memory could weigh down the balance to the other side – and to remember it better Richard narrowed his eyes until he could not see his own reflection in the glass, – and saw instead a picture of Hastings outside a door, a lop-sided grin because the king had pawed a naked whore before his brother. And this picture, looked at with intense concentration, helped to blur another – of a headless corpse on Tower Green, wearing the crumpled but still elegant clothes of William, Lord Hastings.

He opened his eyes, touched the tight, scarlet boil and winced, and he heard Anne stop immediately, then collect herself and start again on her endless woman's chatter. It poured into his ears more comfortably than the appeals of Rotherham and Morton and Stanley, all of them pardoned, even reinstated as a futile defiance of the fate who had demanded the blood of a better man than they. Anne's voice was softer than the voice of Harry Buckingham, certain and energetic, Clarence-like in his suavity, or those other voices – of dear Miles Metcalfe, Tom Howard, Kendall, Catesby, the Archbishop who had taken little York from Westminster to the Tower – the voices of his nephew the king, of Stanley, Ratcliffe, Percy, of the Chancellor and the Privy Seal, the voice of Shaa the Lord Mayor and his brother the Franciscan, the voice of his mother at Baynard's Castle, and the coldest, most adamantine voice of all, that of Robert Stillington, Bishop of Bath and Wells.

Richard shook Stillington out of his head but back came Stillington – jack-in-the-box Stillington – whose voice by now was as unsmotherable as fire in a peat bog.

At last the Bishop had used his voice, and publicly. His arcanum was out for men to puzzle over.

All London had stirred uneasily as the open secret passed from man to man, that Edward the king before his marriage, had been pre-contracted to another, and she no common whore or courtly legs-opener who saw advancement in pleasing the king, but one of his mother's ladies-in-waiting, the respectable, widowed daughter of that fierce warrior against the French, John Talbot, Earl of Shrewsbury. To plight his troth had been Edward's only way to get her to his bed – and Robert Stillington had witnessed a contract which, by Church and Civil Law was binding on them both. But, once his itch was satisfied, Edward overlooked his obligations to the lovely widow and by the magic of his charm persuaded her to accept two manors and let the matter sleep.

The only other witness to the indiscretion he watched with a wary eye, keeping him sweet and silent with rewards – a Bishopric, a Deanery, manors, the Chancellorship; until he had dared to blab to Clarence. Then Stillington had been swiftly tamed by loss of office and a spell in the Tower, and afterwards bound once more through a pardon and reinstatement to most of his offices.

In advancing an obscure, unaccomplished priest to great place and power and then subjecting him to sanctions and menaces to make him hold his tongue, Edward himself gave the strongest evidence of his indiscretion. Stillington's mysterious career bore out the truth of his disclosure. His scrap of paper was less important, for documents were as easily forged as they were written. More telling – and especially to the commons who had adored their Ned and knew him well – was the undeniable fact that he would cheerfully have promised the world to satisfy his lusts, and, like all other men, he had been strictly consistent in his tastes, being caught twice by lovely but stubborn widows, both older than himself.

The tales had spread, giving birth to rumours, some to swell up to grotesque proportions, others to shrivel quickly in the light of common sense. But the plain facts that remained constant were sufficient to keep the citizens on the stir as they waited for something to happen and wondered what the disclosure would signify.

Friar Shaa had told them in one of his roaring sermons preached at Paul's Cross. Because of King Edward's pre-contract with Talbot's daughter, his children begotten on Elizabeth Woodville were set aside as illegitimate; and the next heir in succession, Edward of Warwick, was disabled in law by the attainder of his father, Clarence. 'Bastard slips shall not take root!' the friar had thundered, quoting from Holy Scripture, and a second time: 'Bastard slips shall not take root!'

Richard found he was trembling. Again there was that moist coldness in his groin and beneath his arms. He put up the glass again, wondering if a man acts before his reflection and if, on the contrary, it was a check to self-deception. He looked, but with unseeing eyes, as he wrangled inside himself, accepting or discarding the counsel he gave himself, counting the risks, the possibilities and probabilities, the needs, the rights and wrongs, the cost and sacrifices. Then he found himself looking at his forehead where the brown hair met the sallow skin – a point three inches, no more, no less, above his eyebrows – and he traced an invisible line there from left to right and back again.

A bell broke the pattern of his thoughts – the Angelus from near-by St Helen's. By now they would be executing Vaughan and Grey and that enigmatic earl, Anthony Woodville.

He shivered for the second time. Anne's voice stopped and started once again. He knew she must be watching him, and tilted the glass so that beyond his cheek he could see her anxious face. With his free hand he felt for the amulet he wore about his neck and prayed to the Blessed Virgin of England's Nazareth.

He put down the glass and turned to Anne. She stopped talking. Her hands flew to her mouth.

'Anne,' he said, going to her. 'Tell me how long it will be before this boil matures.'

She looked at it. 'Soon.'

He put his arm about her. 'What if . . .' he began: but knowing what he would say, she laid a finger on his lips.

'Dickon, you are all my life. Whatever is done for England I would have you remember this.'

He kissed her. After a moment he said: 'You remember Dom Edmund's reply to my threat that I should make him bishop.'

She nodded. It had made them all laugh, for Dom Edmund had parried the threat by saying it was no more easy to make a bishop of an unwilling priest than a king of an unwilling duke.

'He was right,' said Richard. 'It is not easy.'

PART FOUR

Proclaimed – Anointed – Crowned

I

On July 6th, the day of the coronation, a warm but strong south wind blew the length of England. It bent the corn in the south lands and up in the north made skitter-skatters of the haycocks. The fine dust it carried overmantled armour and furniture, plate and hangings, but it blew some of the stench from the alleyways of London, and down at Westminster even Ty Bourn smelt sweeter than for many months.

As he walked barefoot to his crowning Richard looked neither to right nor left, and kept his eyes on the long snake of scarlet cloth which stretched the whole distance from Whitehall to the great doors of the Abbey.

A long long way behind him, in her own procession, and also barefooted, Anne struggled in her heavy robes. It had been her intention to pray continuously for Richard, but the suffocating weight of clothing on her frail body took away her concentration and made prayer difficult. Only when they stood together before the High Altar, half-stripped for anointing with the sacred Chrism, and there was a profound silence in the Abbey, did she find herself so conscious of the holiness of what was happening that prayer was easy, and even the necessity to reveal the discoloration of her skin gave her no feeling of shame.

Richard, too, was deeply moved, and prayed that God's Presence in the Chrism, and in the Host he received after the crowning, would always guide the ways of Richard, King of England, France and Ireland. It was also soul-stirring to hear the way his people cheered and double-cheered as he and Anne walked side by side to the palace at Westminster – calling down blessings on the king and queen, and throwing flowers in their way, so many that there could surely be no roses left anywhere between Thorney Island and Tottenham. The warm wind picked up the petals, blowing them in spirals, and soughed away towards the north.

Anne pressed Richard's arm and told him her chief train-bearer swore the wind was England's sigh of contentment because a strong and proved ruler was crowned that day. He smiled at this, for Anne's train-bearer was none other than Stanley's wife, mother to Henry Tudor. 'As neat an idea, madam, as my own,' he whispered. 'That it is her son's moan of vexation blowing in from Brittany.'

A ringing fanfare of trumpets, capped with a flourish of clarions, greeted them to the palace of Westminster, and there on the steps, flanked by household knights, stood the King's Comptroller Sir Robert Percy. He was swiftly joined by the new Lord Chamberlain, Francis Lovell, who had been carrying one of the king's swords of justice in the Abbey. Both he and Robert wore about their necks the coronation gift Richard had given to all his fellowship of the White Boar: collars of gold, worked in roses and suns with a large white boar of Gloucester attached.

They welcomed King Richard and his Queen, and led them to rest in the royal apartments, while Tom Howard, now created Duke of Norfolk and Earl Marshall, and the Duke of Buckingham, made preparations for the coronation banquet.

That evening when all the ceremonies were done, Richard and Anne retired to the king's chamber with the members of their household, and there the queen distributed her coronation gifts.

For the king there was a robe of purple embroidered with insignias of the Garter and the white roses of York. 'You need only wear it on great occasions,' she assured him for she knew his liking for simple doublets of black. 'Not when you would be at ease and comfortable.'

He admired the gown and kissed her cheek, grateful for her gift and for her thoughtfulness.

Then she gave her chief waiting lady, Robert's wife, a gown of blue velvet worked all over with golden lions – the crest of the Percys. For the men there were poniards of hardened steel, sheathed in scabbards of crimson satin, each decorated with the owner's crest: for Percy his rampant lion, for Miles, the Metcalfe crest of a hound with its paw on a shield, for Francis, the Lovell squirrel cracking a nut. It was the same, too, for Tyrell, Ratcliffe, Parr, and John Kendall.

The king had presented all save one of his coronation gifts that morning. He now went to a press to fetch his gift for Anne, took out a package of waxed paper, and watched eagerly as she began to unwrap it. But, as women sometimes will, she stopped to finger its shape and ask Joyce Percy to guess with her what it might contain. This made Richard fidget. Eventually he urged her to open it, and, amused by his impatience, she did so. Inside was a wooden box. It was then his turn to chuckle as she puzzled over it, turned it over and over, searching for a fastening or a keyhole. She begged him to tell her the secret of this magical box. How could she open it?

'Tomorrow, madam,' he pronounced solemnly. 'You shall be told.'

'Oh, no, Dickon, please,' she turned to her waiting lady. 'Joyce, beg his grace for me. I shall not sleep until I know.'

Richard took the box from her, turned it over and pressed one corner with his knuckle. A small piece of wood came away to reveal a keyhole.

He pressed another corner. A second piece of wood came away to disclose a tiny golden key resting in a shaped slot. 'There you are,' he said. 'An ingenious nest made by the Venetians, containing a crimson bird's egg.'

Anne quickly fitted the key to the keyhole and gasped when the lid flew open and she saw the crimson bird's egg. It was a huge ruby – almost as large as the Black Prince's.

'See, Joyce,' Anne showed it to her lady who admired the jewel in a breathless flurry of words – until she remembered its safe-keeping would be her responsibility.

'Madam,' she said uneasily. 'It will attract every rogue in Europe.'

'What matter?' cried Richard. 'Now you have the royal guard of men-at-arms to keep you safe.'

He took Anne's arm and walked her to the window.

'Would you have it made into a brooch, a necklace, or fitted to your crown?'

'I shall keep it as it is a crimson bird's egg in a Venetian box – a memory of today.'

He nodded understandingly. They looked out on to the river. The wind had dropped and the tide was ebbing. The setting sun behind the palace cast long shadows on the mud flats.

Richard took off his fur-trimmed cap of maintenance now circled with a light crown of gold, and held it at arm's length to look at it before setting it on the sill. He sighed. 'A pretty thing.' Another sigh. 'Not heavy save in the burden it suggests. But I was not born to wear a crown as king.'

'Nor I to be a queen,' she put in softly. 'Yet God today has made us so. And England wills it . . .' She laid her hand on his. 'I count it wonderful that you, who never shared your brother Edward's love of pageantry, should have been blessed and crowned by Holy Church in a ceremony more magnificent than any man has ever seen – or heard of.'

He looked away from the crown to meet her eyes. 'Who said this, Anne?'

'The Cardinal of Canterbury.'

As she knew it would, this impressed Richard. From almost any other source he might have discountenanced it, but his uncle was far too old and wise to trouble himself with flattering anyone, and far too secure to feel the need to do so.

'He told me something else,' she added.

'As complimentary?'

'Aye, Dickon; and as true. The kings-at-arms finished their lists before the banquet, and your uncle bade me tell you that never in history have so many of the peerage been present to witness the anointing and crowning of an English king.'

She could see that he was both touched and heartened by this demonstration of loyalty and goodwill. He hugged her elbow and they leant out from the open window breathing the warm summer air.

At length he said: 'I lack two things to cap my own happiness: the presence of our son and dear Dom Edmund – and a skilled physician to cure you of your sickness.'

'But, Dickon, I am content with Master Hobbes.'

He made an impatient gesture.

'He is honest to admit that he does not know the nature of my illness. Candour is rare in royal physicians.'

'How does this help you, or me, or anyone?'

'By giving us confidence,' she replied. 'I know that he will not rest until he has found out what my disease is, and how it may be cured.'

'Then God speed his work,' he muttered, and afterwards, more cheerfully, he added: 'When the kingdom lies quiet I shall take you and Edward to England's Nazareth.' He saw how much this pleased her. 'The Blessed Virgin of Walsingham is generous to her pilgrims, and we shall pray for your health and that Edward might grow into a strong and wise ruler.'

'And much else besides,' she said. 'I would ask her to pray for the blessings of heaven on your reign.'

He tilted her chin, and like a young lover laid his cheek close to hers. 'As England is Our Lady's dowry she will be praying for these blessings from this very day.'

'Dickon,' she whispered. 'I would help you carry your new burdens.'

'And you shall,' he declared. 'By being gentle with Edward's widow. God knows I have no cause to thank her for her conspiracies, but yet she is Edward's widow. Visit her and, if she will receive you, assure her of my goodwill and earnest wish she should leave sanctuary and lead a retired life under my protection. And take her news of our nursery in the Tower.' He frowned. 'I would the children could be with her, or free to do as they wished. But it cannot be. Not yet. They would be snatched away or worse by men who would use them for their own ends.'

Anne regarded him with horror. 'Oh, no!' she breathed.

'Aye, my love. They are declared bastards by the word of Stillington, by a proclamation of the Council and by Act of Parliament – yet for all that they are in peril. Young Edward stands to me as Richard of Bordeaux did to Bolingbroke or poor mad Henry to my brother.' He saw she was still perplexed. 'To those who favoured Bolingbroke and my brother, and to those who favour me we are kings by right of blood, by Act of Parliament and by public acclamation – but to those who do not favour us we are counted as usurpers who have snatched our crowns from living sovereigns. If my nephews were free, Dorset would snatch them up and rend England with civil war. If they were free, the Tudor's agents would scotch them mercilessly – simply because like me they are of the house of York and stand between Tudor and the throne. If they were free, King Louis would steal them away or have them slain – such is his love of intrigue. Any one of my enemies would harm these children in order to harm me, and slip the blame on me as well.' Again his voice thinned into melancholy. 'Poor lads. They are only safe in ward, and that the strongest in the kingdom with my own trusted Brackenbury from Yorkshire in command. Though it is a grey cage indeed for two youngsters . . .' His voice trailed off.

Anne quickly promised to make their cage as bright as possible, and said she would visit the queen in St Margaret's sanctuary the very next day. Then, purposefully, she left the subject, for the strain of the past two months had told heavily on Richard. There were deeper lines at the corners of his mouth, and sometimes a strange look in his eyes that showed he was at the edge of what he called himself 'my own black pit'. He was close to it at that moment, his nerves screwing tighter and tighter like a sodden rope, and she was determined the day should not be spoilt.

She laid her cheek against his again and whispered; 'Dickon, I am weary after the ceremonies and I would rest. Could you not ride out with your fellowship?'

He said no, he would sit with her until supper; but she won him over by suggesting he rode out in his plain doublet. 'As a private gentleman and not as king, racing your friends as once you used to do at Middleham.'

Their race through Tothill Fields was brought to a halt by a marshy tract of land.

'I claim I am first,' shouted Robert.

'To rein in, aye!' panted Miles. 'But look, I am further into the slime.'

They had flushed a snipe or two, and the birds began to drum overhead.

Richard stood in his stirrups. 'There are houses to the left. Our race finishes at the first inn to be found.' With a crack of his whip he was off.

'Wait, wait,' called Francis. 'You have the advantage.'

They followed, thudding over the turf until Richard reined in at the first cottage in a village street. It lost him the race. Lovell galloped past him and yelled when he saw the inn sign – a branch of withered sweetgale hanging before a house.

But Robert was first again.

'Holy blood,' cried Francis, reining in behind him. 'Do you ride a Pegasus?'

Robert grinned and slapped the stallion's neck.

'Whether it has wings or no, it has led us to an ill-favoured place,' said Richard. 'Yet let us try their wares.' He slid from his horse.

Two boys came out to catch their bridles, and a beanpole of a man eyed the strangers with amazement.

'You are landlord of this pot-house?' asked Francis.

'I am, my lord.' The man wiped grease from his mouth. He was dismayed to find such customers at his door.

'Then lead us in, man, lead us in,' said Richard genially.

The taproom was furnished with a trestle table and three benches. It was empty of customers.

'Is your ale so bad no one will drink it?'

'No, no, my lord,' stammered the beanpole. 'Hereabouts we are fowlers and fishermen, and early to bed.'

He offered bread, cheese, meat if they would.

'Your own brew of small ale will satisfy us,' said Richard.

'And plenty of it,' added Robert.

They settled round the table and drank small ale. It proved to be as thin as its manufacturer.

Miles pulled a face. 'Two marks to a groat its base is bog water.'

Richard smiled. 'Aye, it lacks the sting of our northern ale,' he said, and then made them all laugh by adding: 'Could it be the sheep corpses in the becks above Middleham that make all the difference?'

This led to talk of Wensleydale and Richard delighted them by saying he would soon make a royal progress through the country. It was right, he said, to show himself to the people.

'Homing north?' inquired Francis Lovell.

Richard grinned and admitted he felt the need of a headful of air from the dales — 'And better ale than this,' he added, pulling a face. 'Still, I am thirsty.'

They all were. The jug was refilled several times, and eventually the beanpole persuaded them to try his wife's cheeses. There were two; one a soft milk cheese flavoured with horse-mint; the other hard and coarsely redolent of the dairy, almost strong enough to drown the taste of the raw leeks and radishes which accompanied it.

Their thirst sharpened, they ordered more small ale, and the beanpole went off to refill the jug and tell his woman they had strange company that night: great lords by their dress and manner, but willing to drink his small ale which even the villagers called villainous, apparently preferring to sit in the twilight for they had not ordered candles, and chatting in pixie-talk as fast as they could.

She went to listen by the open door and, not understanding the mixture of courtly French and the clacking dialect of the north, she decided they must be imps led out of the marsh by that little pigwidgeon clothed in black. Had she known the truth, that the pigwidgeon talking with his imps was in reality her king discussing affairs of state with three of his councillors, she would have found it even more unbelievable.

When they paid their reckoning and left she watched them go, expecting them to be swallowed up by the marsh from which she believed they had come. But they were soon out of sight, and all she heard was the imps singing lustily – a ballad of some sort it sounded – but eventually even this sound died away.

II

Only the Duke of Buckingham remained in London when the court and council moved to Windsor for St Mary Magdalene's day. He had begged leave to establish himself in his new offices as Constable and Great Chamberlain of England and would later ride west to oversee the government of Wales and the west country.

Windsor in July. There were few fairer places in the kingdom and, consulting with Master Hobbes, Richard and Anne decided that she should rest there for a time and afterwards take the slow and easy route to join the court at Warwick.

On the 23rd the large assembly broke up. Percy of Northumberland led off his northern game-cocks to foray against the Scots. Norfolk returned to hold the reins of central government in London. Richard himself began his progress along the Thames valley. With him travelled attending lords and councillors, his household officers and guard, the keepers of his seals, and the secretariat.

He was moved but not deceived by the warmth of his welcome wherever he went. England not only needed a strong king, she wanted one. Her people remembered the upheavals and disasters caused by Henry VI's minority. They remembered the prophecy from Holy Writ – 'Woe to thee, O land, when thy king is a child.' They knew Richard's reputation as lord of the north and one of the foremost generals in Europe, and though he lacked the spontaneous charm of his brother Ned, they respected his courage and his love of justice and his concern for all his subjects even the meanest. So everywhere along the route of his progress respect and relief made them acclaim him as their king, but when he came to Gloucester, his own city, they showed their love as well. He might now be king but it mattered more to them that for over twenty years he had been Duke of Gloucester.

It was there that Buckingham overtook the royal court on their way to Brecon, bringing the latest news from London and dispatches from the Duke of Norfolk. He also carried three private letters for the king; one from his steward at Crosby's Place announcing that

239

Lord Mayor Shaa had sent a gift of timber for wainscotting the gallery; the second from his mother to say she had decided to move to her manor at Berkhampstead and would like him to take Baynard's Castle for his own; the third from his son, John of Gloucester, begging to be allowed to join the court.

Richard feasted Buckingham with his household, and later asked Tyrell to ride to London, see the Duchess Cecily into her new cell at Berkhampstead, appoint a king's seneschal for Baynard's Castle, and bring young John to meet them in York at the end of August. This done he followed Severn from Gloucester up to Tewkesbury, where as a lad of eighteen he had had to sit in judgement as Constable of England. And in the Abbey he prayed for the souls of his brother Clarence and the duchess Isabel who lay buried before the altar. Unknown to everyone, even his closest friends, he added a quiet prayer for another who lay there in an unmarked grave, Edward of Lancaster, once betrothed to Anne.

The king's progress moved up-river to the city of Worcester, and struck east to Warwick. Anne was waiting for him in the castle which had been one of her childhood homes, and she looked so gay and fresh after her short rest at Windsor that it was hard to remember her illness. He surprised everyone – and visibly scandalized those old-fashioned courtiers who valued protocol – by lifting her in his strong arms to swing her in a circle while Bat yelped and snapped at the hem of her skirt.

Master Hobbes who stood in the throng of courtiers quickly looked away. He felt a tear roll down his cheek, and shook his head angrily, telling himself he was a man of learning dedicated to the science of healing, not a babe to show his feelings because these two young people so much adored each other, and he knew more by intuition and experience than by diagnosis, that one of them was doomed.

The meeting was short and the queen had to return to her apartments because couriers and envoys followed or preceded the king at each stage of his progress and there were many matters of state waiting for him at each halting-place.

Isabella of Spain had sent an ambassador to propose an alliance. He expected to treat with Edward IV, but was entirely content to negotiate with the new king, Richard III, and consider his suggestion of a mutual pact to bear heavily against the strength of France.

The King of France sent a message from his bed of sickness to recognize Richard's assumption of the throne. 'Monsieur mon cousin,' he wrote tersely. 'If I can do you any service I'll do it very willingly for I want to have your friendship. Adieu.'

Secret reports from the French court were more informative. Richard learnt that Louis was endeavouring to drown his terror at the approach of death by busying himself with affairs; sitting up in bed and rubbing his hands like an old usurer whose gold is political intrigue; and making sure Richard should hear that he had sent messages to Henry Tudor and his host Duke Francis of Brittany, and to John Morton, Bishop of Ely.

Richard considered it significant that Louis should want him to know about the messages. He would not be able to resist peppering the diplomacy of Europe before he died, and it was natural for him to write to the Lancastrian pretender at the same time as he wrote to the Yorkist king. But Morton made a strange confidant. Since the Hastings conspiracy the Bishop of Ely had been kept an open prisoner and out of mischief at Harry Buckingham's castle of Brecon, far away from the centre of events. He dictated to a scrivener a succinct reply to Louis's message, saying he was contented to have France's friendship, but he would be obliged if the king would control the French free-booters who were plaguing English merchant shipping. He ended: 'And farewell to you, *Monsieur mon cousin*.'

Afterwards he wrote the letter which mattered most to him – a summons sent to Dom Edmund to bring Prince Edward to Pomfret where they would meet in the third week of August.

III

Talking many years afterwards with a colleague from the University of Salerno, William Hobbes expressed the opinion that King Richard of England had begun to die in spirit on August 24th, 1483.

It was not then noticeable, even to those who were closest to him: but with hindsight the physician could trace the collapse of his master's happiness from the moment when a litter was carried into Pomfret Castle. It contained not the old priest who had been racked and twisted and who found riding painful, but his ward Prince Edward.

Though the shock was great, both his parents managed to stifle their feelings for Edward's sake. Anne took the frail little boy in her arms and kissed him, and Richard, wearing a ghost's smile, told him to prink himself out and wear his brightest doublet for that very night he would create him Prince of Wales and Earl of Chester. By terrible irony, Dom Edmund appeared to be more agile than he had been for years. He slipped from his horse with unaccustomed ease and, without waiting for permission, he took the boy's hand, bade him take leave of his parents, and quickly led him away to the apartment which had been prepared for him. There he left him with a favourite body-squire and returned straight away to Richard and Anne. They had already gone to the solar, accompanied only by Lady Percy, Master Hobbes and the physician who had travelled with Edward from Middleham.

Anne's face was chalk-white as she demanded to know why they had not been informed of the prince's condition.

To the physician's relief, Dom Edmund answered for him, assuring her that Edward had shown no marked signs of deterioration until the day before, and then he had complained of a great tiredness. 'It was my decision that he should travel this last stage of the journey in a litter.'

'Yet not to warn us . . . Why did you not send word?'

'Madam,' said the priest steadily. 'If I had done so you would have imagined him worse than he is. You would have spent fourteen dreadful hours exaggerating his exhaustion into something else and something far worse, for anxiety often breeds fancies and terrors. Is this not so?'

'Yes.' It was Richard who replied. 'He is right, Anne.'

But she said nothing, merely held out a trembling hand to Joyce Percy. The depth of her feelings had moved her own sickness. She began to heave and pressed her stomach.

Master Hobbes said at once: 'Your grace will kindly leave us.' And when Richard did not move but stared blankly at his wife, the physician snapped: 'This is not serious, your grace, but to be plain, your lady will vomit . . .'

Dom Edmund led Richard from the room.

'Jesu! Sweet Jesu!' breathed the king. He was sweating.

The priest said nothing.

'She was so well . . . She had been so, so happy . . .'

'Hobbes said it was not serious.'

'Not now, maybe. Sweet Jesu! Anne and Edward! Edward and Anne! My wife and son!' He began to moan.

Dom Edmund was ruthless. He shook the king physically, and in a hard, sharp voice ordered him to pull himself together. 'By God's mercy you *shall* be a man. You shall, because I will not have my dearest friend so soft in faith, nor my anointed king so abject a whiner.'

Richard tore himself free. 'No man alive dares to insult me so.'

'I do.'

'By God's teeth . . .' began Richard savagely; then abruptly he paused, and the priest knew he had succeeded. Richard had found himself again, or, at least, that part which is shown to the world.

'Punish me for my insolence to your crown,' said Dom Edmund with a smile. 'Though,' he added hastily, 'I will not be a bishop even for you.'

'Instead you shall suffer by remaining with me always, for I need you and your honesty.'

'You shall have it Dickon.'

'I shall?' said Richard. He walked a few paces down the passage, and over his shoulder he said: 'Then let me test your candour.'

Knowing what was coming the priest felt for the Crucifix on his girdle and clutched it tightly.

'You know how dear Edward is to me?'

'I do,' said the priest.

'And you also know from his physician and from your observation that he slowly wastes away.'

'I do.'

'He will not be long my heir?'

'No.'

There was a silence. At length Richard turned to face the priest. 'Thank you, old friend,' he said. 'It is better not to see too many pictures in the sky. Though Rivers did,' he added, linking arms with the priest. 'You knew he was beheaded here at Pomfret?'

Dom Edmund nodded.

'And wrote me a ballad before they topped him?'

'I did not know.'

'He did. I have it by heart – and now some of his verses cry out to me.' Very clearly he repeated them:

> *Methinks truly*
> *Bounden am I,*
> *And that greatly,*
>   *To be content;*
> *Seeing plainly*
> *Fortune doth wry*
> *All contrary*
> *From mine intent.*

Afterwards he was thoughtful and slowly walked Dom Edmund along the passage. Eventually he said: 'Your honesty has made me change my mind. I will not keep you with me. Were I to die I could wish for no more honest or understanding counsellor than you, and I would not deprive my son. Will you serve me by staying with him until the end?'

'Aye, Dickon.'

❊

It was that time of dusk when weak moonlight almost balances the grey western sky. Lovell and Percy had spent three quarters of an hour at the river end of a cockshoot, waiting for woodcock to flight from the woods above Pomfret to the marshes by the Aire. Only two birds had thumped into their net, but this did not matter.

244

They had enjoyed the silence of the evening. It had been an escape. They padded slowly back to the town and neither spoke until they saw Miles and John Kendall walking along the path below the castle mound, their heads close together, quite clearly deep in conversation.

Francis grinned. 'Shall we take them, Robert?'

'Aye, from the rear.'

A sudden thunder of hooves behind them made the two walkers leap for safety. Miles stumbled and fell headlong, but Kendall had his poniard out before the horsemen could turn. Then he recognized them.

'I thought you cut-throats,' he gasped.

'Moon-mazed lunatics!' roared Miles, picking himself up. 'See, my gown is as dusty as a miller's sack.'

Francis laughed. 'You were too nimble. We would have picked you up and carried you home.'

Miles was dusted down. Robert produced a leather bottle from his saddle satchel. They sat on a bank to drink at it in turn.

When Miles had wiped his mouth and passed on the bottle he tugged at the bill of one of the two woodcocks hanging from Robert's belt. 'Have you thought of these rumours while netting your poor wee sparrow.'

'No,' returned Robert. 'We thought of nothing but poor wee sparrows.'

Francis shrugged. 'They are but rumours. And such rumours spring up naturally in Pomfret.' He looked at the shape of the castle in the twilight, and they knew what he was thinking. Only eight weeks before Rivers and Vaughan and Grey had been beheaded there, and somewhere within those curtain walls the deposed king, Richard of Bordeaux, had met his end. 'Rumours of spilt blood breed here like flies in a carcase.'

'But these,' said Miles shortly, 'were bred in Brittany.'

Francis looked quickly at Robert, then back at Miles again. 'You are certain?'

'No!' said Miles. 'I have no proof. But it seems probable.'

He owned that he was worried. His elaborate network of agents and the excellent courier system which, in open weather, made it possible for a message to travel over a hundred miles in a day, now proved that the rumours the king's party had picked up on their way north were not confined to any single part of England. The same talk was springing up simultaneously in towns and villages all over the countryside, and the fact it was so persistent and never varied suggested that it was being fed into people's minds from one source.

'Holy Blood!' breathed Francis. 'I had not dreamed it was so serious a matter. Poor Dick! He is overbattered by events.'

'But why should the source be Brittany?' demanded Robert.

Miles asserted there was only one man in Europe capable of spawning so precise and calculated a plan to defame the king of England.

'Louis of France?' said Francis immediately.

Miles nodded. 'Aye, Louis, who is next to a Saracen in his use of obloquy as a diplomatic weapon, and in Brittany he has an apt pupil.' He drank from the bottle. 'It fits. Only the Lancastrians are disaffected to the king, and there are enough of them up and down the land to spring this tale at an arranged time.'

'I see,' Francis looked again at the castle. 'And what does the king say?'

'At first he was angry,' replied John Kendall. 'But since he has shrugged it off like any other rumour that circulates about a king.'

'He must be made of iron,' said Robert.

'No.' Kendall shook his head. 'In fact I have not yet told him how widespread this calumny is, nor how convincing it has been made to sound.'

'Then you should tell him at once,' urged Francis.

Kendall looked away. 'As you said, he is being overbattered by events. I would not unnecessarily add to this.'

Miles agreed with him. No harm could be done by remaining silent for a little longer. But Francis and Robert were adamant.

Kendall stared hard at them. 'You believe it is my duty to tell him now?'

'Why, man!' burst out Francis. 'He is defamed as a monster, a child butcher who has murdered his nephews. He has a right to know how serious the situation is.'

The secretary sighed. 'Very well,' he said. Then he held out his hand. 'With your leave I shall soothe the matter with a brace of woodcock for his supper.'

'They are fresh-netted, too tough,' said Robert.

'And so is my tale.'

IV

King Richard's smile was half genuine, half false as he acknowledged the welcome of the citizens of York; genuine because he sensed these people belonged to him as no others ever could, and false because he was gorged with frantic anxieties – for Anne, for Edward, for the settlement of King Louis's calumny.

It was five days since a courier had spurred out of Pomfret Castle and by now his nephews would have been walked through London to scotch the slander that had seeped through England. But he longed to hear with his own ears that it was done.

As dearly he longed to know the reasons for Tudor's curious public proclamation that when he had taken England by force he would marry Edward's eldest daughter to unite the white rose with the red. The girl was as much a declared bastard as her brothers in the Tower, and it could not suit Tudor's purpose to deny their bastardy. The announcement was insolent and head-in-air and imbued with the sort of sentimental appeal to be expected from a Welsh mountebank, but Tudor was no fool, and Richard, as he dined with his household, ate very little as he puzzled over many questions which could not be answered until his agents in Brittany sent in their reports.

His train of thought was broken by Francis Lovell who plucked at his sleeve, and bent close to his ear to whisper that Tyrell had that moment arrived from London. Thank God! Richard grunted with pleasure – but then he realized Tyrell would have made the journey in easy stages and could not possibly have the news he wanted. Still, it would be good to see him. Prompt, dependable Tyrell to arrive on the last day of August as he had been ordered; and young John would be with him . . .

Why, he asked Francis, had they not come in to dinner? And the anxiety knotted again deep down in his belly when Francis whispered that Tyrell had grave news. He begged the king to see him at once – and to take Dom Edmund with him. With a slight pressure on his shoulder Francis managed to prevent the king from springing to his feet. In the same low voice he pleaded with him to move naturally, not to arouse comment by too abrupt a departure, not to distress the queen.

This told Richard what he had already guessed. Something had happened to his son. He put a trembling hand up to his forehead, and asked Francis to bid Dom Edmund follow him when he left the hall. His chamberlain bowed and stepped away, and Richard suddenly remembered his mother in her cell – a black-clad figure with the fixed gaze of an oracle denouncing her own blood. Now it was John. Was nothing to be left to him?

Anne was not deceived when he kissed her cheek and feigned an excuse to leave the table, and she noticed Dom Edmund rise at the same time from his place down the hall to follow Richard. Bat slipped after them. She pushed away the dish before her and closed her eyes.

As Richard expected, Tyrell was alone in the privy chamber, but evidently he had not taken the route from London in easy stages. He was travel-stained, red-eyed from lack of sleep. He knelt to kiss the king's hand.

Richard quickly raised him to his feet, and asked in a clipped, flat voice what had happened to his son.

His eyes opened wide with amazement at the reply. John's horse had foundered close by the village of Riccall and Tyrell had judged it best to leave the boy, with two-thirds of the escort, to follow later. He would reach York before sundown.

The relief was too much for Richard, and Tyrell stopped abruptly, bewildered by his sudden rush of tears. Then he shook his head and smiled and cursed himself for a fool to weep before his chaplain and his master of horse in such a way. He caught a little time in which to calm his feelings by offering them wine and pouring it himself. He fussed and played with Bat. He invited them to sit down and shook and plumped a cushion for Dom Edmund. But James Tyrell would not sit. He could not sit, he said – not until he had told his news.

By now Richard had full control of himself. It showed in the way he stood with his legs slightly apart and his chin tilted upwards. He was braced mentally for anything, and it was as well, for without preamble Tyrell bluntly told him that both his nephews were dead.

Dom Edmund climbed to his feet and crossed himself.

The king neither moved nor spoke.

Tyrell hesitated nervously, uncertain how to proceed. Then he found his voice again to say how it had happened; that both boys had been suffocated while they lay sleeping. It was not known who had murdered them. Robert Brackenbury, the Tower Constable, neither wanted nor expected any mercy from the king. It had been his responsibility to hand-pick the jailers, men-at-arms, and servants who attended the two young princes, and his judgement had been faulty. One or more of them had proved to be faithless. Either they had allowed outsiders to murder his charges, or they had done it themselves, and without a thorough investigation which would reveal the murder to the whole world there was no way of discovering who the traitors were. Brackenbury accepted full blame and awaited the king's punishment.

Richard came out of his shocked silence. He crossed himself and asked quietly what had followed the discovery.

Tyrell drank a mouthful of wine, and a second. Brackenbury, he said, had come to him at dawn that same day at Crosby's Place and, under a solemn oath of secrecy, he had revealed the truth. Then together they had ridden out to Berkhampstead, and under the same oath, told the Duchess Cecily her grandsons were murdered. She had barely known the boys because their mother had kept them away from her, but they were of her blood. Her chaplain was summoned, sworn to a confidence as close as the Seal of the Confessional, and at once, at the wall Altar in her cell, he had said a Requiem for their souls.

Richard crossed himself again, thanking God for his indomitable old mother with her first concern for the things that really mattered, and thanking God as well that James Tyrell had had the wisdom to go to her. The Requiem done she had been shrewd and practical, making Brackenbury cringe by emphasizing that the Tower was the strongest fortress in the kingdom, and the princes had been guarded by the king's own men. If their murder were revealed few would believe that the king had had no part in it, and those who wavered in their loyalty between York and Lancaster would be alienated for ever. The rumours that his nephews were dead were already harming the king, but he would be harmed far more if it was known to be true. Therefore the obloquy must be ridiculed, the bodies disposed of.

When her family was at stake the Duchess Cecily did not give advice. She gave commands.

Tyrell and Brackenbury had done the work with their own hands, placing the bodies in a large chest and concealing it as well as they could under a staircase.

Richard was filled with horror but he would not let Tyrell see it. The man had already borne enough in serving him.

For the rest, said Tyrell wearily, silence could never be guaranteed, but by making no investigation and allowing the traitors to go undetected, Brackenbury hoped to keep the matter close. Only he and perhaps three or four others at the Tower knew of the murder. Those who were guilty would not dare to compromise themselves by publishing the fact: the rest could be counted on to keep up the pretence that the princes were still alive.

Dom Edmund showed his distress. He sat down again, clasped and unclasped his hands, looked at the floor. He had seen too many people die to fear death or count it as an enemy, but the callous suffocation of sleeping children moved him deeply; and his heart was wrung by the certain knowledge that if the truth were known Richard could not escape being branded as a bloody tyrant.

The king was thoughtful for a long, long time.

When at length he spoke it was to thank Tyrell for his service, and commend his mother's wise decision to keep the matter close. Beyond Metcalfe, Percy, Lovell and Kendall no one should ever hear of it. No one else at all. Not even the queen. It was too terrible a matter for her to know of. As for Brackenbury, what was done, was done, and the king would always honour him as a worthy gentleman of Yorkshire, a valued councillor, and his Constable of the Tower of London. Would Tyrell tell him this – and take the road south again when he was rested? – for such a message might not be trusted to a courier.

Tyrell knelt to kiss his hand, and, such was his fatigue that when he stood up he swayed slightly. The king steadied him, and ordered him to get something to eat and then sleep.

When he had gone Richard sat beside Dom Edmund, not at first to talk or ask his advice, but simply to suck comfort from his closeness and try to still the whirlpool stirred up in his mind. He put his head in his hands and screwed his eyes up tightly, trying to arrange his thoughts into a coherent order.

Where, where lay the guilt?

Any one of his enemies might have suborned the jailers. Any one.

'Buckingham!' he said aloud. 'Harry Buckingham, as Constable of England, has access by right to all prisoners of state.'

The priest eyed him apprehensively. 'If you cannot trust your own appointed Constable, whom can you trust?'

'Whom can I trust?' repeated Richard. 'If Buckingham was responsible, were his motives hostile – to harm my reputation; or were they friendly – to rid me of a supposed embarrassment. Dom Edmund, I can never now be certain that my dearest friends have not risked their immortal souls by killing these children thinking mistakenly it would be to my advantage.'

'No, no, no.' The priest was horrified. 'It must have been an enemy . . .' He broke off because Richard had jumped to his feet.

'My greatest,' he cried. 'Henry Tudor.'

He was suddenly filled with the conviction that there must be a connection between the murder of his nephews and Tudor's proclamation. Henry would not wed a bastard, yet to deny the bastardy of Elizabeth Plantagenet would legitimize her brothers and place them between him and the throne.

Richard caught his breath. Had his mother been wrong? Could he not have shown his people the slaughtered princes and made them then understand that to him, Richard the Third, with a proved title to the crown, such a monstrous act was both unnecessary and political folly, whereas, to Henry Tudor, it was in all ways an asset?

Richard paced up and down the room, aware that because the decision had been made he was in a cleft stick; that, because no investigation was possible, Tudor's guilt could never be proved – not even to his own satisfaction.

He stopped pacing and seized the priest's hands. 'We can never know, Dom Edmund, where the blame lies,' he cried. Then he added despondently. 'But I know my own share of the guilt: that by moving according to the will of Parliament, I doomed my brother's sons.'

The priest started. 'How so?'

'By taking the crown. I realize now they were condemned to death at the moment of my coronation. Inevitably they followed the way of all deposed rulers – of the second Edward and the second

Richard in our history, and, as I well remember, of poor mad Henry of Lancaster. It is one law of sovereignty.' He sighed deeply. 'Dom Edmund, soon I shall invest my son as Prince of Wales, and then I shall ride south. Will you take him to Middleham for security? And take, too, my wife.' He sighed a second time. 'I shall have mountains to climb, and shall climb them with an easier mind if I know they are safe.'

V

Unless they were personally involved, the commons paid little attention to what was happening that autumn. The great lords of England calmly waited to see what might happen, assessing the advantages and possible moves of each side as though chess were being played, not a battle for England. They found the game altered, and made more interesting, when one royal piece fell out. Louis of France, scheming to his last moment, died horribly at Plessis-les-Tours. His heir to the throne was a sadly deformed youth of licentious habits and doubtful sanity, but the real heir to Louis's cautiousness, his cruelty, his notorious parsimony, even to his liking for shabby clothes and the company of parvenues, was his pupil in statecraft, Henry Tudor.

It was October and King Richard was on his way back to London when Tom Howard of Norfolk sent word to say Kent was up in arms. Lady Stanley and the Duke of Buckingham had shown their faithlessness and were declared traitors. Would the king look to the west and midlands. Norfolk had London in safe keeping.

Richard was angered by the treachery of Stanley's wife who enjoyed high place at court, but as she was Henry Tudor's mother it was understandable. Less believable was Buckingham's bewildering ingratitude. And yet Richard was not really surprised to find him at the head of a rebellion. Buckingham could not hold his tongue and Miles's agents in the west had recently sent in some strange reports. It seemed that Robert Percy had been right in his assessment. The duke was indeed a replica of Clarence: treacherous, ungrateful, insanely jealous of the supreme power.

Scheming at Brecon with the slippery Bishop Morton, an ambitious maggot had eaten at Buckingham's mind. He had come to believe he was a second Warwick. His power had made Richard king. His power could make Henry Tudor king, or even, yes – he, Henry Stafford could be king. The maggot chewed faster almost devouring his mind. He shared with Tudor descent from Edward III through the base blood of the Beauforts, but he also had a stronger claim to England as the direct heir of Edward's youngest son, Thomas of Woodstock. This was unchallengeable. Buckingham's mania swelled . . . He was greater than Warwick, would use Tudor to break Richard and then discard him. So very like Clarence – his own worst enemy.

Richard sat with his small Council and appraised the situation. With God's help Tudor could be kept from landing on the south coast. Only Buckingham, Oxford and a handful of malcontent lords were openly opposed to the crown. The rest would show how they stood when summoned to meet their king. It should be at Leicester, he decided, on the 20th.

Already he was a different person. Though he had shown a brave face to the hints of conspiracies against his crown, and had tried to show indifference to the vicious calumnies of his enemies, he had a plain man's hatred of underhandedness. His manner completely altered once he was faced with action, with physical threats, with armies that could be grappled with. He became zestful, brisk, needle-sharp in his assessment of the military situation and, by a masterly deployment of his forces and knowing when to be patient and when to move rapidly, he threw his enemies into confusion.

The rebellion was squashed like a fly beneath his thumb and without so much as fighting a single skirmish.

Poor Buckingham, who had boasted he would have as many Stafford knots as Warwick had had ragged staves, woke from his manic dream. Men would not break with a strong king to tie their fortunes to a crazed adventurer.

Morton and Oxford bolted to Flanders. Buckingham disguised himself and fled in terror to the west. He was caught and brought to face trial at Salisbury before the Vice-Constable. When condemned, he shrieked hysterically and begged to see the king. But Richard refused. He was disenchanted at last. Even in his cowardice Harry Buckingham was like his brother, and he shared his plausibility. No persuasion should make him see this traitor who had brought the country to the brink of civil war simply to gratify his lust for power. He steeled himself. He would not see his cousin. He ordered the sentence to be carried out at once.

Since that moment two months before when his son was carried into Pomfret Castle Richard had lived permanently in a state of half-panic, for ever in that second of apprehension before a man catches his breath. Now, as he heard the drums rolling for Buckingham's execution, the feeling intensified. The drums rolled and rolled: a thin sound of death, more strident than the thumping of the pile-driver when George was strangled. Drumming and thumping – Harry Buckingham and George of Clarence. The rolling stopped. He heard a faint cheer. And he swallowed hard, gulping at the air, trying to hold back the desolation that was stealing over him.

VI

When the rebellion had been fully crushed, Richard sent for Anne to keep Christmas with him in London, and to bring their son if the journey was not beyond his strength.

The queen was faced with an unenviable decision. Master Hobbes confessed it was unlikely that the prince could survive such a journey, and she knew quite well that, if she left him, she might never see her son alive again. Dom Edmund would not advise her, although once she had made up her mind and prepared to leave for London he told her she had chosen the right way. In the degree of love and duty a husband must come before a child. In her heart Anne agreed. But it was hard. It was very hard. She was denied even the small solace of leaving her son in the expert care of Master Hobbes! The physician was resolute. He had received direct orders never under any circumstances to be parted from the queen. He would accompany her to the royal court.

After they had gone, Dom Edmund would have tried to cheer the fragile boy, but he found it was quite unnecessary.

Edward was not greatly upset by the departure of his mother. He accepted it as inevitable. He had known from the cradle that princes could seldom enjoy the luxury of being with their parents.

Dom Edmund admired the boy's philosophical acceptance of things, but he could not share it. Because he so greatly cared for Richard he would remain with Prince Edward as he had promised, but he longed to break his word and go to the king, principally to chip away part of the crust of guilt which he knew Richard would be building about his soul . . . imagined guilt for his part in the slaughter of his nephews, a guilt made worse because he confessed they were more Woodville than Plantagenet and he had not really cared for either of them . . . imagined guilt for damaging England with the threat of civil war through overtrusting Buckingham . . . even guilt because Tudor's abortive invasion and the unsettled state of the country made it impossible for either Edward or the queen to make a pilgrimage to Walsingham. Better perhaps than anyone alive the priest understood the nature of Richard's tendency to melancholy. He knew that unless he were pushed and prodded the king would be incapable of offsetting his mistakes with his considerable achievements. And his successes were remarkable. Miles and John Kendall kept Dom Edmund in touch with events at court, and he dearly wished to know by what magic Richard had moved his brother's widow to send her daughters out from sanctuary in Westminster, and then leave it herself. It proved beyond any shadow of a doubt that she accepted his good faith and did not believe the obloquy which held King Richard as the murderer of her sons. And Dom Edmund pondered over Kendall's long letters in which he made it clear that Richard was undertaking the government of England with the thoroughness he had once ruled the north, and that he showed an unerring instinct, knowing what was best for the kingdom and the way his policies should be effected.

Yet, despite this good news, Dom Edmund still longed to be with the king, to prod him and push him and make him see how much of his guilt was imaginary, how much misplaced. He was often on his knees praying for Richard and Anne, and for their only child who, quite perceptibly, was growing weaker and weaker.

The day came when, after consulting with the prince's governor and the Middleham physicians, Dom Edmund decided it was his duty to bring the king north. He sent a courier warning the king and queen that the Prince of Wales was not expected to live.

They were at Cambridge when his warning reached them and, though they wasted no time on the journey north, they had only reached Nottingham a few days after Easter when a further message arrived to say their son was dead.

It made small difference that Richard and Anne had long expected Edward to die. Their grief was too overwhelming to be stormy. They found their son's death so unbelievable that, to their household's distress, for twenty-four hours and more they seemed to be deceiving themselves it was untrue. Though they heard Requiems, paid their Mass pennies, lighted candles, accepted formal condolences from ambassadors, and went through all the customary ceremonies of mourning, they did it with the artificiality of dolls.

Francis Lovell loved them too well to let this continue. He tried to be gentle but he was still firm when he told Richard the time had come to nominate his heir to the crown. Anne went rigid and the king blazed up like fused powder, but Francis showed no fear. He kept his

257

eyes steadily on Richard's. At length Richard said: 'Very well. Yes. Later. I shall. Later. Later.'

Thereafter neither Anne nor Richard played the abnormal game of make-believe, but their grief was cold and silent. They would only take consolation from each other, nothing from their friends. Nor did they seek the relief of tears.

When Dom Edmund arrived from Middleham the king was consulting with his chief captains. It was certain that Tudor would try again and again for England and though Richard was already calling Nottingham his Castle of Care, he had decided it should be the centre of his defences.

He broke off the meeting to greet his old friend and hear how the Prince of Wales had been laid to rest. Then, directly, as though to crush his sorrow by work, he bade Dom Edmund go to the queen, and he returned himself to the plans for the defence of England.

Dom Edmund found that Anne had taken to her bed. Master Hobbes told him it was but temporary, a natural reaction; she would soon be up again.

The priest went to her and told her of her son's easy death. At last she wept a little, asked many questions, and then thanked him and asked his blessing.

Outside her chamber he looked hard at the physician. 'Tell me,' he said. 'I am no fool, Master Hobbes, nor am I blind not to see how her grace has altered in these past five months.'

The physician looked away. 'She would have no one know.' He hesitated. 'But as physician to priest I may tell you her disease grows worse. She is given to such weakness that sometimes she has to keep to her bed, and she has chronic pains . . . grave pains. I have blistered her and tried cautery, but to small effect.'

'Poor, poor lady.'

'But this is not all.' The physician sadly shook his head. 'She now shows all the symptoms of a second disease.' He paused thoughtfully. 'It is strange that a hardy and healthy father like the Earl of Warwick should beget such puny daughters.'

Dom Edmund, remembering that Anne's sister Isabel had died of the blood-cough, caught his breath in dismay.

'Aye,' said Master Hobbes nodding. 'She has the blood-cough, too.' He turned an unhappy face to the priest. 'The king does not know, yet for the sake of his own health I should tell him.'

'Not yet. Not until it is really necessary.'

'Very well. But it cannot be long before the queen will be dangerous to him – two months, three.' The physician laid a hand on Dom Edmund's arm. 'I can do so little for her. One of her complaints is beyond my knowledge, the other beyond my skill.'

'Then together we shall do our best for them,' said the priest. 'Come, Master Hobbes, if you and I do not feign smiles, no one at all will wear them.'

VII

For many months they deceived the king, giving him time to set the country in order and prepare against the next invasion from Brittany.

'Not until his own life is in peril,' Dom Edmund urged again and again whenever the physician said he could not bear the responsibility of remaining silent any longer. 'He has two loves – for England and his wife. Though one is dying, let him show his love for the other.'

Anne herself was equally persuasive. She had no fear of death because life was weary now and often painful, but she did fear what would happen to her Richard if he knew the truth. 'You must remain silent for a little longer,' she told the physician.

'Madam, your disease becomes increasingly dangerous,' said the unhappy Hobbes. 'My first duty is to his grace.'

'No. No,' pleaded the queen. 'Until it is truly impossible for him to be with me, keep your silence – for my sake as much as his. Let him continue his good work.'

And so Hobbes had kept his reluctant silence, watching and waiting, turning the king's anxious questions and trying to justify the deception by admitting the undoubted excellence of Richard's government.

In a few months the king confirmed his reputation in Ireland as one of the most benevolent and understanding of English sovereigns. In the north he made a three-year truce with Scotland and reconstituted the council of the north on a fresh basis, with his nephew, and proclaimed heir, John, Earl of Lincoln, as its president. In general affairs he proved himself a far-sighted and original ruler: voluntarily curtailing the sovereign's right to demand loans from his richer subjects; transferring powers from the Exchequer to his own household treasurer; founding an arsenal of artillery; establishing a college of heralds; reorganizing the navy and encouraging shipbuilding; protecting English commerce by clearing the seas of privateers; reforming the whole machinery of the administration of justice.

His closest friends knew that he was burying his personal troubles in hard and constructive work – but it amounted to a funeral of achievements which benefited the country and made the people of England thank God they had a strong and wise king at the head of affairs.

But then on a February day in 1485, Anne took to her bed in the palace at Westminster and from all the signs the physician knew it was for the last time. It was no longer possible to deceive the king, and now no longer possible for him to be with her.

The priest and the physician told him together.

He heard them out in silence. 'You warn me to keep away from my own wife?' he asked coldly.

'Your grace,' said Master Hobbes bravely. 'It is a prohibition not a warning. I am your physician just as I am the queen's. You may not go near her save at peril of your life.'

Although he was small, at that moment Richard gave the impression that he was very tall indeed, and what he said would have daunted most men. But the physician refused to be browbeaten. Affecting to be outraged he used the very last sanction to make the king see reason. He bowed and asked leave to retire.

'No!' snapped Richard. 'I will not have you skulk in your chamber when you are needed.'

'I meant not to my chamber, but from your service altogether. Clearly I can be of no further use to your grace.'

Richard could not believe his ears. He stiffened, leant forward and said between his teeth: 'By the splendour of God! You would not have dared treat my brother Edward in this way.'

'On the contrary.' The physician allowed himself to smile at the memory. 'I did on one occasion, and he was very angry. He threw things at my head.' The smile died. Stiffly he added: 'With your grace's permission I shall leave your service and find other patients – more tractable.'

There was an intense silence.

Then, knowing Richard had given way but would find it difficult to say so, Dom Edmund said: 'Master Hobbes, his grace would wish you to continue caring for the queen.' His eyes told the physician to leave the chamber.

'That I shall, your grace,' said Hobbes in a lighter voice altogether, and bowed himself out.

❊

261

Queen Anne grew weaker and weaker.

Joyce Percy and the queen's other ladies had cut themselves off from the court in order to nurse her, and the petty jealousies and spitefulness which inevitably sometimes ruffled their small community were forgotten in their anxiety to do all that was possible for their mistress.

When she asked after the king they admitted his wretchedness, but they would not dwell on it and quickly spoke of less painful things; that the king's bastard John of Gloucester had been given Hastings's office as captain of Calais, and Sir James Tyrell sent out as captain of Guisnes to act as the boy's deputy until he was old enough to rule himself; how a basket of spring violets and jellies and bletted medlars had come from Berkhampstead with a typically stern message from the Duchess Cecily commanding her daughter-in-law to improve in health at once.

They kept it from her that the king no longer concerned himself with ruling England. Had he been with Anne he would have hidden his misery for her sake. Away from her, there was no point, and almost from the moment he knew that she was dying he stepped into a new life.

John Kendall found his position as secretary impossibly difficult. Very seldom could he persuade the king to sit in council and urgent affairs piled higher and higher. Foreign envoys, eager to see the king, began to show signs of angry impatience. Quite a number of appointments which quickly needed filling were still left vacant. When Kendall tried to urge decisions from the king he was waved away and told to wait. More and more he was leaving affairs of state in the hands of other people.

✳

Only a few hours before Anne died she seemed so well that Joyce Percy and her ladies dared to hope that the physicians had been wrong.

They sent for Master Hobbes and he came at once to find his patient sitting up and talking vivaciously. But to the ladies' indignation he neither examined her nor gave her the usual draught, and when he left the chamber they flocked after him to repeat their belief that their mistress was on the road to recovery.

'Master Hobbes,' protested one of them. 'I have seen new life come into her with my own eyes . . .'

'Yes,' said the physician. 'It is always so with those who have the blood-cough. They appear to have new life just before the end.' And when one of them began to cry, he added gently. 'Deal kindly with your mistress by not showing her you know the truth.'

He went himself to fetch Dom Edmund.

'You have little time,' he said. 'Give her the last Rites, my friend. And then together we shall go to the king.'

Dom Edmund crossed himself. 'He is prepared for it. I am sure he is prepared. Pray God he will take his loss with grace and patience.'

He continued to pray this until, at a little after noon, and when Londoners gaped at the sun in eclipse, Anne died in Richard's arms.

❊

That evening, while bells tolled over Westminster and the city, the king rowed secretly with Francis Lovell from the palace steps to the middle of the Thames, and there he made a weighted bundle of the small Italian casket that contained Anne's crimson bird's egg, and he dropped it in the river. It plummeted through the water leaving no trace.

After a moment Francis bent to the oars to make for the steps again, but Richard stopped him. They drifted and bobbed on the flooding tide while tears streamed down Richard's face. At length he hunched forward, holding his head in his hands, and in his agony he whispered: 'Oh, God! Oh, God! Oh, God!' And then again. 'Oh, God! Oh, God! How weary I am; how weary of it all!'

VIII

The king took up the reins of government once more, but he was too weary to care any longer for the little concerns of humble people. These he left entirely to his almoner and John Kendall.

Wearily he received envoys and ambassadors, and presided at meetings of the Council.

Wearily he sat in the marble chair of King's Bench in Westminster to judge causes and hear pleas.

Wearily he received reports on the state of France and Burgundy, of Scotland and the border country, and wearily he heard from agents in Brittany that it was certain Tudor would come again that summer.

But at least his weariness deadened the hurt he would ordinarily have felt on hearing Henry Tudor's latest calumnies.

There were now two widespread rumours circulating in the kingdom: that God had punished the king for murdering his nephews by striking down his only son, the Prince of Wales; and that Richard had actually poisoned Queen Anne in order to marry his niece Elizabeth.

Tudor, as King Louis's apprentice in cunning, was beginning to outmatch his master.

The second cruel calumny was contrived to cause the most pain and damage to the Yorkist king. It mocked his mourning as hypocrisy and taunted him with littleness of mind in that he would seize the very woman Tudor had said he would marry. It impugned him as a monster who could butcher two innocent children and then lie incestuously with their sister, and, most dangerous of all, it slighted his undoubted right to the crown by insinuating that he needed to strengthen a weak claim by marrying Edward's eldest daughter.

It was Richard's Fellowship of the White Boar who told him all this. They urged him to proclaim a denial because, by his clever device Tudor could shift the allegiance of those who still wavered between York and Lancaster. One after the other they begged him to send Elizabeth right away to the royal household he had established at Sheriff Hutton, and make a swift and vigorous denial that he had any intention of marrying her.

They knew Richard had his share of Neville pride and ordinarily it would not have been easy to persuade him to make such a public acknowledgement of Tudor's importance; but this time he accepted the advice without question, and without spirit. He made the proclamation, and put his niece into Lincoln's care at Sheriff Hutton.

He continued to be so dejected and listless that his friends were seriously worried. Thinking it would recapture a happy moment they persuaded him one afternoon to gallop over Tothill Fields towards the marshes and the inn where, on the night of his coronation, they had drunk too much small ale and eaten cheeses, radishes and leeks. But, to their consternation, far from helping, it served to lower his spirits further. The previous autumn a peat-hag fire had set the inn ablaze. There was nothing there but charred timbers and a floor of tiles all criss-crossed and patterned and cracked by great heat.

Richard looked sadly at the blackened ruin, shrugged his shoulders, turned his horse, and rode silently back to Westminster.

Robert and Francis considered sending in private for Miles, who, since the queen's funeral, had returned north to do his duty as Recorder of York. Miles had always possessed the knack of bringing out the best in everyone, not least the king. But this plan was discarded when Richard announced that when the main preparations had been made against the summer invasion from Brittany he would make a second progress to the North Country. He wanted, he said, to see Middleham again.

His tone told them that they were trying to help a man who, although only thirty-two, had suffered sufficiently to hope that his life was drawing to a close.

IX

Dom Edmund's cramps and pains had returned with greater force
that winter and, because it appeared they had not lessened at all
with the coming of summer, Master Hobbes insisted on examining
his friend. He then prohibited him from accompanying the king on
the royal progress north.

It was a sign of his low vitality that the priest had consented to
the examination, but he still had the spark to say he would do as he
pleased. 'And that,' he said warmly, 'is to go to Middleham.'

The physician threw his hands in the air at such a preposterous
suggestion, called his friend a mule-pate with half a dozen other
names besides, and called on the king to exercise his authority.

'I shall defy you, Dickon,' said the old priest.

Richard pretended to be stern as he tried the familiar threat. 'If
you do I shall make you bishop.'

This time Dom Edmund paid no attention. 'You may have me
elected Pope,' he said crossly. 'I am still going to Middleham.'

The king took Master Hobbes to one side. 'He is determined,' he
murmured.

'Obstinate, wilful and lunatic,' muttered the physician, and added,
'but he is a good good man.'

'He is.' Richard was thoughtful. 'It is impossible?' he asked.

'To accompany you, yes. He would not have the strength.' Master
Hobbes frowned. Then he half smiled. 'But I could take him in
slow and easy stages on the most direct route.'

'You?'

'If your grace wished it.'

'I do wish it, Hobbes, and thank you.' Richard returned to the
priest and told him of the physician's offer.

'He and I together,' chuckled Dom Edmund. 'We shall quarrel,
quarrel all the way north.'

But they only reached Nottingham, and there Master Hobbes's
poppy draughts could no longer prevent Dom Edmund crying out
with pain at every movement.

'We must rest here and wait, Sir Mulehead,' said the physician.

'For what?'

'Until you can prove your strength by boxing my ears, or the king catches up with us, which ever is first.'

Dom Edmund made an enormous effort. 'I undertake to box your ears tomorrow,' he promised.

He could not keep his promise and they were still at the castle when the royal party arrived at Nottingham.

William Hobbes hurried to meet the king and tell him of the priest's condition. Richard immediately threw his reins to a groom and followed him to the little chamber where his old friend lay. He did not stay very long.

Afterwards in the Presence Chamber, he asked the physician outright if Dom Edmund was dying.

'Aye, your grace. He will not see Middleham again. Nor will he leave Nottingham.'

There was a silence. Everyone there had a great affection for the king's confessor.

'We shall miss him sadly,' murmured Richard. 'How rightly I called this my Castle of Care.' He played with Bat's scruff and sighed a number of times, then he determined to remain with Dom Edmund as long as he could. 'It is right that I should, and best perhaps as Tudor will come after harvest.'

He told Robert he might as well send for his wife. Joyce had gone north to prepare Middleham against their arrival. It was no longer necessary. At the same time he commanded Kendall to summon Miles Metcalfe. York would have to do without him.

'We wait here for Tudor,' he repeated.

Stanley caught him in this despondent mood and asked permission to return temporarily to his estates in the north-west.

With the threat of invasion mounting each day it was a strange time for the Constable of England to leave his king, but Richard consented, and was even puzzled when Robert Percy hastily suggested that Stanley's son, Lord Strange, be asked to remain at court to act in his father's interests.

'Aye, if his father consents,' agreed Richard.

Stanley felt obliged to consent.

Later, when the king was alone, Robert Percy went to him and asked why he had given Stanley leave to go. 'You may regret it,' he said. 'When Henry Tudor comes.'

'Eh?' Richard smiled wryly. 'Robert, I declare you have the most suspicious mind of anyone alive. Has he not, John? Stanley has been my friend since I was knighted. Yes. Be sure I shall send for him when there is need.'

The garrison at Nottingham seldom saw their king and then only as a small black figure with a brachet always at his heels. When he was not at Dom Edmund's bedside he was hunting in Sherwood.

It was in Sherwood on August 11th a courier brought the news everyone awaited. Henry Tudor had made landfall, but not at Southampton, where Francis Lovell awaited with a white hot welcome, but in South Wales, at Milford Haven.

'Poor Francis,' was Richard's only comment. He bade his huntsman sound an end to the day's sport, and galloped back to Nottingham.

It was as it had been at the time of Buckingham's rebellion. The king sent couriers to his captains to meet him at Leicester, and calmly discussed his chances with those of his council who were with him. They urged him to march for Leicester, but he said he would not leave until after Assumption Day.

His calmness was broken when a messenger came from Lord Stanley who had been summoned to Leicester with the other captains. Stanley sent his humble duty but the opinion that, in view of the disposition of the rebel forces, he and his brother could best serve the king by remaining where they were to guard the approaches from North Wales.

Richard frowned at the messenger. Then abruptly he ordered the arrest of Stanley's son.

Robert told him Lord Strange was already taken. He had been seen leaving the castle two hours before without the king's leave.

Richard threw him a look of gratitude.

He was as hard as steel when Strange was brought to him. 'If you value your life, my lord, you will plead for it to your father the Constable.'

At Miles Metcalfe's dictation the young man wrote a letter to his father, urging him to join the king with all speed.

That same day another horseman arrived at Nottingham. It was the Serjeant to the Mace of York, to say that the Mayor and Twenty-Four knew of the Lancastrian rebellion, but as yet had no instructions.

The significance was not lost on anyone. Henry Percy of Northumberland should have raised the city days before.

Richard commanded that the best rider and freshest horse at Nottingham should take his orders to York and bid the citizens force-march to Leicester.

The next morning he went to ask Dom Edmund's blessing and say good-bye.

William Hobbes raised the frail old priest on his bed. With trembling hands he traced the sign of the Cross on Richard's head. 'God go with you, Dickon,' said Dom Edmund.

X

The armour-bearer tugged at a strap. 'There is no priest at hand, your grace, to say a Mass.'

Richard smiled at him. 'No matter, lad. If our cause is just, God will protect us – alive or dead.'

Robert looked up from the map that had been sketched out the night before by the chief of the royal scouts. 'You are high-spirited,' he said.

'And should I not be?' Richard drank half a horn of ale and seized a hunk of bread.

'There is meat, your grace,' suggested his squire, John Parr.

'No . . . For fighting, bread!' Richard walked from the pavilion with Bat at his heels and went directly to a vantage point which overlooked the valley. There he chewed at his bread and looked over to the fires of Tudor's camp. Beyond there was a flush of light along the sky. Soon it would be dawn. He eyed the land before him to re-think the strategy he had planned the night before.

The countryside had no grace. It was open, uncultivated, almost treeless, without fences or hedges, shot everywhere with streams which leeched all goodness from the earth. Quagmires were spotted here and there in the scrub of coarse grass tussocks and stunted thorns and alders. A sour, uninviting part of England, not easy to fight over, but Richard had the advantage of the hill on which he stood and Northumberland's levies were encamped on a long ridge to his right. The main battle would be fought down in the valley, but his own men would be fresh from a run downhill, the Welshman's troops short-winded after plodding through the marsh and scrub.

Richard wrapped his cloak tightly round him. The air was keen for an August morning. He looked again at Tudor's camp, wondering if he in turn might be looking up at the royal army.

It struck him at that moment how little he really knew of this Welshman who had spent a lifetime conspiring to win the English crown. He showed two masks to the world: one, painted by his followers, of a handsome, hard-done-by prince, appointed so-to-speak by God Himself to cleanse England of a usurping tyrant; the other, quite as illusory, published by his enemies, of a graceless entrepreneur, as unsavoury in his personal habits as in appearance, who simply to advance a single inch towards his goal would sacrifice anything or anyone except himself. Neither picture represented the truth; and beneath the distortion lay a real man but still a total stranger to the Yorkist king he had come to supplant.

Richard fondled Bat's scruff, regretting that he would never know whether Tudor was a romantic who saw all battle and warfare as chivalric exercise or a realist as he was himself – able to calculate what might befall that day, the chances of death and, worse, of mutilation, as steel chopped through sinews, or maceheads laid open whole areas of flesh, coursers hammered living men into the ground, lance points and bolts and arrows seared into bellies and faces, as cannon shot mixed cloth and metal, blood and fat and muscle and entrails into a nightmare pudding of death.

Richard crossed himself. It must come to some men on that day – for the sake of York or Lancaster, Plantagenet or Tudor, Richard or Henry – and many of his own would die and suffer disfigurement.

They had all come at his bidding – his faithful Yorkshiremen, Brackenbury from London, Francis Lovell with men from the south, Norfolk with his East Anglians, even Northumberland; and, as in answer to prayer, Stanley and his brother Sir William whose forces alone outnumbered Henry Tudor's.

There were steps behind him. It was Robert with more ale. Richard accepted it. 'I told you, Robert, that Stanley would come.'

'To sit like a stoat between two eggs,' was Robert's quick answer. 'See how he lies below us, half-way to Henry Tudor.'

'Which is half-way to us.' Richard grinned at his chamberlain. 'And we have his son.' He threw wide his arms as though to embrace the air. 'I cannot remember how many battles I have fought, but never have I had such strength of arms nor so favourable a position.'

'Dick,' said Robert Percy, suddenly and urgently. 'I beg you to order Stanley here at once. Now.'

'Very well.' Richard eyed him curiously. 'He was once my true friend, and would, I believe, make up for his part in Will Hastings's conspiracy. But do as you will.'

Robert wasted no time. The herald Blanc Sanglier trotted down the hill to Lord Stanley's camp. When he returned with a polite but evasive reply, only the king remained calm, and for a long time he refused to send a second message with the threat that if Stanley and his brother did not muster their forces to the king Lord Strange would be put to death. His friends tried every persuasion, reminding him that Stanley was Tudor's step-father, that he had been proved faithless more than once, but it was Francis Lovell who moved him to agree. Stanley, he said, was most likely to turn his coat simply because Richard had forgiven him his treacheries and heaped him with great offices. He was too small-minded a man to be beholden to anyone.

Richard's face clouded, but he gave the order they all wanted. At the same time he ordered his troop to make ready to move into the plain.

A trumpet sounded from the opposite ridge. The king's captains were riding to meet him for his last instructions. Northumberland came with the suggestion that his men should stand in reserve behind a body of mounted archers and men-at-arms on the ridge. In this way he said he could cover the royal army from any treacherous moves from Stanley or his brother. Richard nodded his agreement. Norfolk looked at his son and then at Lovell. Miles Metcalfe would have spoken a warning and risked the wrath of his king and the king's viceroy in the north, but at that moment Blanc Sanglier rode up with Stanley's last message.

'My lord Stanley bids your grace know that he has other sons, and he is not disposed at present to leave his position.'

There was a gasp. Richard's face was drained of all colour. He shook his head angrily. Then he cried: 'Take Strange's head.'

Everything was altered. He could fight solid enemies but not men with hearts so small they could contain no gratitude, nor fathers who would shed their own sons' blood . . .

But as he struggled to control himself he saw it would be ignoble to share in Stanley's callousness. Abruptly he cancelled the order for Strange's execution.

Forcing a smile he addressed his captains, bidding them God speed. Then slowly, with his household around him, he moved to a commanding position on the ridge to watch Norfolk's vanguard meet the Lancastrians.

The battle began.

Loyal Norfolk went down in the mêlée and his men wavered. Reinforcements were sent in. Richard gave the order Miles dreaded: that the Earl of Northumberland should advance from his position into the main line of battle. The Stanleys had held off to this point, but at any moment they would declare themselves.

Northumberland sent a scurrier to say he believed it was his duty to remain where he was.

Miles and Robert looked at their saddles. They could not meet Richard's eyes.

'Then we ourselves shall ride to seek Henry Tudor,' he cried, and not in rage at Northumberland's treachery, nor in panic because their situation now was desperate, but casually, almost gaily, as though he were a boy again at Middleham proposing a race up the fells.

'Where does he lie?'

John Parr moved up beside him and pointed to a small hillock far away down the valley. A smudge of red and white hung in the sky; the banner of Wales. 'He will be there, your grace. With his household knights.'

'Friends!' Richard rose in his stirrups. 'Will you carve with me a corridor through the centre of our enemies to reach Henry Tudor?'

There was a roar of consent.

Francis Lovell shouted. 'If we scotch this pretender his men will fall off like flies in winter.'

'No!' It was Catesby, showing a side which John Kendall had long suspected: the prudent, fearful lawyer who would not take a chance. His face was grey as he urged the king to take refuge in flight. Only in this way could he save his crown. To cleave through Tudor's army would expose him to Sir William Stanley to the right and Lord Stanley to the left. At any moment one or both of these brothers would move.

Richard gave him a smile; then turned his head so that John Parr could adjust his helm. Catesby slipped away out of sight.

Francis and Ratcliffe took up their place at the king's right hand. To his left were Sir Robert Percy and Miles Metcalfe.

John Kendall, Robert Brackenbury and all the knights and esquires of the body were behind him.

'I would Tyrell were here to make our fellowship complete.'

'Now a fellowship of steel,' said Robert Percy.

'Aye.' Richard smiled at them all, then, nodded at John Parr who

273

closed his visor. Another squire placed a battle-axe in his grip. With his right hand he signalled to the trumpeters, and they sounded a peal as he led his household at a walk down the ridge slope towards the main press of his enemies.

He spurred his white charger to a trot, and at the bottom of the hill to a gallop. With less than a hundred men behind him he thundered straight across Sir William Stanley's front – aiming at the heart of the enemy's reserve and the white and read banner hanging limply from its ashpole.

Richard threw back his head and shouted the battle-cry of the Plantagenets. It was taken up by his friends and his household as they crashed into the mass of cavalry ahead.

Thereafter he was caught in the pattern of hand to hand fighting which he knew so well and when only four things seemed to matter – his arm, as he smashed limbs and bodies with his battle-axe, his mouth, dry and salty, and his ears packed with squeals and screams and the din of pain and energy, and then his mind which swept and soared away from his body, backwards and forwards as though his thoughts were attached to his head by long, long pieces of string. Out they went as he cut open a thigh, then a shoulder, then pulped a breastbone – out, out to make all this reality seem so unreal.

There was Bat leaping a yard or more ahead. Why had they not tied her up in camp, safe from the flying hooves? Anne's gift . . . Aye, Anne. He was so close to Anne, and to Edward, and his brothers, to Warwick and his father, to Peter and poor Tom at Ludlow . . .

The standard of his enemy, the red dragon of Cadwallader was before him, and with a cry he struck at the standard bearer, laying him dead in the dust with the banner on top of him. And there was Tudor – but, out of the corner of his eye, he saw at the same moment on his right flank a dense mass of horsemen in scarlet jackets: Sir William Stanley's cavalry.

Treason . . . *Treason* . . . Dom Edmund was not to see Middleham again . . . Nor he perhaps . . . Calmly, without even wincing he saw Robert Percy die barely three feet from him – his face laid open, his scream quite terrible; then Ratcliffe. And Miles fought and scrabbled on the ground; pulled up to Lovell's pommel . . . *Treason* . . . *Treason* . . . Faithful Brackenbury was down . . . The king beat about him against a hedge of lance points and swords. And now

Kendall was gone . . . his head cut from his shoulders bouncing, once, twice – then kicked aside by a courser's hoof like a ball . . . Such friends. Such friends. His fellowship of steel. . . .

The last of the Plantagenets died in the thickest press of his enemies. But the Tudor was vengeful. By his order they stripped Richard's mangled corpse, put a felon's halter round his neck, laid his naked body across the rump of a pack-horse, and drove it from the field of battle. As the beast crossed a bridge on the road to Bosworth village King Richard's head struck the bridge supports one after the other. It rattled and banged on the stone like a boy's stick against palings, his long brown hair falling downwards streaked with sweat and blood, his eyes open and staring.

Beside the heap of clothes and armour that had been stripped from him lay the bodies of Robert Percy, Richard Ratcliffe, Robert Brackenbury and John Kendall, and the smashed corpse of a small brachet bitch with blood upon her teeth.

England had a new king.

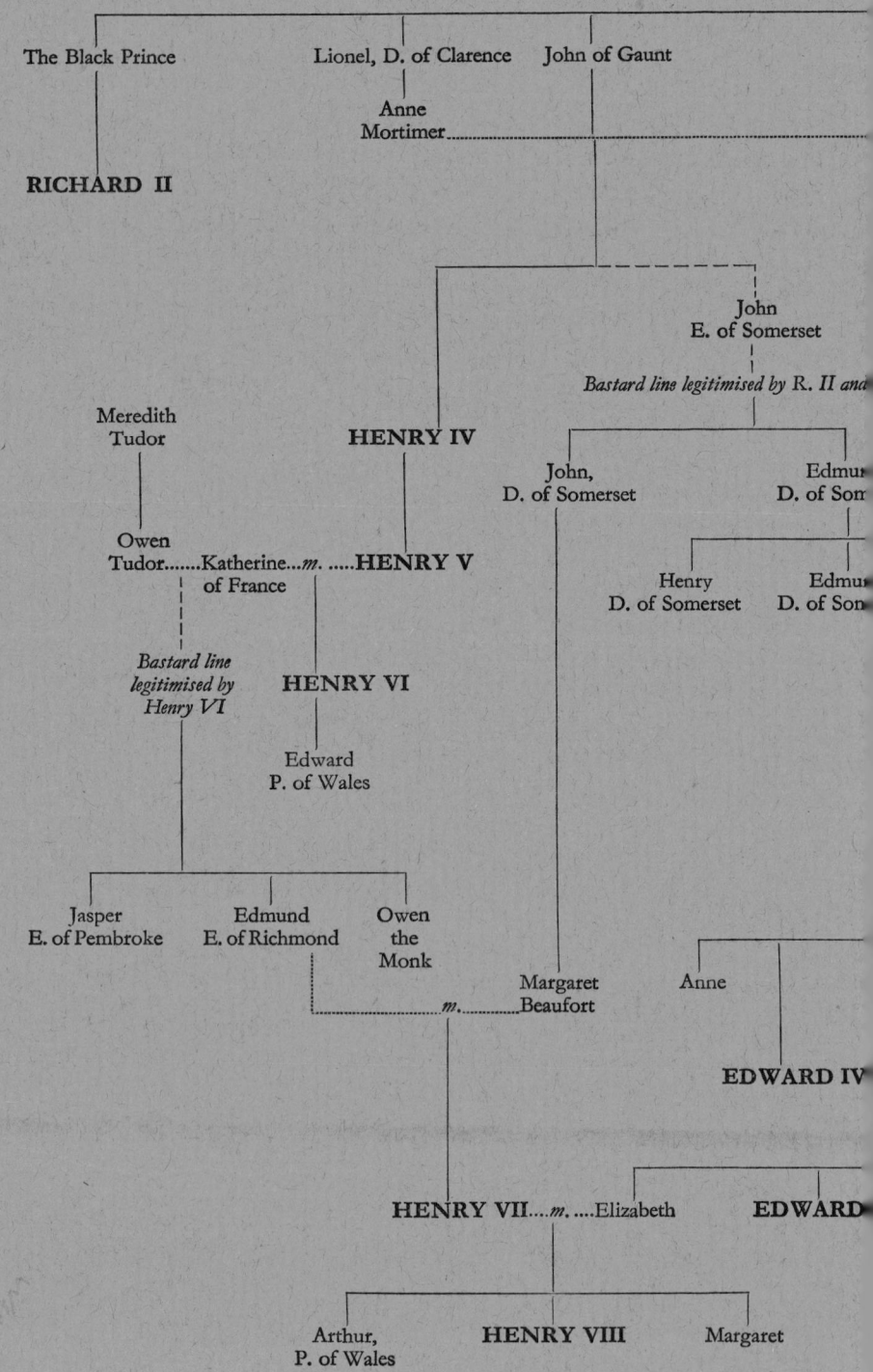

The Black Prince   Lionel, D. of Clarence   John of Gaunt

Anne Mortimer

RICHARD II

John E. of Somerset

Bastard line legitimised by R. II and

Meredith Tudor

HENRY IV

John, D. of Somerset   Edmu D. of Son

Owen Tudor.......Katherine...*m.*.....**HENRY V**
of France

Henry D. of Somerset   Edmu D. of Son

Bastard line legitimised by Henry VI

HENRY VI

Edward P. of Wales

Jasper E. of Pembroke   Edmund E. of Richmond   Owen the Monk

Margaret Beaufort   Anne

m.

EDWARD IV

HENRY VII....*m.*....Elizabeth   **EDWARD**

Arthur, P. of Wales   **HENRY VIII**   Margaret